OXFORD MODERN LANGUAGES AND LITERATURE MONOGRAPHS

Oxford Modern Languages and Literature Monographs

VOLTAIRE: Historian
By J. H. BRUMFITT. 1958

THE PETRARCHAN SOURCES OF *LA CELESTINA*
By A. D. DEYERMOND. 1961

THE TRAGEDIES OF GIAMBATTISTA CINTHIO GIRALDI
By P. R. HORNE. 1962

PONTUS DE TYARD AND HIS *DISCOURS PHILOSOPHIQUES*
By KATHLEEN M. HALL. 1962

PIERRE BAYLE AND VOLTAIRE
By H. T. MASON. 1963

THE GENESIS OF *LE COUSIN PONS*
By DONALD ADAMSON. 1966

RILKE AND FRANCE
By K. A. J. BATTERBY. 1966

LAMENNAIS AND ENGLAND

The Reception of Lamennais's Religious Ideas in England in the Nineteenth Century

by
W. G. ROE

OXFORD UNIVERSITY PRESS
1966

Oxford University Press, Ely House, London W.1

GLASGOW NEW YORK TORONTO MELBOURNE WELLINGTON
CAPE TOWN SALISBURY IBADAN NAIROBI LUSAKA ADDIS ABABA
BOMBAY CALCUTTA MADRAS KARACHI LAHORE DACCA
KUALA LUMPUR HONG KONG

PRINTED IN GREAT BRITAIN AT
THE UNIVERSITY PRESS
ABERDEEN

PREFACE

To be pedantically accurate, perhaps this study should be entitled *England and Lamennais*. For it is concerned less with the part played in Lamennais's life by England and the English than with the effect of Lamennais's ideas and example in England.

It is a study not of the influence of a set of persuasive and coherent ideas upon the thought of another nation, but rather of English reactions to several of the key themes of nineteenth-century thought as they were expressed by one man. The subtitle speaks of the 'reception' of Lamennais's religious ideas in England rather than of their 'influence'; for influence is difficult to prove, and not always illuminating, even when it is proved. I have aimed at showing the relation between, on the one hand, Lamennais's thought and his character (which in many ways was more significant to Englishmen than his thought) and, on the other, the many different movements in nineteenth-century England and the personalities who dominated them.

The subtitle then refers to Lamennais's 'religious' thought. Much that he wrote was political and moral in intent. What separates him from many politicians and moralists of his day and of ours is his persistence in treating everything as a religious issue and with religious fervour. He was not a trained theologian, and no attempt is made in this study to enter into the byways of theological speculation. He had, however, the poet's eye for the ideal, and this made him one of the most 'religious' spirits of his age.

The words 'England' and 'English' are almost as unmanageable as the word 'Catholic'. Scots and Irishmen abound in the following pages, but only where they operated mainly in England or their work took a natural place in the pattern of contemporary English culture have they been included. Thus the Irish-born Sir Charles MacCarthy appears, although O'Connell does not. Much could be written of the political affinities between those who struggled for emancipation in Ireland and continental liberal Catholics, but it would not fall within the scope of this essay.

My gratitude is due to many librarians, archivists and owners of unpublished papers, who helped by telling me where material about Lamennais was *not*. I am particularly grateful also to the following: to Lady Crewe and the Master and Fellows of Trinity College, Cambridge, for permission to use the papers of Lord Houghton and Sir Charles MacCarthy; to the librarian of the Cambridge University Library for access to the Acton papers and to Lord Acton's library; to Mrs. Sheed (Maisie Ward) and Mr. N. A. Middleton for access to Wilfrid Ward's papers; to His Eminence the Cardinal Archbishop of Westminster for permission to quote from the archives of the Archdiocese; to Father C. Stephen Dessain for permission to quote from letters in the archives of the Oratory, Birmingham, and to Dr. Louis Allen who first drew my attention to these letters; to Mr. A. Coombe Tennant for permission to quote extracts from the papers of Gertrude Tennant; to Professor J. Seznec and Dr. A. R. Vidler for much helpful criticism and comment; to the Committee for Advanced Studies, without whom the publication of books in this series would be impossible; to the Monographs Committee of the Board of the Faculty of Modern Languages at Oxford, and in particular to Mr. A. D. Crow, Professor T. B. W. Reid, and Dr. R. A. Sayce, who read typescript and proofs with a sharp eye and made many valuable suggestions. Finally, I owe a special debt to Dr. Enid Starkie, who supervised my work before it was presented as a doctoral thesis and who has been unsparing with help and encouragement.

W. G. R.

CONTENTS

ABBREVIATIONS

A.A.	*Articles de L'Avenir*, 7 vols., Louvain, 1831-2
Affaires	Lamennais, *Affaires de Rome*, 1836-7
Boutard	C. Boutard, *Lamennais: sa vie et ses doctrines*, 3 vols., Paris, 1905-13
Cottu	ed. Comte d'Haussonville, *Le Prêtre et l'ami, lettres inédites de Lamennais à la Baronne Cottu 1818–1854*, Paris, 1910
Des progrès	Lamennais, *Des progrès de la révolution et de la guerre contre l'église*, 1829
Essai	Lamennais, *Essai sur l'indifférence en matière de religion*, 1817–23
Essai d'un système	Lamennais, *Essai d'un système de philosophie catholique*, ed. Y. Le Hir, Rennes, 1954
Garnier	Lamennais, *Paroles d'un croyant Le Livre du peuple*, *Une Voix de prison*, *Du passé et de l'avenir du peuple*, *De l'esclavage moderne*, and *Mélanges*, Paris, n.d.
L. à Bruté	ed. H. de Courcy, *Lettres inédites de J.-M. et F. de la Mennais adressées à Mgr. Bruté*, Nantes, 1862
L. à M.	ed. E. Forgues, *Lettres inédites de Lamennais à Montalembert*, Paris, 1898
M. à L.	ed. G. Goyau and P. de Lallemand, *Lettres de Montalembert à La Mennais*, Paris, 1932
Mozley	ed. A. Mozley, *Letters and Correspondence of J. H. Newman*, 2 vols., London, 1891
O.C.	Lamennais, *Œeuvres complètes*, 12 vols., Paris, 1836–7
O.I.	ed. A. Blaize, *Œeuvres inédites de F. Lamennais*, 2 vols., Paris, 1866
O.P.	ed. E. D. Forgues, *Lamennais: Œeuvres posthumes*, Paris, 1859
Paroles	Lamennais, *Paroles d'un croyant*, 1834
Portefeuille	ed. G. Goyau, *Le Portefeuille de Lamennais*, Paris, 1930
Tradition	Lamennais, *Tradition de l'église sur l'institution des évêques*, 1814
Vidler	A. R. Vidler, *Prophecy and Papacy*, London, 1954

I

LAMENNAIS AND HIS TIMES

ALTHOUGH Lamennais was an outstanding figure in the politics, literature, and religion of the nineteenth century, he is not now well known in England. By turns a monarchist, an ultramontane, a liberal Catholic, a religious democrat, and a messianic revolutionary, he was a restless visionary who contributed something to many quite different streams of nineteenth-century thought, but who never remained content with any one of them.

These remarkable changes of outlook have made his influence difficult to assess: no sooner had he sown the seeds of that ultramontanism which was later to triumph in the decrees of the first Vatican Council, than he was advocating that independence of the spiritual from the secular power which in many countries is only now coming to be accepted as desirable; and no sooner had those ideas in their turn obtained powerful support, than he was addressing himself in vague and apocalyptic terms to the general mass of the people. No one followed him through all the phases of his turbulent life. His course changed so frequently and so unmistakably that it would have been difficult to do so with sincerity. Yet there was no lack of sincerity in him. Some have attributed his development to pride and self-seeking[1] (others said the same of Newman a few years later). But the underlying consistency of his life, his care for the welfare of society and his willingness to suffer loneliness, hatred, and imprisonment, give the lie to that judgement.

This combination of politics, poetry, and religion, and of different approaches to religion, within one personality, makes him more representative of the many conflicting forces of his century than any other single person. 'In him', wrote W. S. Lilly, 'we see more fully and clearly than in anyone else, the working of the spiritual forces of his times: more fully and clearly than

[1] See J. C. Versluys, *Essai sur le caractère de Lamennais*, Paris-Amsterdam, 1929, pp. 151–4.

in De Maistre, or Bonald, or Chateaubriand, or Comte—all true representatives and exponents of the *Zeitgeist*.'[1]

As a representative of the spirit of his times Lamennais was known, both personally and by his work, to a great variety of people in England in the last century. To study the extent of this contact not only throws some light on the value and appeal of Lamennais's own thought; it also shows that widely differing and apparently unconnected ideas associated with the Oxford movement, the growth of English Roman Catholicism, and popular radicalism were not totally isolated phenomena. At bottom they were all concerned with the nature of authority, the nature of belief, and the destiny of man. And of all the influential figures in nineteenth-century France, it was Lamennais who pursued these questions the most relentlessly.

Félicité Robert de la Mennais was born in 1782.[2] Since his mother died when he was five and his father (who survived until 1828) was preoccupied with business affairs, his education was largely undertaken by his uncle, M. des Saudrais, who taught him by the simple method of letting him read what he liked. This combination of a lack of parental love and an undisciplined education had a great effect on his emotional and intellectual outlook in later years. He was not pressed to take a job. He had no need to earn money. He spent the years of his youth in reading, in co-operating in his uncle's literary projects, and in groping his individual way towards the faith of a Christian. In this he was helped by his elder brother, Jean, who was destined for the priesthood. Gradually, after extensive study, it became clear to the two brothers that their vocation was to invigorate the Church, which had recently concluded a concordat with the State, and to stiffen its theological backbone by passing on some of their laboriously acquired learning.

This they did in two books, *Réflexions sur l'état de l'église en France pendant le xviiie siècle, et sur la situation actuelle* (1809)

[1] W. S. Lilly, *Studies in Religion and Literature*, London, 1904, p. 155.

[2] Biographical details of the first part of Lamennais's life may be checked from A. R. Vidler's *Prophecy and Papacy*, London, 1954, which supersedes and corrects earlier biographies. The later part of his life has not been adequately dealt with. Both Duine (*La Mennais: sa vie, ses idées, ses ouvrages*, 1922) and Boutard (*Lamennais: sa vie et ses doctrines*, 3 vols, 1905–13), although sympathetic and fair, were ecclesiastics more interested in his life before 1834 than in the time he spent outside the Church.

and *Tradition de l'église sur l'institution des évêques* (1814). Lamennais did not include *Tradition* in his *Œeuvres complètes*, which is probably an indication that he regarded it as quite as much his brother's work as his own. In any case, it dealt with a domestic problem of little interest in the England of the time.[1] *Réflexions* on the other hand clearly bore the stamp of his style and was of sufficient general interest to be sold in England.[2] Not that it could have been comfortable reading. England, 'cette éternelle ennemie de la France',[3] was denounced for its Protestantism; the Reformation was condemned for giving the people the idea that sovereignty was in their hands, and for making the individual judge of his own faith.[4] But these comments were incidental to an attempt to jerk a Church, persecuted by the revolution and manipulated by Napoleon, back to life, and to arouse the country from its materialism and apathy about religion. To this end Lamennais emphasized the need for more efficient ecclesiastical organization and greater freedom for the Church in the running of her affairs.[5] He made many practical suggestions for retreats and Church conferences, for measures to combat the ignorance of the clergy, for parish communities, and for means of stimulating the flow of recruits for the priesthood. He pleaded for a more thorough training of priests. He stressed the importance of missions and the need for more outward expression of religion.[6]

Not only did the *Réflexions* sound the authentic note of a prophet calling the Church to renewal (much of it might have been written today), but it contained the germ of many of the ideas which later appeared in the *Essai sur l'indifférence*: the emphasis on the glory and continuity of the Church, the reasoned hatred of Protestantism, a hatred which lasted all Lamennais's life, even when he himself was outside the Roman communion, and the opposition to all forms of religious liberalism and democracy.

[1] So afraid was Lamennais that the *Tradition* would be censored that he suggested to Jean that the printing (already started in Paris) should be transferred to London (*O.I.* i, p. 162—26 July 1814). When this was shown to be impossible he persisted in a desire that the place of printing should appear on the title-page as London (*O.I.* i, p. 167). When it finally appeared in August 1814 it claimed as its place of origin, by way of compromise, Liége.

[2] It cost 10*s*. (*Blackwood's Magazine*, September 1819, pp. 745 f.).

[3] *O.C.* vi, p. 47.

[4] ibid., p. 6.

[5] ibid., p. 88.

[6] ibid., p. 110.

These works, *Réflexions* and the *Tradition*, achieved some fame for the brothers in France, although they did not sell sufficiently well to provide a living. So Félicité, having discovered his talent for writing, turned to journalism. This not only paid but also provided a means of broadcasting his ideas. He remained an indefatigable journalist to the end of his life. Throughout all the stages of his career he was never for very long without a newspaper or magazine as a forum for his ideas. He started by writing in the moderate Gallican *L'Ami de la religion et du roi* articles which were translated and published in England. In 1819 he collaborated with Chateaubriand in the *Conservateur*, the mouthpiece of the Ultras. The next year he was concerned with the *Défenseur* of Genoude and Bonald. For some time the Ultra *Drapeau blanc* had contributions from his pen. These were followed by the *Mémorial catholique*, the organ of ultramontane opinions, and then by the *Avenir*, one of the most influential Catholic papers of nineteenth-century France. Of the many papers he used during the latter part of his life we need only mention *Le Monde*, of which he was the editor for a time, *Le Peuple constituant*, which brought him great fame in 1848, and *La Réforme*, which he edited in 1849. Much of Lamennais's reputation was based upon his ability as a journalist, and the degree of publicity which he received from those media has perhaps not been taken sufficiently into account when his influence has been analysed.

He was also a provocative publisher of pamphlets. One which he wrote in 1814 about the University may have been a contributory factor in his decision to flee to England in 1815. The story of his brief stay in Kensington is told in greater detail later.[1] Its principal outcome was that, as a result of his contact with the abbé Carron in London, he sought ordination. This was accorded him remarkably swiftly. Having left London in November 1815, he was already a sub-deacon by the end of December. He was ordained priest at Vannes on 9th March 1816, barely four months after his return to France.

The next milestone in his life was the publication of the *Essai sur l'indifférence en matière de religion* (1817–23), with which 'Lamennais steps straight into the centre of the stage of French church history'.[2] The *Essai* was written with great clarity and style, and is now a classic in the history of apologetics, lauded but

[1] See below, pp. 60 ff.

[2] Vidler, p. 68.

largely unread. In it Lamennais started to come to grips with the philosophy of his time, and his arguments had great repercussions within his own communion.[1]

The first volume, published in 1817, was written with all the passion of Lamennais's new-found commitment to the faith. It was intended to be, and in this it succeeded, a frontal attack upon the rationalism of contemporary philosophy and theology. It was a brilliant attempt to reassert the claims of religion, not merely as something which merited the consideration of intelligent men, but as the very mainspring of society. In it Lamennais castigated as indifferentists those who believed that they could stand apart from the faith which they professed: the sceptics who maintained that religion was a political institution necessary for the preservation of good order among the people[2]; the Deists, who, while admitting the necessity of religion for all, refused to commit themselves to anything more definite than natural religion[3]; and the Protestants (among whom he included most Englishmen), who made themselves so far independent of the faith as to be able to choose for themselves which dogmas to accept and which to reject.[4] There is only one faith, he proclaimed, and that faith is essential to the life of every individual and even to the life of society; lack of it is injurious even to God himself.[5] Such fervent theology had not been written since the seventeenth century. It had the authentic ring of prophecy. No wonder the second volume was eagerly awaited.

When it finally appeared, however, in July 1820, it had a mixed reception. Lamennais was always much better at attack than defence, and now that he had embarked upon an exposition of his positive ideas, he had less success. He started by examining the concept of certitude. Committed as he was to the claim that religion was the very principle of society, that it was impossible to stand apart from it or to treat it as an object, he was obliged to find a means by which man could be certain that this was so. This means he found not in the the powers of human reasoning, which he distrusted, not in human feeling, but in the 'consentement commun', the 'sensus communis' of all peoples at all times.[6] With this weapon in his hand he proved the existence of God and

[1] C. Maréchal, *La Mennais: La dispute de l'Essai sur l'indifférence*, Paris, 1925.

[2] *Essai*, i, chs. 2 and 3.

[3] ibid., chs. 4 and 5.

[4] ibid., chs. 6 and 7.

[5] ibid., ch. 12.

[6] *Essai*, ii, ch. 13.

of one true religion which was absolutely necessary to salvation. But in order to discern where this one true religion was to be found and what its conditions were, something more than the 'sensus communis' was necessary. It was possible for Lamennais to point to the common consent of mankind to the existence of God, and even to the existence of one true religion, but it was not possible for him to press the argument any further upon that line. He then had to show, by elaborate demonstrations of the fallibility of man's reasoning powers and feelings, that man's principal function lay not in what he himself could decide or achieve (the Renaissance ideal so abhorrent to Lamennais), but in his ability to obey, to submit to authority. And in submitting to authority, said Lamennais, he would find his true self and discern the true religion: 'la vie éternelle n'est qu'une éternelle obéissance.'[1] The second volume ends by pointing to the Roman Catholic Church as the spiritual society which claimed that very authority, and the teachings of which could be known, by common consent, to be certainly true.

These two themes of the 'sensus communis' and authority were elaborated in volumes 3 and 4 (1823), in which it was shown by a superabundance of evidence that the marks of the true religion attested by the consent of all were those very marks which distinguished the Roman Catholic Church. Since this Church claimed to exercise the authority of God, and since obedience to the laws of God was the foundation of all society, earthly and divine, then it was evident that submission to the Church of Rome was the only possible course open to men and societies of good will.

By this time Lamennais's fame was prodigious. He was held in such esteem by Pope Leo XII that it was later widely believed that the Pope had made him a Cardinal *in petto*.[2] Yet he remained a man of very simple habits, frequently in financial difficulties, and, what is often forgotten, willing to give generously of his time to those who came to him for spiritual counsel, and to the many people with whom he was in correspondence. He translated Thomas à Kempis's *De Imitatione Christi*, and derived some income from its proceeds for the rest of his life.

He was not only a religious and philosophical figure, but also a political one. His works reflect an increasing prophetic appreciation of the rise of democratic power and an attempt to harness it

[1] *Essai*, ii, ch. 20, p. 286. [2] See below, pp. 127 ff.

to the Church. *De la religion considérée dans ses rapports avec l'ordre politique et civil* was published in 1825 and 1826, when he was still a monarchist because monarchy was stable and orderly. He abhorred democracy because it was changeable and could in time destroy Christianity.[1] Society, he wrote, was an organism which could have moral standards. It could be Christian or not, as it chose.[2] French society of 1825 was, according to him, atheist, and he was particularly concerned that the malady of atheism was spreading from political and civil life into the life of the family.[3]

The reason for this state of affairs was the gradual submission of the Church to the tyrannical demands of the State, its steady decline to the status of a government department, and its slow assumption of the character of a State Church, something which Lamennais regarded as a contradiction in terms.[4] Against all these dangers Lamennais erected a bulwark, the Pope. This was the logical conclusion of his argument in the *Essai*. Without the Pope there could be no Church, without the Church no Christianity, without Christianity no religion, and without religion there could be no society.[5]

De la religion was the watershed between Lamennais's earliest views and his increasingly uncompromising ultramontanism. On the one hand, he still held by the monarchy, since the monarchy stood for stability and order,[6] but at the same time he claimed that if the King ceased to be the representative of the power of God in the State and started to wield power as if it were his own, then the people had a right to overthrow him.[7] On the other hand, we see the Pope assuming much more importance in Lamennais's thought.[8]

In *De la religion* he had not resolved the difficulty of knowing how far allegiance was due to the Pope and how far to the King. He was aware of a third and menacing force, the people, which he could only push aside for the time being. That it troubled him was evident from the conclusion, where he indulged some of his apocalyptic fancies and envisaged disorders and disasters which could only end either in complete destruction or in the rise of a new society founded on the Church.[9]

[1] *O.C.* vii, pp. 18 f.
[2] ibid., ch. 2.
[3] ibid., ch. 3.
[4] ibid., chs. 4, 7, and 8.
[5] ibid., ch. 6.
[6] ibid., pp. 18 f.
[7] ibid., pp. 169 f.
[8] ibid., especially pp. 232 ff.
[9] ibid., p. 299.

De la religion marked Lamennais's last attempt to cling to monarchy as a workable system of society. It based the power of the Pope, much more firmly than that of the King, on authority, and did no more than note the rising tide of democracy.

Des progrès de la révolution et de la guerre contre l'église (1829) tipped the balance in favour of the Pope and took the power of the people, which by this time was rising everywhere, much more into account. The doctrine of the 'sensus communis' was having its effect upon Lamennais. Everywhere he could see Roman Catholic countries ready to rise in revolt against their kings. Kings, he reluctantly agreed, stood for tyranny and oppression, while the revolutionaries stood for democracy and freedom. From his position in the Church he could see two, equally disastrous, ways of dealing with the situation. The first was liberalism, the sovereignty of the individual reason, which excluded all superior authority and led to anarchy and atheism (these two in Lamennais's mind amounting to the same thing). The second was Gallicanism, the ecclesiastical version of reaction, submission to the monarch, be he heretic or no, 'un esclavage profond, inévitable, éternel'.[1] In this there was nothing really new. Lamennais had always hated political liberalism, just as he had always hated Gallicanism. The new formulation of his beliefs was the result of a clearer realization of the implications of both ways of thought in the present situation. The most urgent need was a means of knowing the divine will. An infallible Pope was the only solution to the evils of the day. The discouragement of religion on the one side by political liberals whose principles led them to atheism, and on the other side by Gallicans who were anxious to subject the Church to the State, was creating a situation which was deteriorating and could be put right only be giving the Church its freedom. This was the new development in Lamennais's politico-ecclesiastical thought. A situation had arisen similar in many ways to that in England, where it was no longer possible to identify the Church with the State. Some dividing line had to be drawn between the two, and in order to do this more easily Lamennais proposed measures for the strengthening of the Church. Priests should isolate themselves from an atheistic society[2]; there should be a revival of the study and teaching of sound theology[3]; there should

[1] *O.C.* ix, p. 39.
[2] ibid., p. 188: 'Soyez évêques, soyez prêtres, et rien de plus.'
[3] ibid., pp. 190–4.

be a closer connection between the clergy and the Pope,[1] to whom the clergy should look more steadfastly for guidance[2]; above all the Church should have liberty of teaching, discipline, and practice.[3]

This conclusion prepared the way for the complete separation of Church and State to be fought for in the *Avenir*. But here the emphasis was slightly different. Lamennais was calling on the clergy to rely entirely on their priestly office to combat the evils of the world, and not to try to use the methods of the civil power. Towards the end of 1828 a new religious community, the Congrégation de St. Pierre, was founded with these aims in view. Lamennais was its Superior, and for many years it was a powerful means of spreading the ultramontanism of 1829 and 1830. By the time of the *Avenir* it became clear to him that the only way for the Church to fulfil its mission was for it to be completely free of the State.

Until now very little has been said about democracy. In the *Essai* Lamennais had been opposed to it because he believed that it enthroned the will and the passions of the individual.[4] But now a subtle change had taken place. In *Des progrès* Lamennais observed that those countries which were ready to revolt were all Roman Catholic.[5] The Protestant countries were less eager. By his former principles this should have proved that the Protestants alone were true Christians. But the principle of the 'sensus communis' of the faithful pointed him steadily to the conclusion that the political situation was wrong and that the people were right.[6]

The 1830 revolution confirmed Lamennais in his belief that the regeneration of society could not be entrusted to monarchies. With the departure of the monarchy went, in his mind, all connection of the Church with the State. He could not ignore the fact that the forces of revolution were in general opposed to the Church.[7] He was in sympathy with their desire for liberty, and yet, in accordance with the principles of the *Essai*, he realized

[1] *O.C.* ix, pp. 181 f.
[2] ibid., p. 182.
[3] ibid., p. 183.
[4] *Essai*, i, ch. 10, pp. 345 f.
[5] *O.C.* ix, p. 22.
[6] ibid., pp. 24 f.
[7] F. Isambert in 'L'attitude religieuse des ouvriers français au milieu du xixe siècle' (*Archives de sociologie des religions*, iii, No. 6, July-December 1958, pp. 7–35) calls in question traditional interpretations of the attitude of the proletariat to the Church in 1830 and 1848. As a generalization, however (and Lamennais dealt in generalizations), the traditional interpretation holds.

that the revolution would destroy one form of order without being able to replace it. The only principle of order which he knew was religion, by which he meant Catholicism.

Accordingly he founded the daily newspaper *l'Avenir*, which had as its subtitle 'Dieu et la Liberté'. Around him he had gathered a band of young and enthusiastic men with similar, though not identical, aims.[1] Among them were Montalembert, Lacordaire, and Maurice de Guérin. The influence of their thought, which in these months of 1830 and 1831 was dominated by their master's personality, spread throughout Catholic Europe.

Lamennais summarized the doctrines of the *Avenir* in an article which appeared on 7th December 1830.[2]

The first doctrine was the unity of the Church. This was Lamennais's old principle that there was no such thing as a national Church, that the Church was one and indivisible. From this it followed that complete submission was owed to the Pope, for without the Pope there could be no Church. A corollary of this was the infallibility of the Pope, which Lamennais here declared uncompromisingly. The *Avenir* recognized the French government of the time, with all the proper reservations, and demanded of it that it should grant to the French people liberty of conscience, religion, teaching, the press, and association. It also demanded that Church and State should be separated absolutely.[3]

In all this could be seen the one constant element in all Lamennais's thought: the desire for order in society and the belief that order could be obtained only by the realization of man's dependence on God. In the revolutionary State he saw a danger to the principles of religion, and although his concern was for society as a whole, a fact which had made him cling to the connection between Church and State until only a short time before, he realized that religion in France would drown in the revolutionary flood if it were not severed from the State. 'Catholiques, comprenons-le bien, nous avons à sauver notre foi, et nous la sauverons par la liberté.'[4]

[1] See P. Stearns on the heterogeneous elements in the *Avenir*, *American Historical Review*, July 1960, pp. 837–47.

[2] *Articles de l'Avenir*, Louvain, 1831–2, i, pp. 382–9 (*O.C.* x, pp. 196–205).

[3] *A.A.* i, pp. 23–30 (*O.C.* x, pp. 149–59), 'De la séparation de l'église et de l'état' (18 October 1830).

[4] *O.C.* x, pp. 154 f.

In coming to this conclusion Lamennais had to abandon many of his former ideas. Liberty of conscience had to be permitted if the true religion was to be preserved. This meant that those dissenters against whom Lamennais had directed so much of his energy had also to be allowed freedom of conscience—although the *Avenir* did not stress this aspect of the problem.[1]

Freedom of education was a demand which sprang naturally from the separation of Church and State.[2] This, too, had wide implications. It meant acquiescing in the atheism of public educational institutions, so much attacked in the past, while obtaining for Catholics the liberty to educate their children as they wished.

To carry out this revolutionary policy Lamennais took several practical steps. He called upon the priests to give up their State salaries in order to assert their independence.[3] He was one of the founder members and the chairman of the 'Agence Générale pour la défense de la liberté religieuse', an organization which fought against any infringements of the rights of the Church.[4] The *Agence* published details of all such cases in the *Avenir* and provided funds for legal action where necessary. The principle of liberty of education was emphasized by an attempt to open a private school with Montalembert and Lacordaire as its teachers. The ensuing prosecution gave the *Agence* unprecedented publicity.[5]

Such doctrines were inflammatory. They had to be expressed in the form of repeated calls for liberty. They also necessitated detailed reporting of the condition of Catholics in other countries. The *Avenir* supported the cause of the Belgian and Polish Catholics and raised a fund for the relief of Roman Catholics in Ireland.[6]

[1] *O.C.* x, p. 321 (28 June 1831), *A.A.*, v, p. 166.

[2] Lacordaire, 'De la liberté de l'enseignement' (*A.A.* i, pp. 14–18, 31–34, 112–16). Lamennais's view is expressed briefly on 27 January 1831 (*O.C.* x, p. 238; *A.A.* ii, p. 325).

[3] *O.C.* x, pp. 155 f. (18 October 1830), *A.A.* i, pp. 28 f.; also 'De la suppression du budget du clergé' (*A.A.* i, pp. 124–7, 155–8, 179–83, 197–200) and 'Le clergé doit-il renoncer à sa dotation? Le peut-il?' (*A.A.* i, pp. 250–4).

[4] *A.A.* i, pp. 455–8 (18 December 1830).

[5] Vidler, p. 177 and the references he cites.

[6] On 9 June 1831 the *Avenir* received letters of support from two Irish priests. On the 13th it announced the opening of a fund to be sent to the Lord Mayor of Dublin's distress fund. In three months over 70,000 fr. were raised. Several letters from Irish priests and bishops were printed.

There was only one way of reconciling Lamennais's newly-defined sympathy with the people and their desire for political liberty with his old conviction that only in religion could men find that fixity and order necessary to society. That way was the union of all Catholics under the Pope. It was in the *Avenir* that Lamennais's ultramontanism reached its peak:

La civilisation chrétienne, à l'étroit dans ses anciennes limites, presse sur tous les points la barbarie qui cède et recule devant elle. Bientôt une parole puissante et calme prononcée par un vieillard, dans la Cité-Reine, au pied de la croix, donnera le signal, que le monde attend, de la dernière régénération. Pénétrés d'un esprit nouveau, conduits à la science par la foi, à la liberté par l'ordre, les peuples ouvriront les yeux et se reconnaîtront pour frères, parce qu'ils auront un Père commun, et fatigués de leurs longues discordes, ils se reposeront aux pieds de ce Père, qui n'étend la main que pour protéger, et n'ouvre la bouche que pour bénir.[1]

Opposition to these views was so great that Lamennais and his companions decided to appeal to Rome. The story of that journey of the 'pélerins de Dieu et de la liberté' has often been told and bears upon it the stamp of all the great crises of religious history.[2] Their journey was surrounded by intrigue: Metternich was kept fully informed of their movements, and the ambassadors of the principal European countries reported home to their governments. But the pilgrims were received coldly. Gregory XVI was on the edge of a volcano. If he approved of their programme he would be accused by all the established rulers of reactionary Europe of fomenting rebellion. If he openly condemned them he would be undermining his own power.

Gregory's first step was, in 1832, by the publication of his encyclical *Mirari vos*, to condemn the doctrines of the *Avenir* without actually naming their author, but at the same time to approve that general aim for which Lamennais had striven earlier in his life, the elimination of indifferentism in religion.

On 11 November appeared a letter signed by nine Irish Roman Catholic bishops, a copy of a letter to the *Dublin Evening Post* (1 November). According to the French translation, this had called the *Avenir* a 'journal véritablement chrétien' (*A.A.* vii, p. 92).

[1] *A.A.* i, p. 479 (22 December 1830).

[2] See how it dominates Mrs. Wilfrid Ward's novel *Out of Due Time*, below, pp. 149 f.

This condemnation produced a tense period in Lamennais's life, which has been sensitively studied by M. Harispe[1] and which was brought to an end by the sensational publication of *Paroles d'un croyant* in 1834.

Unlike its predecessors, this work did not rely simply upon its grace of style and cogency of argument to convey its ideas. It was a poem couched in biblical language and arranged in chapters and verses suggestive of the Bible. It began with the invocation of the Holy Trinity and continued:

2. Gloire à Dieu dans les hauteurs des cieux, et paix sur la terre aux hommes de bonne volonté.
3. Que celui qui a des oreilles entende; que celui qui a des yeux les ouvre et regarde: car les temps approchent.
4. Le Père a engendré son Fils, sa Parole, son Verbe, et le Verbe s'est fait chair, et il a habité parmi nous; il est venu dans le monde, et le monde ne l'a point connu.
5. Le Fils a promis d'envoyer l'Esprit consolateur, l'Esprit qui procède du Père et de lui, et qui est leur amour mutuel; il viendra, et renouvellera la face de la terre, et ce sera comme une seconde création.[2]

This is not the merely political work which he claimed it was,[3] but a new expression of his religion. It is dominated by his apocalyptic visions of the reign of peace and goodness which will follow the return of the Messiah. It is an attempt to translate the atmosphere of the early years of the Church into the political situation existing eighteen centuries later. Not only is its style totally different from all Lamennais's previous work but the thoughts in it burst the limits which had hitherto confined them.

With the *Paroles* Lamennais gave up the position he had formerly held. He no longer viewed humanity from the standpoint of formal religion, but showed his concern for humanity itself and for the sufferings of the people.[4] From the theological point of view this had the result that, whereas in his earlier

[1] P. Harispe, *Lamennais: drame de sa vie sacerdotale*, Paris, 1924.

[2] *Paroles d'un croyant*, ed. Y. Le Hir, Paris, 1949, p. 79.

[3] On 29 April 1834 Lamennais wrote to Mgr de Quélen: 'Je n'écrirai donc désormais, ainsi que je l'ai déclaré, que sur des sujets de philosophie, de science et de politique. Le petit ouvrage dont on vous a parlé est de ce dernier genre' (*O.C.* xii, p. 170).

[4] His relations with the Church remained ambiguous for some time: 'from his point of view there was no one moment when he ceased to be a catholic' (Vidler, p. 257 and references).

writing he had been preoccupied with the doctrine of the Church, in the *Paroles* and in the books which follow he turns to the doctrines of the trinity, the atonement, and the incarnation. It is significant that Christ takes a more prominent place in his theology than before. The *Essai* contained very little Christology—a grave defect in a work of apologetic for Christianity.[1] The *Paroles*, however, would be incomprehensible without Him.[2] The *Avenir* was the last of Lamennais's many attempts to reform society by strengthening the unifying influence of institutional religion. The *Paroles* is a new departure.

Lamennais's new view was that society was to reform itself, not by submitting to the influence of a liberated Church, but by rooting out sin in mankind. The emphasis moved from discipline to conscience. The restraints imposed by the papal obedience were now swept away, and the absolute freedom of conscience claimed originally for Catholics was now extended to all men. In the same way, Lamennais's sympathy for the oppressed stretched out beyond those who had been fighting mainly for religious liberty, the Irish, Belgians, and Poles, to all oppressed peoples, including the English. William IV took his place among the European tyrants. The misery which Lamennais described was not now the misery of those who could not worship God as they wished, but the misery of those who were starving.[3]

It would, however, be quite wrong to say that at this critical point in his development Lamennais had abandoned the firm outlines of Catholic doctrine in favour of the vague visions of a sentimentalist. On the contrary, the *Paroles*, at which many pious hands were raised in horror, contained much Catholic teaching, and the point of view from which it saw the world was still recognizably Catholic. The hope which Lamennais advocated was still the Christian hope. The happiness he promised was neither material prosperity nor vague visions of spiritual perfection: it was the vision of Christ exalted at the right hand of God.[4]

[1] One chapter of the *Essai* (iv, 35) is devoted to Christology. It reads well by itself, but it has little integral connection with the argument.

[2] This is not to claim that Lamennais was more religious or orthodox in later years. Lamennais, like St. Paul, dealt with those subjects he believed to be most important at the time and subject to misunderstanding. The lack of a sound Christology was evident only from later events.

[3] *Paroles*, XXXIII, 18.

[4] *Paroles*, II, 28, XXIII, 40 and XLII, 18.

He still had a profoundly trinitarian view of the Godhead[1] (and he continued to express himself in trinitarian terms to the end of his life, despite his changed beliefs about the nature of God). The doctrines of creation,[2] of evil,[3] and of the atonement[4] are all explicitly stated. There are even moving examples of devotion to the Blessed Virgin Mary.[5] His most significant departures from Catholic teaching occur in his treatment of the Church. Of the doctrine of the Church or of the priesthood he makes no mention, but individual Popes and priests are bitterly depicted as weapons of Satan.[6]

Whether the *Paroles* was 'orthodox' or not is difficult to say. It was certainly more apocalyptic than contemporary theology was wont to be, a characteristic which it shared with many parts of the New Testament. It might easily have been written by a zealous visionary sympathetic with the sufferings of the people. Equally it might have been written by a Deist clothing his imaginings in Christian terms. The most that can be said is that there was little in it which was contrary to orthodox belief, and much which would have given hope to the ordinary Christian of the day.

Although at the time the *Paroles* was found to be inflammatory in the extreme, the 'practical' religion advocated in it was in striking contrast to the passions which it actually aroused. Lamennais exhorted his readers to patience, courage, confidence in God, prayer, and love.[7] He proclaimed peace and tolerance and hatred of sin.[8] Although he allowed resistance when it was necessary to overcome evil,[9] he never claimed rights without reminding his

[1] See especially *Paroles*, XI and XLII.

[2] e.g. *Paroles*, XII, 14, and XVIII, 7–9.

[3] He distinguishes three sources of evil: the Devil (XXXIV, 1), rebellious man (III and VIII, 2–3), and the conditions produced by man's rebellion (IX). This emphasis upon man's responsibility for his rebellion and even for the wickedness of the tyrant is more evident here than in later works: 'Voulez-vous travailler à détruire la pauvreté, travaillez à détruire le péché, en vous premièrement, puis dans les autres, et la servitude dans la société' (IX, 12).

[4] *Paroles*, V, 5–7, X, 1–3, XIII, 12–14, XX, 13, XXIII, 40.

[5] *Paroles*, II, 16 and XXV, 19–22.

[6] Popes Alexander VI: *Paroles*, XXX, 20–24; and Gregory XVI: XXXIII, 53–58; priests: XIII, 39–42.

[7] *Paroles*, XVII and XXXVIII, 1; VI, 16 and XXI; XVII and XXV; XVIII; IV, 1–4 and XV, 1–2.

[8] *Paroles*, XVI; XII, 13; IX, 12.

[9] *Paroles*, II; IV, 9; VI, 14–15.

readers of the corresponding duties.[1] It is quite understandable that opinions about the *Paroles*, in both England and France, should have been so much divided.

From this religious view of life flow certain social principles, which from this time onwards become more clearly defined in Lamennais's mind, although they never achieved the tidiness of a 'system'.

Lamennais preferred to rearrange the slogan of the Revolution to read: 'Égalité, Liberté, Fraternité.'[2] For him, equality was a fact to be recognized, not a goal to be achieved: 'In the city of God all are equal; none has the pre-eminence, for there justice alone reigns with love.'[3] By taking a theological view of equality and refusing to exhort his readers to fight for it Lamennais differed from most of the socialists of his day. From this principle of equality proceeds the practical realization of liberty. Liberty is the theme of the *Paroles* as it was of the *Avenir*.[4] Fraternity, the third abstraction of the revolutionary trinity, is the necessary corollary of liberty. There can be no rights without duties. Liberty is a right and love is a duty; fraternity is the love of man for his neighbour.

It is not necessary to trace this theme throughout the *Paroles* because it appears in nearly every chapter. It needs only to be pointed out that Lamennais did not regard the principle of love as a vague sentimental idea floating in a utopian system, as some of his contemporaries probably did; for him it was the action of the third person in the Christian Trinity in the universe.[5] Love unites. Hatred divides.[6] Society is sacred. Once we are divided we are lost. This is the same principle (although differently applied) which he had employed in the *Essai*, and which he preserved to the end of his life. It is more extensively analysed in the lectures which he gave to his pupils and disciples at Malestroit, Juilly, and La Chênaie, which were extracts from his *Essai d'un système de philosophie catholique*, which itself eventually became the *Esquisse d'une philosophie*.[7]

[1] e.g. *Paroles*, XIX, 2–3; XXII, 2.
[2] *Du passé et de l'avenir du peuple*, Garnier, p. 262.
[3] *Paroles*, XXXIV, 13.
[4] *Paroles*, XX.
[5] *Paroles*, XLII, 10.
[6] *Paroles*, IV, 5.
[7] See *Essai d'un système de philosophie catholique*, edited by Y. Le Hir, Rennes, 1954.

One final point is important for an understanding of Lamannais's political position. Much of his notoriety sprang from a popular belief that he was a socialist or even a communist in priest's clothing, a belief which seems to be justified by the words from the *Paroles*: 'Dans la cité de Dieu, chacun possède sans crainte ce qui est à lui et ne désire rien de plus, parce que ce qui est à chacun est à tous, et que tous possèdent Dieu qui renferme tous les biens.'[1] Since this verse was capable of an interpretation which Lamennais probably never intended, in the fourth edition he added a chapter which made his position clear.[2] In this he wrote that the poor were those without property. The solution to their problem was not to deprive those who had in order to give to those who had not, but to give to those who were without an opportunity to acquire it. In order to achieve this, either men had to be enabled to acquire property by their labour, or the rich, influenced by the spirit of love, had of their abundance to give to the poor.[3] Poverty and evil were inevitable and only charity would overcome them.[4]

Moderate and commonplace though many of these ideas now seem, they were expressed not in the form of a manifesto, but as a biblical poem. It was this fusion of religion and sympathy for the sufferings of the people, of art and ideas, within the context of the Europe of 1834, which gave the *Paroles* its influence and its electrifying effect.

It was no wonder that from this point onwards Lamennais was closely identified with the people in their struggle for freedom. His connection with the Church was virtually severed. He was never formally excommunicated, and, like Saul of Tarsus, whom he resembled in many ways, he never completely left his past. The rupture with organized Christianity, however, was complete. He was condemned in exceptionally violent terms in the encyclical *Singulari nos* of 25th June 1834. It is almost certain that by that time he had ceased to say Mass.[5] He may, however, have continued to go to Mass until as late as October 1836.[6]

[1] *Paroles*, XXXIV, 14.
[2] This is the present chapter X of the *Paroles*, written on 31 May 1834 (*Paroles*, ed. Le Hir, p. 125).
[3] *Paroles*, XV, 16.
[4] *Paroles*, XXXVI, 41. The ambiguity of 'charité' is deliberate.
[5] Vidler, p. 254.
[6] A. Roussel, *Lamennais d'après des documents inédits*, Rennes, 1893, ii, p. 258.

By this time he had great popularity with the people, in spite of his association with the Church in an anti-clerical age. He was called upon, with Carnot, Pierre Leroux, and others, to act as one of the counsel for the defence of the survivors of the Lyons massacre of 1834, who were accused of republicanism. He accepted the invitation (although, not being a lawyer, he was allowed to play little part in the trial) and later wrote an account of the whole affair under the title *Du procès d'avril et de la république* (1836) which was published by E. D. Forgues in 1856.[1]

Lamennais's next published work was *Affaires de Rome* (1836–7). Much of this is not relevant to a consideration of his religious ideas, since it is mainly an account of the fateful journey to Rome, written soberly and with many passages of great beauty, but it has a peculiar importance for England because it was the means of introducing Lamennais to much of the English thinking public. Through the narrative of the journey shine many comments indicative of Lamennais's current beliefs, which gave rise to Newman's complaint of a certain 'ill flavour'[2] about his doctrine.

In the first place the book, which is not the product of one phase of his thought, gives the uniform impression of impending disaster. In the section entitled 'Des maux de l'église et de la société et des moyens d'y remédier',[3] which was composed from observations made on the journey, he declared that the world was ready to pass from one condition to another; all were agreed that there should be a change, and it was the duty of the Church to be prepared for it.[4] After examining the condition of the Church in Italy, Spain, Portugal, and France, he concluded that the world's disorder could be cured only by the reformation of the Church.[5]

Secondly, and linked with this premonition of disaster, was his repeated demand for progress by the Church and for development in religious ideas. This was vaguely hinted at in those parts of the book which were written the earliest: he demanded that religion should be more closely associated with the people; that the priest should be first 'l'homme de Dieu', and then 'l'homme

[1] *O.P.*, *Mélanges*, pp. 307–438. A later text has been published by L. Scheler under the title *La Liberté trahie*, Paris, 1946.

[2] *British Critic*, October 1837, xxii, p. 283.

[3] *Affaires*, pp. 185–273.

[4] ibid., pp. 188–93.

[5] ibid., pp. 200 ff.

du peuple'[1]; and he warned the Church that if she failed in this task, she would be guilty of providing no counterbalance to a power which would overturn the world.

In the part of *Affaires de Rome*, however, which was written after the *Paroles*,[2] he broke all restraint. He saw only three possible ways of bringing order into the existing state of chaos. The first was unity under the Pope, once proposed but now rejected. The second was unity under kings, similarly rejected. The third was the triumph of the people, which now seemed to him the only workable solution.[3] This decision was typical of Lamennais's all-or-nothing mentality. He remained an authoritarian, for he combined his break with the Papacy with a vigorous condemnation of Protestantism as a 'système bâtard'.[4] The people, and not popes and kings, were now regarded by him as instruments of God's power.

In the *Affaires* he gave the outline of what was virtually a new religion. Christianity, he believed, was a religion of the past. His new religion developed from it. Its first law was the law of progress, and its first precept incessant activity.[5] This alone was true religion because it was based upon the only valid authority, 'la race humaine'.[6] These seeds were later to grow into the astonishing religion which formed the background for all his later works, and which was fully described in the *Esquisse*. These later works, although superficially similar to the *Paroles*, which was still intelligible to Christians, were really quite different. His thoughts were no longer moulded by Catholic dogma but by beliefs which he imagined to be imposed by the authority of the people.

For the next few years Lamennais lived in a succession of ill-heated and obscure rooms, emerging only occasionally to associate with George Sand and other literary and political celebrities. Most of his energy was spent in writing letters and publishing newspaper articles and small aphoristic works within the range of the more intelligent members of the proletariat.

Among these was *Le Livre du peuple* (1837),[7] the first full statement of the new religion, based upon an elevated interpretation of

[1] *Affaires*, p. 196.
[2] ibid., p. 275.
[3] ibid., p. 292.
[4] ibid., p. 302.
[5] ibid., p. 296.
[6] ibid., p. 302.
[7] References are to the Garnier edition of his later works, *Paroles d'un croyant*, *Le Livre du peuple*, *Une Voix de prison*, *Du passé et de l'avenir du peuple*, *De l'esclavage moderne*, and *Mélanges*, Paris, n.d., cited as 'Garnier'.

the formula 'Equality, Liberty, Fraternity'. In it Lamennais taught that the aim of mankind was to construct, by uninterrupted labour, the city of God. Man was perfectible, and union with God would be achieved as a result of man's own striving.[1] But, as before, no right could be claimed without its corresponding duty.[2] Love and forgiveness are the primary virtues in the new society. The sanctity of marriage must be observed. Children must honour father and mother. The liberty and property of all must be held sacred. All thoughts of revenge must be put away.[3] In this connection Lamennais could still write of Christianity as the religion of love, fraternity and equality, of mildness, equity, and humanity.[4]

This state of perfection would be hastened by the application of certain practical measures: excessive dependence upon the rich would be overcome by association[5]; property would be created for those who were without it, not by redistribution, but by the abolition of monopoly and by the future diffusion of capital[6]; punishment would be restorative, not vindictive, for when the law kills it commits murder.[7]

Gone are the firm statements of the Christian hope which characterized the *Paroles*. No longer are the people encouraged to seek the vision of God; now they look forward merely to a 'more perfect existence'.[8] This life is still transitory and miserable, but after it comes rest, true joy, and the certain reward of duty thoroughly finished.

The *Livre du peuple* fixes the connection between Lamennais's new social philosophy, already foreshadowed in the *Paroles*, and the new religion. The remaining popular works are only variations on this theme. A volume of essays reprinted from the *Revue des deux mondes*, *Le Monde* and the *Revue du progrès* under the title of *Politique à l'usage du peuple* (1839) added little except that it showed that Lamennais was still an apocalyptist. He believed that the rise of the people would be violent and awe-inspiring: 'un grand tremblement, comme si la face de Dieu leur apparaissoit'.[9]

[1] Garnier, pp. 109 f.
[2] ibid., pp. 113 f.
[3] ibid., pp. 135 f. and p. 157.
[4] ibid., pp. 155 ff.
[5] ibid., pp. 161 f.
[6] ibid., p. 165.
[7] ibid., p. 169.
[8] ibid., p. 172.
[9] *Politique à l'usage du peuple*, 1839, ii, p. 91.

His next pamphlet, the greatly admired *De l'esclavage moderne* (1839), argued that present inequality was in effect slavery; since the end of all religion was simply to do the will of God, and since the improvement of society was undoubtedly the will of God, then, he claimed, social duties and religious duties were the same.

In the following year (1840) he published his revolutionary little brochure, *Le Pays et le gouvernement*, in which he inveighed against the government and the police. For the people, he wrote, the only escape from slavery was by fighting and by reconstituting society with justice, duty, and right. He demanded immediate reform while it could still be peaceful, in order to avert possible violence.[1] In the last few lines he gave himself over to the familiar apocalyptic vision of the triumph of the people.[2] This pamphlet earned him a year in the prison of Sainte-Pélagie, during which he wrote feverishly and produced *Du passé et de l'avenir du peuple*, *Une Voix de prison*, *Discussions critiques*, and the section, *De la religion* of the *Esquisse d'une philosophie*.

Du passé gives the fullest account yet of Lamennais's new religious position. In it he tries to set Christianity in its historical perspective and to explain his own relationship to it. He sketches the origins of society according to his, by now, familiar principles, illustrating from biblical history the sources of the desire for love, marriage, property, and union with God. He shows how the conception of liberty progresses in Greek and Roman culture, but that it could not develop fully without the aid of Christianity. In his religious scheme Christianity represents a synthesis of all previous religions: the monotheism of the Jews and the polytheism of the pagans are combined in the Christian doctrine of the Trinity. But in making this synthesis Lamennais claims that Christianity made its fatal mistake—and it is here that we see that he has not only broken completely from his former religion, but fabricates false charges against it in the interest of his own later beliefs—Christianity erred in setting itself in opposition to nature and in encouraging excessive spirituality. Christianity, he writes, excludes the religion of nature and therefore is powerless to organize society.[3] Its aim is the restoration of man to a supernatural state. Christianity is separate from the world. This has

[1] *Le Pays et le gouvernement*, Paris, 1840, p. 50.
[2] ibid., p. 52.
[3] Garnier, p. 278.

led to a dualism of Church and State, for the Christian has always been forced to live in two societies.[1]

At the Renaissance this cleavage between Christianity and humanity was deepened. Science developed along its own lines, independent of religion. This led Lamennais to believe that the time had come for a synthesis of the two streams of thought, for a complete dogma or 'science' of God. In spite of his scorn for the faculty of reason, the idea of intelligence always played an important part in his thought: in earlier days the curriculum of the Congrégation de St. Pierre had been based upon the belief that human reason was a reflection of the Intelligence of the Son in the Trinity.[2] In *Du passé* he weaves this old thread into his new pattern by exhorting the human race to seek liberty through the simultaneous development of intelligence and love, the principles he takes to be fundamental to both science and Christianity.[3]

His new relationship with Christianity thus stands clearly revealed. He claims to be the prophet who is helping to bring this synthesis about, and who is enabling society to see that once his principles are recognized, the new religion is inevitable. He concludes that the only possible way for the individual to obtain complete emancipation is by faith,[4] but by a faith made active by the removal of all legal, intellectual, and material hindrances. This faith is not easy to define precisely[5]; but its very imprecision is an indication of the state of Lamennais's religious thought. For him, now, faith is trust in the power of the people to bring about their own emancipation and to be more closely united with God, through the God-manifesting principles of power, intelligence, and love.

Another product of his time in Sainte-Pélagie was *Une Voix de prison*, originally published separately as the last part of *Amschaspands et Darvands*[6] but later issued by itself. It has been

[1] Garnier, pp. 274–6.

[2] See especially *Essai d'un système*, ed. Le Hir, 1954, ch. 5, pp. 24–27.

[3] Garnier, p. 284.

[4] His precise formula, elaborated in later pages, is: 'La Religion, c'est-à-dire la connoissance du dogme ou des lois nécessaires de l'Être absolu et des êtres créés, et la foi au dogme, est une condition indispensable de la réalisation du droit' (Garnier, p. 309).

[5] He speaks vaguely of 'la foi au dogme' (p. 309), 'la foi au droit et au devoir' (p. 311), 'la foi religieuse' (p. 311), 'une foi puissante' (p. 316). He ends 'VOTRE FOI VOUS SAUVERA' (p. 316).

[6] *Amschaspands et Darvands*, Paris, 1843, takes the form of a dialogue between good and evil spirits, derived from Persian mythology. It was

justly pointed out[1] that Lamennais here recovers a little of the biblical inspiration which made the *Paroles* such a success. As in the *Paroles*, visions, allegories, exhortations and lyrical scenes are mingled together, but the note is less strident. There is less talk of equality, liberty, and fraternity and more awareness of the power of God and of the people's duty to Him.

Lamennais's gaze rests not so much on the plight of the poor as on the forces of evil which afflict them. This little book shows what happens to a naturally religious mind when it is released from the discipline of intellectual obedience. It paints a more vivid picture of Christ than any of his previous works: Lamennais imagines the Son of Man, who had nowhere to lay his head, looking down in holy anger on those hypocrites who despise the poor,[2] and later he describes Christ upon the cross and his resurrection from the dead.[3] But Christ is now, for Lamennais, only a picture in the mind, a device intended to direct the people's earthly endeavours towards a heavenly end.

Lamennais's religious development reaches its logical conclusion with *Discussions critiques*,[4] also written in prison. The preface to this collection of articles explains that they were intended to demonstrate the change in his views. The familiar themes of liberty, intelligence, and love reappear in such a way as to be in contradiction to all forms of contemporary organized belief. He demolishes communism because, he says, it produces not collective liberty but individual slavery; Catholicism because it produces not only collective certainty but also individual intellectual slavery; and Protestantism because it produces not only individual liberty but also collective anarchy. He speaks of the 'flux divin' which unites men with God in a way which no conventional religion has yet discovered.[5] And he proposes his own solution to the problem: the denial of a supernatural order altogether.[6] Religion, he claims, has returned to the realm of

little noticed in England and adds nothing to what is already known about Lamennais's religious ideas of the time. It does, however, show how remote from Christianity his thought was when it was shorn of conventional Christian terms.

[1] Y. Le Hir, *Lamennais—Une Voix de prison*. Paris, 1954, p. 21.

[2] ibid., p. 71.

[3] ibid., p. 83.

[4] *Discussions critiques et pensées diverses sur la religion et la philosophie*, Paris, 1841.

[5] ibid., p. 28.

[6] ibid., p. 16.

purely natural laws and consists in the proper development of the divine element inherent in all men.

A full exposition of this theory appeared in the *Esquisse d'une philosophie*. The theme of the *Esquisse* is that society is the finite expression of God. Progress consists in movement towards unity with God, the finite with the infinite. This principle is carried into physical science, aesthetics, and many other branches of learning. But it finds its most famous expression in *De l'art et du beau* (1841).

In this section of the *Esquisse* Lamennais starts from the idea that the True is the equivalent of the infinite Being, who is God. The Beautiful is also equivalent to God but only inasmuch as it is the means whereby the True manifests itself. The Beautiful is therefore infinite. Art is the finite manifestation of the Beautiful. The True is the source from which finite beings are derived. The Beautiful is the source from which finite forms are derived.[1]

Art for art's sake is therefore an absurdity, Lamennais says.[2] He divides man's activity into three phases: industry, when man seeks what is useful; art, when he seeks what is beautiful; and science, when he seeks what is true.[3] Art is therefore not the supreme form of man's activity. It is only one stage in his quest—a quest which culminates in the attainment of truth by means of science. Through science man feeds on truth, the supreme intelligence, God Himself. . . . 'D'où l'on voit que, pour lui, se développer c'est s'unir à Dieu, et que le terme de son développement, s'il étoit possible qu'il eût jamais un terme, seroit l'union parfaite avec Dieu.'[4]

The religious consequences of this are considered in the section characteristically entitled *De la société première et de ses lois, ou De la religion* (1848). In religion nothing is fixed. As society progresses, dogma and science converge: man achieves greater unity with God.[5] This means that it is not necessary to believe that God was made man or other 'fables surannées',[6] because religion is only the finite expression of the divine law. According to Lamennais, all formal religions are an expression of egoism, a means of separating self from the rest of mankind. True religion,

[1] *De l'art et du beau*, Paris (Garnier), 1909, p. 2.
[2] ibid., p. 10.
[3] ibid., p. 344.
[4] ibid., pp. 352 f.
[5] *De la société* &c., bk. ii, ch. 4.
[6] ibid., p. 90.

on the other hand, is the link not only between God and man, but between man and man also.[1] Religion is the law of life itself.

Despite foreshadowings of the debate about 'natural' and 'supernatural' religion, which still continues, this theory is outwardly an attempt to cloak in religious terms moralizations about the duties of men to each other and to abstract principles. Most of Lamennais's later religion amounts to this. But there are hints that his personal beliefs went further. In spite of his denial of what he calls the supernatural order and his attempt to synthesize the spiritual and the scientific, he admits that there must be some sort of future life where all beings will enter into a closer relationship with each other and with God.[2] Death is a transformation which allows love, the principle of unity, to work in the individual unfettered.[3] This Lamennais believed when he refused the ministrations of the Church on his deathbed. His faith in some sort of God never wavered, but the development of his philosophy of the universe made him deny the reality of any supernatural existence.

He had a passion for unity. From believing that it could be achieved by the submission of the earthly power to the heavenly, he passed, when he saw that the tide had turned against this idea, to demanding that the Church should equate her struggle with that of the people. When the Church steadfastly refused, he drifted away from her, devoting himself more and more to the cause of the people, and finally convincing himself that true religion was to be found, not in the teachings of the Church, but in this cause alone.

After the 1848 revolution, for which he had been steadily working and of which he was one of the principal architects,[4] Lamennais was elected to sit as a deputy for the département de la Seine. A measure of his popularity is that he polled 104,871 votes, while Lacordaire, Hugo, Leroux, Eugène Sue, and Michelet were all rejected with much smaller totals.[5] Shortly after this he was also elected to a small committee of the Assembly which was

[1] *De la société* &c., bk. ii, ch. 8. [2] ibid., ch. 6.

[3] ibid., bk. iii, ch. 8, pp. 231–8.

[4] J. Plamenatz, *The Revolutionary Movement in France, 1815–71*, London, 1952, p. 50. A glowing appraisal of Lamennais's influence ends: 'France had not exactly wanted the republic, but that she accepted it with so good a grace was largely owing to Lamennais.'

[5] These details appeared in the *Annual Register*, 1848, p. 262, in the daily newspapers and in the *Westminster Review*, v, 1848, p. 206.

convened to draw up a new constitution. This resulted in the *Projet de constitution de la république française* (1848). The committee's proposals were, however, rejected in favour of something more moderate, a 'preposterous constitution, organized for deadlock and manacled against change,'[1] a constitution which made it possible for Louis Bonaparte, once elected President, to seize fuller powers. In the Paris elections to the new Constituent Assembly on 12th and 13th May 1849, Lamennais was once more elected, this time with 113,331 votes.[2] He was, however, ineffective in the Chamber because of the weakness of his voice, and he viewed with increasing disquiet the activities of Louis Bonaparte. With the *coup d'état* of 2nd December 1851, he withdrew from politics and devoted the rest of his time to a translation of Dante's *Divine Comedy*. After a short illness during January and February 1854, he died on 27th February. He refused the ministrations of a priest, and stipulated that his body should be carried to the cemetery without any church ceremony. He was buried in a common grave at Père Lachaise. The spot where he lay was marked simply by a stick and a scrap of paper bearing the words 'La Mennais'.

It was a dramatic end to a life which had been in the centre of the European stage for nearly forty years. Lamennais was not a great leader. He was not even a great original thinker (although his style and eloquence enabled him to launch ideas which more profound philosophers had been unable to bring to the light of day). But he saw penetratingly into the needs of his time and followed his vision with no regard to himself. He who was always poor was consistently generous to those who needed him[3]; and he who was so often accused of public violence and intolerance was tender and attentive to his friends.[4]

[1] H. A. L. Fisher, *History of Europe*, 1936, p. 910.

[2] *Westminster*, ii, 1849, p. 488.

[3] In spite of his poverty, his name was nearly always to be found on subscription lists for the oppressed. In the British Museum is a subscription list in favour of eight Spanish officers of the democratic party who in 1849 had been forced to emigrate without any means of support. It is signed by a number of French liberal politicians, most of whom gave 2 fr. Lamennais gave 3 fr. (B.M. Add. MS. 40015, fo. 51b).

[4] The increased loneliness and public bitterness of his later years made no difference to this characteristic. See, e.g. Magda Martini, *La dernière amitié féminine de Lamennais*, Geneva, Lille, 1956, and his correspondence with the tailor Dessoliaire (*Nouvelle Revue rétrospective*, July-December 1903, pp. 73–96, 309–12).

It was (and probably still is) impossible for anyone to comprehend all the diverse elements in his life and to see how they could be contained within one personality; but we come nearest to understanding the mystery when we realize that he saw everything in terms of religious faith. It was this viewpoint which gave him his important position in nineteenth-century history, and his insight into the problems of belief and society which made him a figure of unique interest to the men of his time, and for many years after his death.[1]

[1] See, e.g. M. Mourre, *Lamennais, ou l'hérésie des temps modernes*, Paris, 1955, and an article in *Europe*, February-March 1954, pp. 3–26 by L. de Villefosse, 'Lamennais, dans son époque et dans la nôtre'.

II

LAMENNAIS'S REPUTATION IN ENGLAND

It is scarcely possible for one brought up in an atmosphere of total warfare to appreciate the indifference with which England regarded her French neighbours with whom she was at war at the beginning of the nineteenth century.

The war (wrote Dr. Trevelyan) was in the newspapers, but it scarcely entered the lives of the enjoying classes. No young lady of Miss Austen's acquaintance, waiting eagerly for the appearance of Scott's or Byron's next volume of verse, seems ever to have asked what Mr. Thorpe or Mr. Tom Bertram were going to do to serve their country in time of danger. For in those happy days the Navy was a perfect shield to the safety and to the amenities of island life.[1]

For long, however, the shield was not only a protection but a barrier, and no one acquainted with the literature of the second half of the century or with the affairs of the present time finds it easy to understand English insularity before 1820. This cautious passage from the *Christian Observer* of June 1820 is more tolerant than most and yet it still speaks of the Continent as of an almost inaccessible jungle:

The restoration of that intercourse with the continent which a warfare of twenty years had nearly closed, has been followed by a familiarity with continental countries, opinions and manners, which, however on some accounts it may be regretted or feared, has been productive of much gratification and advantage. To the Christian it was particularly interesting to inquire into the state of religion, both among Catholics and Protestants.[2]

It is not surprising, therefore, that the emergence of Lamennais on the French political and religious scene went almost unnoticed. The first volume of the *Essai sur l'indifférence* (1817), which caused such a stir in France, was ignored in England. Although,

[1] G. M. Trevelyan, *English Social History*, 2nd ed., 1946, p. 466.
[2] *Christian Observer*, June 1820, p. 399.

it is true, Helen Maria Williams, the Paris friend of the Shelleys, referred, in a book published in 1819, to Lamennais's opposition to the distribution of Bibles in French, she gave no hint of his reputation in his own country.[1]

It was 1820 before the *Essai* received any serious consideration. The *Monthly Repository*, a magazine unitarian in religion and radical in politics, was indignant at Lamennais's 'violent, implacable hatred' of Protestantism and portrayed him as the representative of the extreme bigots who also had their supporters in England.[2] The *Quarterly*, the most influential of the English reviews and a barometer of Lamennais's reputation, called it a work 'characterised by some eloquence, much fanaticism and still more intolerance'.[3] An Englishman, probably Sir John Bowring, one of the founders of the *Westminster Review*, wrote a refutation of it and sent it with a polite note to Lamennais.[4] Henry Crabb Robinson, the garrulous and radical diarist, was offered a copy by a professor while travelling by coach from Grenoble to Marseilles,[5] read it six weeks later in a coach to Norwich,[6] and found it to be an 'eloquent and very able work' although the author did not in the slightest degree accommodate himself to the spirit of the age.[7] A guide to French literature written for English readers quoted one opinion which accused the *Essai* of a 'deplorable spirit of intolerance' and another which agreed with one responsible Review[8] in praising its style and its author's 'great talent'.[9]

[1] Helen Maria Williams, *Letters on the Events which have passed in France since the Restoration in 1815*, London, 1819, pp. 113 f.

[2] *Monthly Repository*, June 1820, p. 325, article on 'Ultra-Catholicism in France'; pp. 327–32 are on Lamennais.

[3] *Quarterly Review*, July 1821, p. 561.

[4] D'Haussonville, *Le Prêtre et l'ami, lettres inédites de Lamennais à la Baronne Cottu 1818–1854*, Paris, 1910, p. 97 (18 August 1820).

[5] ed. T. Sadler, *Diary, Reminiscences and Correspondence of Henry Crabb Robinson*, 1872, 3rd ed., i, pp. 387 f. (2 September 1822).

[6] ibid., p. 389.

[7] ibid. Crabb Robinson was sufficiently interested in Lamennais to talk to Goethe about him (*Diary*, ii, p. 75; cf. E. J. Morley, *Life and Times of Henry Crabb Robinson*, 1935, p. 164, for a slightly different account).

[8] *The Eclectic Review*, July-December 1822, p. 466, which quotes approvingly from *Europe*, by a Citizen of the United States, London, 1822, pp. 97–99.

[9] L. T. Ventouillac, *The French Librarian or Literary Guide*, London, 1829, p. 32.

Both Lamennais and his brother believed that an English translation had been made,[1] but this never appeared. The only book to bear any resemblance to it was *The Semi-sceptic; or The Common Sense of Religion Considered* (1825) by the Rev. J. T. James, M.A., a country vicar in Bedfordshire who later became Bishop of Calcutta.[2] After taking a good degree at Oxford and acting for some time as a tutor at Christ Church, he travelled abroad from 1813 to 1816. During his travels he became acquainted, as few other clergymen of his day were,[3] with Continental theology. He set to work to prepare a volume of his own, and although he never as much as mentioned Lamennais's name, he clearly built on his foundations. He took Lamennais's principal theses: the categories of indifferentists, the fallibility of human reason, the pre-eminence of Christianity, Christianity as a development of older religions. He then deprived them of their Gallic sting and clothed them in Anglican generalities. The result was a curiosity of Anglican apologetic which became lost in a sea of ecclesiastical bickering as the Roman Catholic controversy grew.

Between 1825 and 1829 Lamennais became increasingly well known in England as an extreme exponent of ultramontanism, an attitude which found sympathy only among Roman Catholics; all other opinions, ecclesiastical or literary, were either hostile or derisive.[4] This may partly be attributed to the lack of sympathy

[1] H. de Courcy (ed.), *Lettres inédites de J.-M. et F. de la Mennais adressées à Mgr. Bruté*, Nantes, 1862, p. 143 (Jean, 11 May 1818) and p. 151 (Féli, 30 November 1818).

[2] Edward James, *Brief Memoirs of the late Rt. Revd. John Thomas James, D.D.* &c., London, 1830.

[3] A notable exception was Connop Thirlwall, later to become Bishop of St. Davids. On 11 April 1826 he wrote to W. J. Bayne: 'But there is still left a very important part of French literature which is absolutely necessary for everyone who wishes to understand the present state and future prospects of the nation. This is composed of the works of a class of writers who have been called up by the reaction which followed the Revolution, and who are accused of wishing to restore the old régime. There are among them several men of very great genius and reasoning powers. I should particularly recommend Fievée [*sic*], Bonald and Le Maistre [*sic*]. Chateaubriand and La Mennais I can only mention.' (*Letters Literary and Theological of Connop Thirlwall*, ed. J. J. Stewart Perowne and L. Stokes, London, 1881, p. 88).

[4] 'Very powerful, very ridiculous and very generally hated' (*New Monthly Magazine*, xv, 1825, p. 510); 'little solid reasoning' and 'more pretension than power' (apropos of *De la religion* in the *Christian Observer*, December 1825, p. 751. This long review reveals the current desire to uncover the weaknesses of Popery; it sees in Lamennais's invective a

with current French politics reflected in these words of the *Monthly Magazine* for January 1824: 'Everything connected with Bourbon France is in such bad flavour in England that, if we had any French literature of importance to announce, it would be considered as "good out of Nazareth".'[1] By most Lamennais was treated as a leader of the Jesuits,[2] a word of great emotive significance in England,[3] and as a fanatic. He was, however, often allowed some merit as a writer.[4] By some he was regarded as a figure of fun. The *New Monthly Magazine*, which numbered some of the more celebrated literary figures of the century among its contributors, in a series of articles painted a picture of him as a fanatical abbé preaching some new religion, they knew not, and they suspected the abbé knew not, exactly what, and doing the rounds of Parisian society, arousing the jealousy of husbands by converting their wives.[5] But by most he was seen as the colourful leader of the ultramontanes in France, doing battle with the equally colourful leader of the Gallicans, the Comte de Montlosier.[6] Although even his pamphlets were sold in England,[7] and uneasiness was expressed that his principles were obtaining a stronger

sign that Popery is on the decline); 'he takes very high ground on the side of pontifical power' (*Christian Guardian and Church of England Magazine*, July 1826, p. 261); he 'reduces everything to a servile dependence on the Pope' (*Christian Examiner and Church of Ireland Magazine*, ii, 1826, p. 484, also p. 76); 'absolute despotism' (*Foreign Quarterly Review*, September 1828, p. 185); 'paradoxical and unphilosophical' (*Foreign Review and Continental Miscellany*, iv, 1829, p. 68).

[1] *Monthly Magazine*, January 1824, p. 552.

[2] *Blackwood's*, December 1825, p. 716; *New Monthly*, xiii, 1825, p. 587; xv, 1825, pp. 270 f.; xvi, 1826, p. 321; xvii, 1826, pp. 303 f.; *Christian Observer*, August 1826, pp. 508 f.; *Edinburgh Review*, September 1826, p. 423; *Westminster*, January 1827, p. 71.

[3] The *Gentleman's Magazine* for June 1826 called them 'pestilential bigots' (p. 555).

[4] Eloquence: *New Monthly*, xv, 1825, p. 271; *Westminster*, January 1827, p. 70; *Foreign Review and Continental Miscellany*, iv, 1829, p. 68. On the other hand the *New Monthly* also called his style 'often imposing though sometimes tiresome' (xiii, 1825, p. 587) and 'obscure' (xvi, 1826, p. 320).

[5] *New Monthly*, xvi, 1826, pp. 320–3.

[6] *Westminster*, January 1825, p. 48; January 1830, p. 213; *Edinburgh*, June 1826, pp. 160 f.; *Christian Observer*, August 1826, pp. 508 f.; *Quarterly*, October 1830, p. 581.

[7] *Des progrès* cost 7*s*. 6*d*. (*Foreign Quarterly Review*, April 1829, p. 345), his first and second letters to the Archbishop of Paris (1829) 1*s*. 6*d*. and 2*s*. respectively, and the abbé Affre's reply to Lamennais's *Des progrès* and his two letters, *Essai historique et critique sur la suprématie temporelle du Pape et de l'église*, 8*s*. (*F.Q.R.*, August 1829, p. 695).

hold on this side of the Channel,[1] for the most part the serious issues in the dispute had little effect, so little that Lady Morgan, who was the Aunt Sally of serious-minded reviewers, but whose travel books were livelily written and widely read, speaking of the 'theological set' which taught 'the dogma of the deceptive tendencies of sensation and of the weakness of human reason', gaily proclaimed: 'At the head of this school are Lemaistre [*sic*] whose work on indifference in matters of religion had considerable temporary vogue [*sic*]; La Mennais, the *proneur* of the Pope; and the Baron Eckstein.'[2] Less cavalier but equally significant are these words from *Blackwood's:* 'To us English, who are so far removed in principle and feeling from the field of such a controversy, it is interesting to contemplate these struggles of the thinking men of a nation, without a creed, in want of one, and in dubiety where to fix.'[3]

The development of Lamennais's ideas in a liberal direction was not closely observed in England, although he was steadily becoming a more familiar figure.[4] Whereas the conflict of ultramontanism and Gallicanism raised issues relevant to the Roman Catholic question, the alliance of political liberalism with ultramontanism aroused little particular sympathy except momentarily[5] among some leaders of the Oxford movement. The *Avenir* was, however, fairly well known to the English public before its condemnation. *The Times* often carried extracts from its columns and reported its frequent brushes with authority.[6] Several other periodicals mentioned the new turn that the abbé's opinions had taken. The *Christian Observer*'s first reports were not very clear, but subsequent observations were admirably sympathetic in their description of Lamennais's aims.[7] The unitarian *Monthly Repository* was equally sympathetic.[8] The *Christian Examiner*

[1] *F.Q.R.*, April 1829, p. 283; see also *Christian Observer*, March 1829, p. 184. Already in 1825 Julius Hare had stated his preference for J. de Maistre over Lamennais (H. Crabb Robinson, *Diary*, 1872, ii, p. 3).

[2] Lady Morgan, *France in 1829–30*, London, 1830, i, p. 286.

[3] *Blackwood's*, December 1825, p. 717.

[4] By 1833 he already ranked as an 'eminent native' of Brittany (*Gentleman's Magazine*, June 1833, suppt. to ciii, pt. I, p. 629; *Monthly Review*, March 1833, p. 454).

[5] Below, pp. 97 ff.

[6] *The Times*, 20, 29, 30 November, 1830; 4, 14 February, 10, 16 May, 14 October 1831.

[7] *Christian Observer*, November 1830, p. 723; December 1830, p. 784.

[8] *Monthly Repository*, June 1831, pp. 403 f.

took note of the new development without apportioning praise or blame.[1] *The Foreign Quarterly Review* thought it worth mentioning that the hero of a novel it was reviewing was an adherent of the ideas of the *Avenir*.[2] Henry Lytton Bulwer's description of Lamennais in the office of the *Avenir* was published in 1836[3] and reprinted in the *British Critic*.[4] The influence of the *Avenir* in Belgium was also recognized in England.[5]

It was the *Paroles d'un croyant* which really brought Lamennais into prominence. The 1830 Revolution had made a great impact in England, and English attention was now more sensitively turned to France than it had been hitherto. 'The habits of friendship, mutual intercourse, and assimilation between Great Britain and France', wrote a British clergyman in 1833, 'appear daily to strengthen and extend.'[6] England was made aware of the *Paroles* at the end of May 1834 by *The Times*, which called it an 'unexpected sortie of his against crowned heads'.[7] On 11th June *The Times* gave it more extensive criticism. It acknowledged its importance and described it as 'a fireship launched in the midst of the moral world'.[8] On 5th August the Foreign Correspondent took note of its influence in Belgium, adding: 'I have heard it openly asserted as the opinion of some that the truths of the work were indisputable, and that its only fault was its appearance twenty years too soon.'[9] The *Morning Post* seized upon the Pope's comparison of Lamennais with Huss and Wycliffe.[10] The *Morning Herald*, which was bitterly opposed to the *Paroles*, said that it had excited throughout Rome a feeling of surprise and disgust and called it 'a melancholy proof of the aptness with which the most exalted talents may fall into the most pernicious and absurd errors when they lend an ear to the dictates of self-love and of

[1] *Christian Examiner*, January 1831, p. 76.

[2] *F.Q.R.*, April 1833, pp. 435–41.

[3] H. L. Bulwer, *The Monarchy of the Middle Classes*, London, 1836, pp. 132–4.

[4] *British Critic*, xix, 1836, pp. 305 f.

[5] J. Emerson Tennent, M.P., *Belgium*, London, 1841, i, p. 265, and a review of this work in the *Church of England Quarterly Review*, x, 1841, p. 289; *Westminster*, April 1834, p. 437; *British and Foreign Quarterly Review*, iii, 1836, pp. 13 f.

[6] J. Davies, B.D., *First Impressions* &c., London, 1835, pp. 3 f.

[7] *The Times*, Friday 30 May 1834, p. 4.

[8] *The Times*, Wednesday 11 June 1834, p. 3.

[9] *The Times*, 5 August, Foreign Correspondence, p. 3.

[10] Cited *The Crisis*, 26 July 1834, p. 128.

unbridled confidence in their own strength'.[1] It prophesied that the *Paroles* would soon be a prohibited work, not because it preached republicanism, but because it aimed at the subversion of all authority and the undermining of Christianity.[2] *Bell's New Weekly Messenger*, the predecessor of the present *News of the World*, gave it sympathetic attention, but the Radical journals as a whole were slow to realize its importance, presumably because its being written in French prevented it from having any effect upon the working classes.[3]

The magazines and reviews were divided in their opinions of its literary and moral merits, although most of them were horrified at it. John Wilson Croker, the chief contributor to the *Quarterly*,[4] was invited to write an account of the *Paroles*. The result was considered so blasphemous by the publisher, John Murray, that he wrote to Lockhart, the editor, suggesting that it should be toned down. Lockhart, however, stood his ground,[5] and the article appeared with only a few minor modifications. Croker called

[1] *Morning Herald*, Thursday 12 June 1834, p. 4.

[2] Below, p. 165.

[3] ibid.

[4] For Croker's life and works see Myron F. Brightfield, *John Wilson Croker*, Berkeley, California, 1940.

[5] The relevant parts of his letter cast some light on the way the English mind worked:

> 'My dear Murray,
>
> It is always agreeable and often useful for us to hear what you think of the articles in progress. Croker and I both differ from you as to the general affair, for this reason simply, that Lamennais is to Paris what Benson or Lonsdale is to London. His book has produced and is producing a very great effect. Even religious people there applaud him, and they are re-echoed here by old Jerdan [below, pp. 35 f.], who pronounces that, be he right or wrong, he has produced "a noble sacred poem". It is needful to caution the English against the course of France by showing up the audacious extent of her horrors, political, moral and religious.' ....
>
> 'Mr. Croker, however, will modify and curtail the paper so as to get rid of your specific objections. It had already been judged advisable to put the last and only blasphemous extract in French in place of English. Depend upon it, if we were to lower our scale so as to run no risk of offending any good people's delicate feelings, we should soon lower ourselves so as to rival "My Grandmother the British" in want of interest to the world at large, and even (though they would not say so) to the saints themselves' (Samuel Smiles, *A Publisher and his Friends, Memoir and Correspondence of the late John Murray*, 2 vols., 1891, ii, pp. 233 f., dated 'November 8th 1826', which should read '1834').

the *Paroles* 'a silly and profane rhapsody', 'a ludicrous and disgusting masquerade',[1] 'laboured rhetoric and frigid bombast',[2] 'an absurd and detestable production'.[3] The *British Critic* called it 'insane follies' and 'unholy parodies' and rejoiced that, although an English translation had been made, no British publisher could be found for it.[4] This was not in fact true, but it is an indication of what a small circulation the first translation must have had.[5]

Also among the adverse critics was the poet and humorist D. M. Moir, writing in *Blackwood's Edinburgh Magazine*.[6] His comments were not as violent as Croker's, but they expressed the dismay and apprehension which must have come upon many intelligent Britons when they read the *Paroles*. He represented Lamennais's work as a typical example of the type of revolutionary thought which was having a pernicious effect upon England: it undermined the authority of the Bible and the Church, and set in its place the authority of human pride and the course of moderate opinion. The very fact that this radicalism was expressed so vaguely was an important factor in this new movement of thought. It was symbolic of the replacement of the old clear-cut dogma by the new ill-defined pseudo-scientific aspiration.[7] Moir's article influenced the tone of *Blackwood's* for some time. Thereafter it was repeatedly warning its readers about the dangers of French influence.[8]

There was, however, a section of the public which welcomed the *Paroles*. One of the leading literary journals, *The Literary Gazette and Journal of Belles Lettres*,[9] which was under the editorship of William Jerdan, a lion of contemporary criticism, called it 'a fine religious poem'.[10] It judged it to be beautiful as poetry, unobjectionable as doctrine, but unsound as politics. According to Lockhart,[11] Jerdan himself was the author of the

[1] *Quarterly*, lii, 1834, p. 358.
[2] ibid., p. 359. [3] ibid., p. 360.
[4] *British Critic*, xix, 1836, p. 305.
[5] For translations of the *Paroles* see below, pp. 164 f., 181 f.
[6] *Blackwood's*, September 1835, p. 332. I am indebted to Mr. G. D. Blackwood for identifying unsigned articles from the records of *Blackwood's*. [7] ibid., pp. 333–6.
[8] It was particularly sensitive to French anticlericalism and democracy (*Blackwood's*, xxxviii, 1835, pp. 54–65, 249, 389, 503 f.).
[9] *Autobiography of William Jerdan*, 4 vols., London, 1852–3.
[10] *Literary Gazette*, 25 October 1834, pp. 717 f.
[11] Above, p. 34.

article, but it is not difficult to see behind his enthusiasm the hand of his assistant editor, the poetess Letitia Elizabeth Landon,[1] whose poems, although much in favour at the time, have been described by a recent critic as 'gush' and 'sentiment'.[2] She spent five weeks of the summer of 1834, just at the time when the *Paroles* was making a sensation, in Paris with Odilon Barrot, Chateaubriand, Heine, Sainte-Beuve and others, and could not have failed to notice it nor to hear it discussed at that time.[3] If it was indeed she who brought the book to the notice of Jerdan, and if it was her approval that Jerdan was expressing in his article, then this is some indication that what nowadays seems ineffective rhetoric appeared in 1834 to literary connoisseurs as fine poetry, and was therefore much more likely to have an influence than we would at present allow.

It is significant that in England there was nowhere a *via media* between these opposing views. The *North American Review*, however, which although published in America was also read in England, was less passionate than its British counterparts.[4] It regarded the *Paroles* as a symptom of the disease of Europe. It approved of Lamennais's attempt to secure liberty by means of the sincere worship of God, but took him to task for failing to teach the French a love of constitutional liberty.[5] It is unlikely that this very American outlook was understood at the time.

For several years after the *Paroles*, the general impression of Lamennais which prevailed was that he was a dangerous and a powerful man of doubtful principles. His association with George Sand[6] and *Le Monde*[7] was widely quoted in support of this view

[1] Laman Blanchard, *Life and Literary Remains of L.E.L.*, 2 vols., London, 1841.

[2] G. Sampson, *Concise Cambridge History of English Literature*, Cambridge, 1941, p. 647.

[3] Blanchard, op. cit. i, pp. 108–16; Jerdan, op. cit. iii, pp. 187–206.

[4] *North American Review*, Boston, April 1835, pp. 269–98 (a review of *Words of a Believer*. Translated from the French, New York, C. de Behr 1834).

[5] ibid., p. 295.

[6] *British and Foreign Quarterly Review*, vi, 1838, p. 362; Edith J. Morley, *H. Crabb Robinson on Books and their Writers*, 1938, ii, p. 545; *Athenaeum*, 25 April 1846, p. 421—Browning objected to this linking of George Sand's name with Lamennais's (*Letters of Robert Browning and Elizabeth Browning*, 1899, ii, p. 108); Thackeray, *Paris Sketch Book*, Oxford (1908), pp. 237–40; *Quarterly*, lxv, March 1840, p. 441; Thos. Raikes, *Journal*, 1856–7, iv, p. 356.

[7] *Fraser's Magazine*, January 1838, p. 51; February 1838, pp. 218 f.; *F.Q.R.*, xix, July 1837, p. 235.

of him, and lengthy articles, couched in almost hysterical terms, were devoted to him in the *Athenaeum* and the *Foreign Quarterly Review*. Jules Janin in the *Athenaeum* wrote:

This priest—this invalid—this lonely man—this breathless and exhausted voice—this earthward-bowed mortal, suddenly lifts up his voice, his words break forth, he reveals himself. He calls unto him all the griefs, all the humiliations, all the miseries, all the sufferings, and all the opinions of disordered humanity. He proclaims himself the priest, the apostle, the infallible Pontiff (and he *is*) of all who are in wretchedness, exile, or revolution in the world. He writes with a pen of iron—a pen at once of poet and politician—the catechism of all revolutions to come.... M. de la Mennais is the most powerful politician of our age.[1]

The *Foreign Quarterly Review* was just as passionate but less sympathetic. It concluded that he was a 'lunatic luminary'[2]:

We must now sum up our estimate of M. La Mennais. With much apparent earnestness but no sincerity; much of display but little sound learning; dogmatory without knowledge, declamatory without zeal, and copious and fluent without real eloquence or vital warmth: assuming, insidious, superficial, ill-judging, inconsiderate, interested and vain; a mere dreamer in action, and opposed to society simply because unpurchased by it:—the Abbé is neither worth buying over, nor converting, nor answering—for he misleads, misapprehends, misapplies everything. Common sense would extinguish,, and only idiots meddle with, this lighted firebrand, courting a purchaser. His admirers, in or out of St. Luke's,[3] may well deem him invaluable; for, in truth,—What is he worth?[4]

The only one of his works to receive any close attention before 1840 was *Affaires de Rome* (1836). It was never translated into English, although it might have played a significant part in the Catholic controversy if it had been. John Henry Newman's attention was quickly drawn to it[5] (*Affaires* was published in November 1836 and Newman's article appeared in October 1837), and his article brought it to the notice of other Tractarians,[6]

[1] *Athenaeum*, 22 April 1837, p. 282. Mrs. Trollope, however, believed that Lamennais was no longer the pre-eminent man he had been (*Paris and the Parisians in 1835*, p. 386).

[2] *F.Q.R.*, xxi, April 1838, p. 131.

[3] A famous lunatic asylum of the day.

[4] *F.Q.R.*, xxi, 1838, p. 131. [5] below, p. 108.

[6] Wm. Palmer, Gladstone and R. W. Church, below, pp. 106 f., 111.

although it is probably an exaggeration to say, as has been said,[1] that it produced a sensation in Oxford. F. D. Maurice read the book and was most impressed and disturbed by it.[2] Thomas Raikes, the diarist and dandy, was convinced of its importance and described it in meticulous detail in his journal.[3] The most prominent periodical to review it immediately was *Blackwood's* which devoted a whole article to it in February 1837.[4] This review, written by a Mr. O'Donnel of Paris, is interesting for its two conclusions: that *Affaires de Rome* showed that Romanism was not as conducive to civil liberty as was claimed by English Roman Catholics,[5] and that it showed the danger of combining the philosophy of utilitarianism with the fanaticism of revolutionaries and the religious strains of millenarianism.[6] It seemed to O'Donnel that *Affaires de Rome* was good evidence both for the hypocrisy of Romanism and for the dangerous tendencies of radicalism, but he consoled himself with the thought that the British were unlikely to fall prey to these subversive views.[7]

Nearly two years passed before the *Quarterly* noticed it,[8] and in this time it came to much more definite conclusions than *Blackwood's*. The reviewer was Dr. A. McCaul,[9] a Low Churchman who was the first man to be offered the Anglican Bishopric of Jerusalem. In his opinion, *Affaires de Rome* showed quite clearly that the battle of the *Avenir* was directly linked with the ascendancy of Roman Catholicism in Ireland and Belgium. He even went so far as to say that the editors of the *Avenir* had had direct relations with Roman Catholics in England and Ireland, and played an important part in the Roman Catholic controversy in England.

By 1840 Lamennais was so well known in England[10] that on 5th November *The Times* thought it worth mentioning that two

[1] H. L. Stewart, *A Century of Anglo-Catholicism*, 1929, pp. 89 f.

[2] Below, p. 156.

[3] Thomas Raikes, *A Portion of a Journal kept from 1831–1847*, London, 1856–7, iii, pp. 176–8.

[4] *Blackwood's*, February 1837, pp. 251–7.

[5] ibid., p. 251. [6] ibid., p. 253. [7] ibid., p. 257.

[8] *Quarterly*, lxiii, January 1839, p. 110.

[9] For details of the authorship of unsigned articles in the *Quarterly* I am indebted to Sir John Murray. On Dr. McCaul see the Revd. J. B. McCaul, *Memorial Sketch of the Revd. Alexander McCaul*, London, 1863.

[10] Abraham Hayward, who did much to increase British understanding of the Continent (H. E. Carlisle, *Selection from the Correspondence of Abraham Hayward, Q.C., from 1834 to 1884*, 2 vols., London, 1886), called him the 'celebrated Abbé de la Mennais' (*Quarterly*, lxv, March 1840,

new (and seditious) works entitled *Aux armes* and *Évangile du peuple* had been published and were erroneously attributed to Lamennais.[1] When Lamennais was eventually tried for the publication of *Le Pays et le gouvernement*, *The Times* described the charges and added this interesting comment:

> Notwithstanding his unquestionable 'civisme' the Abbé is threatened, it appears, with the fate experienced by other revolutionists in other times by their corevolutionists. 'He has received', says the *Universe*, 'notice, that sentence of death has been pronounced upon him by one of the secret societies for opposing the principle of a division of property.'[2]

Readers of *The Times*, at least, would not fall into the error that Lamennais had allied himself with the most extreme socialists.[3] Both the *Morning Herald* and the *Morning Post* had brief reports of the sentence.[4]

The trial did not go unnoticed in the magazines. The *Athenaeum* seemed surprised that so much fuss had been made about it.[5] *Blackwood's*, which had already warned its readers several times against the dangers of French influence in England, lost no time in reviewing *Le Pays et le gouvernement*, and citing it as yet another example of the moral and political evils of 'the wild doctrines of universal levelling preached up by the Republican party, with the Abbé de Lamennais at its head'.[6] Both *Blackwood's* and the *Annual Register* for 1841 pointed to one fact which had, surprisingly, been overlooked by the newspapers. It was that Lamennais's pamphlet was responsible for some of the prevalent anti-British feeling in France. In it he violently attacked the Treaty of London, and accused Guizot of selling France to her

p. 441); T. Adolphus Trollope (*A Summer in Brittany*, ed. Frances Trollope, 2 vols., 1840, ii, pp. 22 f.) 'the well-known Abbé de Lamennais'; a handbook of French literature put him among the favourite authors in the 'Moral Sciences' (A. Albites, *The Authors of France*, &c., London, 1839, p. 66).

[1] *The Times*, Thursday 5 November 1840, p. 4.

[2] *The Times*, Thursday 26 November 1840, p. 4.

[3] *The Tablet* reproduced both of these reports almost word for word without acknowledgement (7 November, p. 412; 28 November, p. 460).

[4] *Morning Herald*, Thursday 26 November 1840, p. 4; *Morning Post*, Wednesday 25 November 1840, [p. 2].

[5] *Athenaeum*, 28 November 1840, p. 947.

[6] *Blackwood's*, xlix, January 1841, p. 108. The author was H. Longueville-Jones.

enemies.[1] This *Blackwood's* saw very clearly and continued to urge that Britain should establish closer links with the Teutonic countries and not lean too heavily upon alliance with the French.[2] The *Annual Register*, while not impugning the abbé's personal character, pointed in a very gentlemanly way to the close connection there was between the publication and condemnation of *Le Pays et le gouvernement* and the hordes of students marching through the streets and shouting 'Death to the English! Down with Guizot!'[3]

Lamennais's year in prison set the seal on his reputation. Between 1840 and 1848 he was regarded by some as an eloquent religious demagogue serving the cause of democracy, and an extremist with dangerous influence,[4] and by others as a rather unpleasant but comparatively harmless republican. One Review wrote that the vague utopianism of his and other socialist thought made no appeal in this country.[5] Milman, then Rector of St. Margaret's, Westminster, and later Dean of St. Paul's, wrote about Lamennais's effect on France as if it were something which did nothing to ruffle England's ecclesiastical waters,[6] and another writer in the *Quarterly* made detached and academic allusions to the possibility of Lamennais's leading a European revolution.[7] The *Edinburgh* refrained from comment except upon some strictly historical aspects of the teaching of the *Avenir*.[8] Other Reviews found opportunity for curious comment but little cause for fear or applause: some continued to regard him as a good Christian soul[9] and to speak of him with affection and sympathy.[10]

[1] F. Lamennais, *Le Pays et le gouvernement*, Paris 1840, especially pp. 17–23.

[2] *Blackwood's*, January 1841, pp. 97–99.

[3] *Annual Register for 1841*, London, 1842, p. 236.

[4] *Fraser's*, December 1842, p. 739; January 1843, p. 103; April 1843, p. 413.

[5] *Church of England Quarterly Review*, xviii, 1846, p. 386.

[6] *Quarterly*, lxvii, March 1841, p. 431; lxxvii, March 1846, p. 461 (an article on Newman's *Development*).

[7] *Quarterly*, lxxiv, June 1844, p. 165.

[8] *Edinburgh*, lxxxi, April 1845, p. 410.

[9] *British Quarterly Review*, iii, May 1846, p. 266; *Westminster*, xliv, December 1845, p. 531; *Christian Remembrancer*, January 1846, p. 135.

[10] *Church of England Quarterly Review*, xviii, 1845, pp. 71 f.; xx, 1846, p. 133—a comparison of Abelard and Lamennais: e.g. 'No one who remembers the enthusiastic and kind-hearted little author of the *Paroles d'un Croyant* during his residence at Kensington, his sojourning in Brittany, or his feverish career in the capital, will ever be disposed to imagine that, for his sake, there ever existed the Heloise who could ask herself—"What means this tumult in a vestal's veins?".'

In spite of this uncertainty about Lamennais's importance, there was at least one person who was disturbed about the influence he was having in England. In the summer of 1841 Thomas Carlyle wrote to the editor of the *Edinburgh Review* offering to write an article on what Goethe called 'the literature of desperation', as it was represented by G. Sand, Lamennais, Mazzini, and others.[1] 'The taste for it', he wrote, 'among Radical men, especially among Radical women, is spreading everywhere.'[2] He intended to go to Wales to write this article, but unfortunately he failed to settle there, and he returned to Chelsea without carrying out his project.[3] He still, however, remained worried about their influence, although he recognized that much of what they said was sound.[4] Undoubtedly much popular radicalism was expressed in terms of sentimental religiosity, but there is little evidence apart from Carlyle's assertion that this stemmed from G. Sand and Lamennais. There is considerably more to show that Mazzini had a large hand in it, and it is probably indirectly through Lamennais's influence on him that the sentimentalism which is today recognized as one of the many characteristics of early Victorianism flourished.

In the more serious realm of philosophy Lamennais, like most of his contemporaries, was still unknown. A writer in the *Edinburgh Review* for 1840 had this to say:

> At a time when the prevailing tone of French speculation is one of exaggerated reaction against the doctrines of the eighteenth century, French philosophy, with us, is still synonymous with Encyclopedism. The Englishmen may almost be numbered who are aware that France has produced any great names in prose literature since Voltaire and Rousseau; and while modern history has been receiving a new aspect from the labours of men who are not only among the profoundest thinkers, but the clearest and most popular writers of their age, even those of their works which are expressly dedicated to the history of our own country, remain mostly untranslated, and in almost all cases unread.[5]

Although professional philosophers had noticed Lamennais (as early as 1837 Sir James Mackintosh had accused him of building religion upon scepticism and of pushing his system to such

[1] *Selections from the Correspondence of the late Macvey Napier, Esq.*, 1879, p. 348. [2] ibid. [3] ibid., p. 349.
[4] Ed. A. Carlyle, *New Letters of Th. Carlyle*, 1904, i, p. 264.
[5] *Edinburgh*, lxxii, October 1840, pp. 1 f.

extremes that his reasoning became invalid,[1] and a few years later Sir William Hamilton had placed him at the end of a long line of 101 philosophers who had propounded the theory of the general reason[2]), it was not until the publication of J. D. Morell's *Historical and Critical View of the Speculative Philosophy of Europe in the 19th Century* (1846) that he came to the notice of a wider public.[3] Morell's thesis was that nineteenth-century scepticism had grown from earlier sensationalism and idealism. Of French scepticism he distinguished three types, of which the 'most decisive' was the scepticism of authority, exemplified by Huet, de Maistre, and finally Lamennais.[4] His account of Lamennais was more than a frigid philosophical analysis; it was lively, almost passionate observation of a thinker with whom he could sympathize but not agree:

> His restless weariness at the delusive glare of human beings; his contempt for the errors, the failings, the follies of mankind; his disappointment over the frailty of his own cherished hopes; all these will ever touch a chord of sympathy in many a heart which has struggled through the same experience, and arrived, perhaps, at the same results.[5]

It must be admitted that his account was not very profound, that he made much of the obvious contrast between Lamennais's use of reason and his derision of it, and that he unjustifiably lumped together Bonald, J. de Maistre, Lamennais, Ballanche, and Eckstein, all with the label of 'sceptics', but in spite of this, it is interesting to note that he seemed to be interested in only one of these, Lamennais. Although the book was published in 1846, it traced the development of Lamennais's ideas no further than the *Paroles*. This fault was pounced upon by *Fraser's Magazine for Town and Country*, ever keen to keep Lamennais's name before the public eye. It trounced Morell thoroughly in robust,

[1] *Miscellaneous Works of Sir James Mackintosh*, i, 1846, p. 299 (dissertation published in 1837).

[2] *Works of Thomas Reid*. Preface, notes and supplementary dissertations by Sir William Hamilton, Bt., Edinburgh, 1863, pp. 770 f. and 801 (the body of the dissertation was written 1841-2).

[3] The author of an article on Moral Philosophy in France (*British and Foreign Quarterly Review*, xv, 1843, pp. 353–406) had confessed himself unable to make much of Lamennais's philosophy, warmly as he admired him as a man and a poet (p. 384). The writer's difficulty seems to have been caused by his attempt to distil philosophy from Lamennais's later works without considering his earlier and more substantial thought.

[4] Morell, op. cit., ii, p. 229.

[5] ibid., pp. 235 f.

nineteenth-century terms and derided him for apparently being ignorant of the *Esquisse* and of Lamennais's other works after the *Paroles*.[1]

These few words had their effect, and when the second edition appeared a year later, in 1847, Morell had made considerable additions and corrections to the account of Lamennais. The footnotes were enlarged, the little popular works were included, and, most important of all, there was a long analysis of the *Esquisse*.[2] This second edition was generally welcomed,[3] although the *Church of England Quarterly Review* was eager to know still more.[4] Only the *Westminster* made no mention of Morell's treatment of Lamennais: it was more interested in German philosophy and did not take him seriously as a philosopher.[5]

By 1848 Lamennais was familiar in England as a social reformer, religious idealist, republican, philosopher, and writer of distinction.[6]

In spite of his apparently modest share in the complicated course of the 1848 Revolution in France, which attracted so much anxious attention in England, he still figured largely in any consideration of the French scene. J. W. Croker, the erstwhile opponent of the *Paroles*, in an article in the *Quarterly* on politics in France and England, sought to discern three parties in the new assembly: Legitimists, Jesuits and what he called the 'radical or revolutionary Catholic party'.[7] This, he alleged, was led by Lamennais, whom he described with his customary passion and whom he declared to have more influence over men's minds even than Rousseau.[8] Although this assessment of Lamennais's position in post-revolutionary politics was well wide of the mark, it erred in the direction of exaggerating his influence. The High

[1] *Fraser's*, October 1846, p. 408.

[2] Morell, op. cit., 2nd ed., 1847, ii, pp. 292–300.

[3] e.g. *Oxford and Cambridge Review*, v, July–December 1847, pp. 374–7; *Tait's Edinburgh Magazine*, xiv, October 1847, p. 700.

[4] *Church of England Quarterly Review*, xxii, 1847, p. 459.

[5] *Westminster*, xlvii, 1847, pp. 11–44.

[6] Philosophers especially were united in their opinions of his merits as a writer. *The British and Foreign Quarterly Review* (xv, 1843, p. 384) called his language uniformly splendid; Morell (1st ed., ii, p. 234)—'this remarkable writer' of 'learning, power and eloquence' (p. 240); Mackintosh (op. cit., p. 299)—'a fine writer'; Hamilton (op. cit., p. 770)—'the eloquent Abbé De La Mennais'.

[7] *Quarterly*, lxxxiii, June-September 1848, p. 212.

[8] ibid., p. 213.

Church periodical, the *Ecclesiastic*, in its article on 'The Church and Revolution', attributed even more influence to Lamennais than Croker had done.[1] But its argument was better founded. It made the wise and justifiable distinction between the current figure of Lamennais the democrat and the still-remembered Lamennais of the *Essai*, *Des progrès*, and the *Avenir*. The former had become 'a pure republican, and a mere speculative religionist, out of the Communion of the Church',[2] but the latter, one whose 'doctrines have been and are silently working in the minds of many who had not energy to push them at once to their extreme consequences'.[3] Both Croker and the better-informed contributor to the *Ecclesiastic* see Lamennais's ideas as one of the mainsprings of the 1848 Revolution, but they place the emphasis not on the idealistic socialism, which was recognized by the English Chartists,[4] but on his early Christianity. To the Englishman, therefore, his place in the turmoil of French politics must have been very uncertain. He was claimed as the advocate of both Pope and people.

Some of this uncertainty was removed in the reports of the elections to the 1848 Assembly. *The Times*, calling him a 'moderate republican',[5] reminded its readers that in spite of his title, still widely used, he was scarcely to be regarded as a defender of Catholic interests, since he was a schismatic and a seceder.[6] It mentioned his appointment to the commission for drawing up a new constitution.[7] The Anglican paper, the *Guardian*, also followed events closely,[8] and even went into more detail than *The Times*. On the front page it printed a rumour that Pope Pius IX had removed Lamennais's state of excommunication (he had, in fact, never been excommunicated) and given him his blessing as a 'philosophical Christian'.[9] For supporting such a dangerously revolutionary measure as income tax it dubbed him an 'ultra-republican'.[10] *Tait's Edinburgh Magazine* refused to restrict itself to any cut-and-dried description of his political leanings. In

[1] *The Theologian and Ecclesiastic*, v, 1848, p. 268.
[2] ibid., p. 288. [3] ibid., p. 277.
[4] below, pp. 167 ff.
[5] *The Times*, 27 April 1848, p. 4. *The English Churchman* (4 May 1848) described him in the same way (p. 294).
[6] *The Times*, 1 May 1848, p. 3.
[7] *The Times*, 20 May 1848, p. 8.
[8] *Guardian*, 15 March, p. 169; 24 May, pp. 330 and 339; 12 July 1848, p. 441. [9] ibid., 31 May 1848, p. 345.
[10] ibid., 6 September 1848, p. 569.

general it classed him with the extreme republicans, with the qualification that, although extreme in his aims, he was moderate in the means he proposed to use—a fair and accurate comment.[1] The *Literary Gazette* welcomed his election, not on political grounds, but because he would represent the republic of letters in the new Assembly.[2]

The 1849 elections received the same attention. When Lamennais was elected thirteenth in the list of candidates for the Seine, the *Westminster* called him a 'socialist known by his writings in favour of the practical application of Christian doctrine to the amelioration of the condition of the mass of the people',[3] a further indication that in English eyes he never wholly detached himself from that Christianity from which he had sprung. The *North British Review*, which at that time resembled the *Westminster* in philosophy and politics, judged him similarly—'the ex-priest Lamennais, believing with hazy eye, in a mystic Future unlike all the Past'.[4]

More conservative journals, however, were less eager to point to the Christian aspects of his teaching. The *Guardian*, recording his second election to the Assembly and his great popularity with the French army (he received more votes than Hugo, Murat, Cavaignac, Coquerel, or Leroux), noted that he belonged to the 'violent party'.[5] J. Palgrave-Simpson in *Blackwood's* painted a dramatic picture of him snarling and growling and uttering low imprecations.[6] The *Annual Register* described him simply as a socialist.[7] British readers were able to judge for themselves the extent of his socialism from an article, written after an interview with him, in the *British Quarterly Review*.[8] The author, who was unsympathetic to socialism, was determined, in spite of his fascination for Lamennais, to prove him a socialist. He was, however, perplexed by Lamennais's doctrine of property[9] and summed up the views of many by saying: 'Out of France, readers must always find it difficult to follow the course of the author's thoughts'.[10]

[1] *Tait's*, xv, 1848, p. 373.
[2] *Literary Gazette*, 1848, p. 330.
[3] *Westminster*, li, 1849, p. 488.
[4] *North British Review*, x, February 1849, p. 272.
[5] *Guardian*, 23 May 1849, p. 333.
[6] *Blackwood's*, March 1849, p. 281.
[7] *Annual Register*, 1849, pp. 245 f.
[8] *British Quarterly Review*, ix, May 1849, pp. 501–16.
[9] ibid., pp. 510–12.
[10] ibid., pp. 509 f.

For him, as for most other observers, certainly those in England, the difficulty lay in the persistent religious undertones to Lamennais's thought.[1]

All this goes to show that by 1849 he had become a renowned figure, 'the famous abbé'.[2] The *Guardian* reproduced an interesting account of his early life up to the publication of the first volume of the *Essai*, which, it claimed (and this was in 1849), would 'outlive the whole religious literature of our time'.[3] It pursued the story no further than 1817 because, it said, Lamennais's subsequent history was 'too well known to repeat here'.[4]

His fame was not simply a matter of political notoriety or religious speculation.[5] There were signs that his life was beginning to be seen in perspective. His early work was not being eclipsed by his later activity. *Fraser's Magazine*, which had been consistently faithful to him,[6] produced a balanced comparison of him with J. de Maistre.[7] This is the more remarkable since it appeared at a time when Lamennais was at the height of his political prominence. *Fraser's* adroitly uses this to point back to other times and other philosophies: 'The name of Lamennais is a familiar one everywhere. De Maistre's is scarcely so well known as it ought to be in France, and deserves to be better known than it is in England.'[8] In pursuance of the same policy it reminded its readers of the 'kindly Breton's' patronage of the young Lamartine when he was a struggling poet.[9] It even quoted him with approval in a discussion on authority.[10]

[1] *British Quarterly Review*, ix, May 1849, p. 513.

[2] *Guardian*, 23 May 1849, p. 333.

[3] ibid., 9 May 1849, pp. 293 f.

[4] ibid.

[5] Mrs. Foster's *Handbook of Modern European Literature*, 1849, reported that Lamennais's religious speculation had attracted universal attention (p. 216).

[6] e.g. *Fraser's* (May 1847, p. 552) has a touching reflection on the misfortunes of authors who, having presented a work of theirs to a friend, find it on a second-hand bookstall: 'I remember once having purchased the first volume of *Affaires de Rome*, with this inscription, "A Monsieur B. de L. . . . Hommage et respect de son obéissant serviteur, F. de Lamennais". This volume and the precious autograph cost me just *one franc!*'

[7] *Fraser's*, April 1849, pp. 383–96.

[8] ibid., p. 385.

[9] ibid., February 1849, p. 214.

[10] ibid., February 1850, p. 240—this in spite of the fact that the book under discussion, G. Cornewall Lewis's *Essay on the Influence of Authority in Matters of Opinion*, London, 1849, makes no allusion to Lamennais.

Some began to contrast Lamennais's ultramontanism with his current socialism[1] and to try to bring the two into some sort of harmony. Others cast a glance back to the days of the *Avenir* and reminded their readers that the Church in France in 1849 owed its vitality to the Lamennais of 1830.[2] Although the influence of the *Avenir* had been frequently acknowledged, it is significant that it should be especially noticed at this time when Lamennais was so much before the public eye as a politician. The *North British Review* drew attention to his influence on Gioberti[3], and the *Ecclesiastic* had some interesting things to say about his influence upon the theology of development.[4]

Between 1849 and his death in 1854 Lamennais retired from the public view and devoted himself to his translation of Dante. Even this did not escape English notice. The *Critic* observed that for a man whose proposed constitution had been rejected and who had watched the whole fabric of republicanism crumble, Dante was fit company: 'Lamennais's translation will, no doubt, be a fine one, like all that comes from his pen.'[5]

Shortly before his death Lamennais was visited by a contributor to a publication of American origin, *Putnam's Monthly Magazine*.[6] In an account which appeared a few months later Lamennais was described with a succinctness which eluded English reporters of the time, as 'very sincere but very green', and the conclusion of his second visit to Rome as the time when Gregory 'sent him away with a big flea in his ear'.[7]

When he died on 27th February 1854 there was a flood of obituary comment in the newspapers and magazines. *The Times*,[8] the *Morning Herald*,[9] the *Examiner*,[10] the *Morning Post*,[11] and the *Globe*[12] all reported the circumstances of his death and assumed their readers to be well acquainted with the details of his career.

[1] *Edinburgh*, xcvi, October 1852, p. 322; *British Quarterly Review*, xiii, May 1851, p. 568; *North British Review*, xii, November 1849, p. 163.
[2] *Christian Remembrancer*, July 1849, pp. 151 f.
[3] *North British Review*, xi, 1849, p. 396.
[4] *Ecclesiastic*, vii, 1849, pp. 368–70.
[5] *The Critic, London Literary Journal*, xi, 1 October 1852, p. 513.
[6] *Putnam's Monthly Magazine*, New York, May 1854, pp. 466–73.
[7] ibid., p. 469.
[8] *The Times*, Wednesday 1 March 1854, p. 10; Thursday 2 March, p. 9.
[9] *Morning Herald*, 1 March 1854, p. 5.
[10] *Examiner*, Sunday 4 March 1854, p. 135.
[11] *Morning Post*, 2 March 1854, p. 5.
[12] *Globe*, Thursday 2 March 1854, [p. 2].

Papers of left-wing sympathies, the *Patriot*,[1] the *Sun*[2] and *Bell's New Weekly Messenger*,[3] gave accounts of his last days. *The Leader*, another paper with democratic leanings, carried a long and glowing description of his life's work.[4]

The literary papers were even less sparing in their praise. The *Athenaeum* linked his earlier work with his later and attributed to him that impulse of 'speculative independence' which was appearing at the time.[5] *The Critic* was quite uncritical in its adulation; it called him 'a man who ought to be held in perpetual remembrance as a philosopher and a lover of his kind'. 'To this man', it said, 'France owes more than she is at the present moment at liberty to avow'.[6] William Jerdan's *Literary Gazette*, although it spoke of Lamennais's later opinions with distaste, yet gave an accurate and even moving description of 'one of the most distinguished of her [France's] sons'.[7] If Lamennais's popularity and appeal could be measured in inches, it would be worth noting that this obituary took over two columns, while Chateaubriand's, in the same journal, was less than a sixth of that length.

Among the religious papers, the Roman Catholic *Tablet*, in recording his death, gave a short account of his career since 1848 without mentioning religion at all.[8] Just as Wiseman had used Lamennais's fall as a stick with which to beat Newman,[9] so *The Tablet*, unlikely though it may seem, turned the manner of his death against Lord Aberdeen. In a leading article the following week it compared the way in which Lamennais had been deprived of a priest at his death with the fact that Lord Aberdeen and his government had refused to provide Roman Catholic priests for ships of the Royal Navy. 'The tragedy of Lamennais is to be enacted again and again on board the Royal Navy': a strange comment but one which illustrates the vividness of Lamennais's situation in nineteenth-century minds.[10] The *Catholic Standard* was

[1] *Patriot*, 2 March 1854, p. 139.

[2] *Sun*, Tuesday 28 February, [p. 2], 1 March, [p. 2] and 2 March 1854, [p. 3].

[3] *Bell's New Weekly Messenger*, Sunday 5 March 1854, p. 2.

[4] *The Leader*, 4 March 1854, v, No. 206, p. 209; see also pp. 194 and 198.

[5] *Athenaeum*, 4 March 1854, p. 279.

[6] *The Critic*, 1 April 1854, p. 187.

[7] *Literary Gazette*, No. 1938, 11 March 1854, pp. 231 f.

[8] *The Tablet*, 4 March 1854, p. 130.

[9] See below, p. 108.

[10] *The Tablet*, 11 March 1854, p. 154.

charitable and restrained,[1] and the *Guardian* called him 'one of the greatest geniuses France has in these latter years produced'.[2] The *Church of England Quarterly* was less warm. It attributed his fame to the *Paroles* and to his political enthusiasm, and said that he had lately become a bigoted infidel.[3] The *Christian Times* was factual and non-committal.[4]

One of the most interesting obituaries was that written by his old opponent J. W. Croker in the *Quarterly*. It appeared two years after Lamennais's death and is a suitably inaccurate parting shot:

> Lamennais died in retirement, not to say obscurity, in Paris, on the 27th February, 1855 [*sic*] at the age of seventy-three [*sic*], of a long and painful illness, and, as his last biographer intimates, without, as might have been hoped, any visible regret for the scandal which the anarchical reveries of his later life had created.[5]

During the second half of the century, France and things French became much better known in England than hitherto:

> Germany (wrote a contributor to the *Saturday Review* in February 1863) has nothing to say on the thoughts which now most haunt and perplex the minds of men. Therefore France and French thought have now an importance for England which is, in a manner, accidental, besides the permanent importance which one of the two great nations of the West can never fail to have for the other.[6]

It might have been supposed that the positivism of Comte and his followers and the scepticism of Renan were the salient features of French philosophy in 1863. But the writer in the *Saturday Review* thought otherwise: 'It is through France that we practically know what Catholicism is.'[7] Samuel Wilberforce, Bishop of Oxford, writing at about the same time, declared: 'Separated, therefore, even as we are from others, we cannot safely disregard

[1] *Catholic Standard*, 4 March 1854, p. 7; 11 March 1854, p. 5.
[2] *Guardian*, 8 March 1854, p. 190.
[3] *Church of England Quarterly Review*, N.S., ii, 1854, p. 524.
[4] *Christian Times*, 3 March 1854, p. 130.
[5] This is a footnote (p. 540) to much wild comment on Lamennais in Croker's review of Montalembert's *Political Future of England* in the *Quarterly*, March 1856, pp. 534–72.
[6] *Saturday Review*, 14 February 1863, p. 196, an article on 'French Thought', with special reference to Matthew Arnold's article on M. de Guérin in *Fraser's*, January 1863, pp. 47–61.
[7] ibid., p. 197.

the ebbs and flows of religious belief on the other side of the Channel.'[1]

This was the time when Matthew Arnold was attracted by the Church in France. It was largely his sympathetic interest in the Roman Catholic Church, and particularly in the Church in France, which helped to moderate the traditional English mistrust of Catholicism. As an educationalist he admired Lacordaire. In 1859 he visited a school run by him at Sorèze, and in the subsequent account of his visit[2] he showed that he appreciated that much of Lacordaire's effort sprang from the enthusiasm engendered by the *Avenir* and from a specifically religious attitude to life.[3]

This, for Arnold, was the heart of the matter. He believed that the Roman Catholic Church was more democratic in character, more capable of imparting to its children a religious attitude to life, than was the Church of England. He was no admirer of ultramontanism, but he warmed to a Church which had so much popular appeal.[4] It is significant that he pointed to this essential difference between the Church of England and the Church of France in a letter to Newman, which was occasioned by the latter's essay on Lamennais in *Essays Critical and Historical* (he refers particularly to pages 121 and 123):

Do not you think that what is Tory and anti-democratic in the Church of England (and undoubtedly her Tory, anti-democratic and even *squirearchical* character is very marked) is one of her great dangers at the present time; and a danger from which the Catholic Church, with its Gregories and Innocents of whom you speak, is much more exempt? I mean, though the R. Catholic Church may in fact have been anti-democratic in modern times on the Continent, there seems nothing in her nature to make her so; but in the nature of the English Church there does; and is not this an additional peril, at the present day, for the English Church?[5]

[1] S. Wilberforce, *Essays contributed to the Quarterly Review*, London, 1874, ii, p. 44. (The essay was first published in October 1865.)

[2] M. Arnold, *A French Eton* (*The Works of Matthew Arnold*, xii), London, 1904.

[3] In his *Popular Education in France*, 1861, he quoted with approval some early words of Lamennais against the secularization of the University and schools (*Democratic Education*, volume ii of the *Complete Prose Works of Matthew Arnold*, Michigan, 1962, p. 62).

[4] See the preface to the 2nd edition (1874) of *Higher Schools and Universities in France* (*The Works of Matthew Arnold*, xii), pp. 101–19.

[5] *Times Literary Supplement*, 31 March 1921, p. 211. The letter is dated 29 November 1871.

Newman replied that both he and R. H. Froude had agreed with this analysis and concluded: 'Perhaps La Mennais will be a true prophet after all.'[1]

Arnold's view of the democratic potentiality of the Church of Rome did not gain general favour, but his sympathetic appreciation of the character of Lamennais did. One of the dominant figures in his articles on the poets and diarists Maurice and Eugénie de Guérin[2] was 'the well-known Abbé Lamennais'.[3] Swimming against the tide of popular belief about Catholicism, he appealed to his public by describing the fervour, the simplicity, the severity, the freedom, the genius, the sincerity, and the lack of sacerdotalism which characterized La Chênaie:

> It is not the spectacle we most of us think to find in France, the France we have imagined from common English notions, from the streets of Paris, from novels: it shows us how, wherever there is greatness like that of France, there are, as its foundation, treasures of fervour, pure-mindedness, and spirituality somewhere, whether we know of them or not—a store of that which Goethe calls 'Halt'; since greatness can never be founded upon frivolity and corruption.[4]

These essays on Maurice and Eugénie sent the English reading public to their journals and letters. According to Browning, they produced an 'outcry of wonder and praise on every side'.[5] In the process Lamennais came prominently to the fore, and the note of deep admiration for his genius which Arnold had struck was sustained in all quarters. The *Saturday Review* spoke of the 'deep and admiring attachment which Lamennais inspired in so many hearts'.[6] The *National Review*, which, as Arnold acknowledged, had first introduced Eugénie to the English public in 1861,[7] included Lamennais with Corneille, Shakespeare, St. Augustine,

[1] *Times Literary Supplement*, 10 March 1921, p. 160. The letter is dated 3 December 1871. See below, pp. 101 f.

[2] On Maurice de Guérin: *Fraser's*, January 1863, pp. 47–61, reprinted in *Essays in Criticism*, 1st series (5th ed., 1896), pp. 80–120; on Eugénie de Guérin: *Cornhill Magazine*, vii, 1863, pp. 784–800, reprinted in *Essays in Criticism*, 1st series (5th ed., 1896), pp. 121–55.

[3] *Essays in Criticism*, 1st series, p. 85.

[4] *Fraser's*, January 1863, p. 49, *Essays in Criticism*, pp. 86 f.

[5] ed. E. C. McAleer, *Dearest Isa. R. Browning's Letters to Isabella Blagden*, Austin, U.S.A., 1951, p. 173.

[6] *Saturday Review*, 21 February 1863, p. 242.

[7] *National Review*, xii, 1861, pp. 145–51. The article, 'Eugénie de Guérin', makes no allusion to Lamennais.

Pascal, and Bossuet in the list of great thinkers who had nourished the masculine thought which underlay Eugénie's work.[1] These and other notices[2] testify to the respect and admiration felt for Lamennais, even in circles out of sympathy with his views. His genius, tenacity, and brilliance appealed to many.

The English translation of Mrs. Augustus Craven's much admired[3] *Récit d'une sœur*, which appeared in 1868, with its portrayal of Lamennais's 'strange mixture of fury and tenderness',[4] contributed to the same impression. When Arnold read it, as he did as soon as it appeared,[5] it must have confirmed him in the view of Lamennais and La Chênaie which he had already expressed and which was now widely held in England.

The careers of Lamennais's former associates were also attracting some attention at this time, and their connection with Lamennais was rarely overlooked. Sainte-Beuve's relations with him, although important, were not a dominating influence in his life. Yet they were recalled in England.[6] And a connection as slender as a common Breton origin was sufficient to link the priest with the sceptic Renan.[7]

It was, however, Lacordaire and Montalembert who provided English reviewers with the best opportunities to write of

[1] *National Review*, xvi, 1863, pp. 242 ff.

[2] *Christian Remembrancer*, xlvii, January 1864, p. 4; *Edinburgh Review*, cxx, July 1864, p. 253; *Theological Review*, iii, 1866, p. 504; *London Quarterly Review*, xxvi, April 1866, p. 194 (not as sympathetic as the others, but it still acknowledged that Lamennais was an 'extraordinary man').

[3] In 1898, George Tyrrell (still untouched by rumour of unorthodoxy) wrote: 'Catholicism is seen at high-water mark in Mrs. Craven's celebrated *Récit d'une sœur*.' (*George Tyrrell's Letters*, London, 1920, p. 256.)

[4] Mrs. Augustus Craven, *A Sister's Story*, translated by Emily Bowles, 3 vols., London, 1868, p. 213. Miss Bowles was a close associate of and sympathizer with Newman.

[5] *Matthew Arnold's Notebooks*, London, 1902, p. 57.

[6] In 1863 Browning told Isabella Blagden that Sainte-Beuve's main subject of study was Lamennais (ed. E. C. McAleer, *Dearest Isa*, 1951, p. 173). *Atlantic Monthly*, No. 17, April 1866, pp. 436 f. makes a suggestion which was later more closely applied by C. Maréchal in *La Clef de Volupté*, Paris, 1905, that Sainte-Beuve's relations with Lamennais were the key to his novel, *Volupté*. See also *Quarterly*, cxix, January 1866, pp. 91 f. (H. Marzials) and cxli, January 1876, p. 190 (A. Hayward); *North British Review*, li, 1869, p. 595; and *The Academy*, 13 November 1869, p. 31 (M. Arnold).

[7] *Fraser's*, November 1862, p. 587; *London Quarterly Review*, January 1864, p. 470; Francis Espinasse, *Life of Ernest Renan*, London, 1895, p. 11; *Atlantic Monthly*, March 1896, p. 429.

Lamennais. Lacordaire, who died in 1861, had visited England and was well known as a popular preacher, a social reformer, and the reviver of the Dominican Order in France. Mrs. Oliphant's account of him in *Blackwood's Magazine* dwelt at length on Lamennais's brilliance and Lacordaire's association with him.[1] The comments of H. Marzials in the *Quarterly* for 1864 gave the impression that the Lamennais of the *Avenir* still dominated the French religious scene and that he certainly had been the guiding influence in the career of Lacordaire.[2] Dora Greenwell's biography of the Dominican (1867) contained a long and moving poem about Lamennais. A popular novelist of the day, Dora Greenwell had obviously felt Lamennais's tragedy so deeply that she distilled her feelings into verse.[3] So prominently indeed did Lamennais figure in these accounts, and in others published in France, that Roman Catholics were much embarrassed.[4]

The history of Lacordaire's connection with La Mennais (wrote Bishop Hedley) is given in these pages [Foisset's *Lacordaire* and Montalembert's *Testament du Père Lacordaire*] with a fulness that will seem to some readers tedious. But a historian of a man who has been so much traduced for Lamennaisian principles as the author of the French Dominican revival, may be excused for trying to make the proofs of Lacordaire's rectitude of intention and loyalty to the Holy See as complete and convincing as possible.[5]

Montalembert was even better known in England than Lacordaire.[6] During Lamennais's lifetime, while there was still no knowing what he might do next, little attention was drawn to Montalembert's friendship with him.[7] His death, however, brought him more to the reviewers' notice and his inspiration was perceived in much of the Count's work. Croker, in the article in the *Quarterly* already referred to, tried to discredit Montalembert's opinion that

[1] *Blackwood's*, xciii, February 1863, pp. 169–87.
[2] *Quarterly*, July 1864, pp. 111–43.
[3] Dora Greenwell, *Lacordaire*, Edinburgh, 1867, pp. 272–4.
[4] *The Month*, v, 1866, pp. 221–40; *Dublin Review*, October 1870, pl 368; H. L. Sydney Lear, *Henri Dominique Lacordaire. A Biographica. Sketch*, London, 1882, p 67.
[5] *Dublin*, July 1870, p. 247.
[6] 'In England his [Montalembert's] name is as highly honoured as it is widely known' (*Edinburgh*, cxiv, October 1861, p. 318).
[7] e.g. the reviews of his *Des intérêts catholiques au xixe siècle* produced little comment on Lamennais: *Quarterly*, December 1852, pp. 137–56 (W. E. Gladstone); *Edinburgh*, xcvii, January 1853, pp. 221–30; *Dublin*, March 1853, pp. 139–74 (J. B. Robertson).

the Church of England was a Protestant Church by making it appear that he (Montalembert) was perpetuating the ideas of that 'unhappy madman'[1] 'of deplorable notoriety',[2] Lamennais. The *Edinburgh* also linked Montalembert closely with Lamennais but was less partial in its judgement.[3] After the publication of *Les Moines d'occident* (1860–7) Montalembert's fame increased. *Blackwood's* published an account of an interview with him by Mrs. Oliphant, in which she admitted that Lamennais was a greater figure than the Count.[4] Two years later appeared Mrs. Oliphant's own memoir of him in two volumes.[5] The hero of this work is not so much Montalembert as Lamennais, of whom she speaks with sympathy and respect. This affected Abraham Hayward's review of the work in the *Quarterly* so much that he traced Montalembert's views about Church and State back to Lamennais as their perspicacious but extreme and intolerant originator.[6] In this way, over the course of twenty years, the memory of Lamennais's early battles in the Church did not die but revived.

From France continued to come a steady stream of books by or about Lamennais, which gave English writers an opportunity to assess the extent of his achievement. Among these writers was R. W. Church, Rector of Whatley in Somerset, later to become Dean of St. Paul's.[7] He was interested in the development of Lamennais's character, for he saw in it a microcosm of the age in which he lived: the violent opposition of faith and despair. He reviewed both Forgues's edition of Lamennais's *Correspondance* and Blaize's *Œuvres inédites de Lamennais* for the *Saturday Review*.[8] Church was a Tractarian who did not attempt to ride

[1] *Quarterly*, March 1856, p. 540. [2] ibid., p. 539.

[3] *Edinburgh*, April 1856, p. 562; see also the *Contemporary Review*, May 1866, p. 21. [4] *Blackwood's*, April 1870, pp. 522–30.

[5] Mrs. M. O. W. Oliphant, *Memoir of the Comte de Montalembert*, 2 vols., London, 1872.

[6] *Quarterly*, cxxxiv, April 1873, pp. 415–56, reprinted in A. Hayward, Q.C., *Sketches of Eminent Statesmen and Writers*, i, London, 1880, pp. 264–328.

[7] For Church see B. A. Smith, *Dean Church: the Anglican Response to Newman*, London, 1958.

[8] 24 January 1863, pp. 116–18; 16 March 1867, pp. 337–9, reprinted in R. W. Church, *Occasional Papers*, 2 vols., 1897, i, pp. 301–33. The *Œuvres inédites* were reviewed *twice* in the *Saturday Review*. Church's account was preceded by a shorter but reasonably detailed notice on 5 January 1867, p. 29.

any Tractarian hobby-horses. He had presumably been drawn to the study of Lamennais by his Tractarian interests, but he represented him to a wide British public, not as a debating point in any current dispute, but as a deeply significant and tragic character on the contemporary scene.[1]

Another contributor to Lamennais's reputation was Edward Dowden (1843–1913), the critic and poet. As a young man he showed an interest in, although he was not exactly attracted by, Lamennais's theory of aesthetics as set forth in *De l'art et du beau*.[2] He found that the work had the incomprehensibility of genius and the logic of pure reason, 'which we empirical English have never had the good fortune to possess'. This led him to write a study of Lamennais's character for the *Fortnightly Review*.[3] It was the development of Lamennais's mind that Dowden, like Church, found most fascinating.

Lamennais's ability as a translator and commentator was noticed at about the same time. In October 1866 the *Westminster* published what was little short of a eulogy of Lamennais's translation of and notes on Dante's *Divine Comedy*. It called it 'one of the most eloquent, just and profound criticisms ever written upon the Divina Commedia'.[4] The article did not restrict itself to consideration of the work's merits as a translation. Although it praised the beauty of the style and admired the master's hand that had moulded it, it showed itself to be just as interested in the character and opinions of the translator himself. It made a striking and not unfavourable comparison between Lamennais and Dante.[5]

Just as neither Church nor Dowden had been satisfied to write only once about Lamennais, but had each gone on to amplify his portrayal of his character in another article, so the *Westminster*

[1] The *Saturday Review* was convinced of the contemporaneity of many of Lamennais's views. The issue for 12 September 1857 carried a powerful passage about the influence of Lamennais within the Roman Church, which concluded, 'she excommunicated Lamennais but quietly took his advice' (p. 234). In 1863 his name turns up frequently and in unexpected contexts.

[2] *Contemporary Review*, i, 1866, p. 300.

[3] *Fortnightly Review*, N.S. v, 1869, pp. 1–26 (vol. xi, old series), reprinted in E. Dowden, *Studies in Literature 1789–1877*, London, 1878, pp. 311–56.

[4] *Westminster*, xxx, October 1866, p. 393.

[5] ibid., p. 372.

followed the account of his Dante with a general one of Lamennais himself.[1] It would be gratifying to record that this showed a still deeper appreciation of his work; but it did not. It was inaccurate and only tolerably sympathetic. It did give, however, yet another account of his life and pin-pointed at least one typical reaction to the *Paroles*: it was, it said, very un-English to make such a fuss about liberty, for, on the one hand, liberty is too much a matter of necessity to be defended by declamation, and, on the other, experience has shown that its advent does not automatically banish selfishness and pride.[2]

In the next two decades very little appeared about Lamennais in print in England. As early as 1873 a famous unitarian divine, Charles Beard, wrote of him and his companions of the *Avenir* as if they were practically unknown.[3]

Towards the end of the century there was a minor revival of interest in him. This seems to have been started by an obscure pamphlet by a Christian Socialist, Alfred Tapley.[4] So little attention did this pamphlet receive that there was only one notice of it, in the *Toynbee Journal and Students' Union Chronicle* for December 1885. This notice, however, was not without its importance, for the following words were taken up and acted upon: 'When will Lamennais find an English translator? It is an incalculable loss to our public to be debarred from the pregnant thought of the "Past and Future of the People" or the Isaiah-like revelation of "The Words of a Believer".'[5] In response L. E. Martineau undertook a translation of these two works into English 'in the hope of making the English working classes acquainted with the character and teachings of the great French apostle of Democracy'.[6] This, too, went practically unnoticed, but F. T. Marzials, a promoter of French literature in England, claimed that nevertheless Lamennais still had something to teach the present generation. 'The man (he wrote) was assuredly a great man, great in influence, great in single-mindedness and

[1] *Westminster*, N.S. xv, 1869, pp. 512–34.

[2] ibid., p. 531.

[3] *Theological Review*, July 1873, pp. 339–64; January 1874, pp. 70–98, 'A Group of French Friends'.

[4] *Lamennais, Prophet of Democracy* (1885); see below, pp. 159 f.

[5] *Toynbee Journal*, i, 1885–6, p. 23.

[6] *Words of a Believer and The Past and Future of the People*, by F. Lamennais, translated by L. E. Martineau, with a Memoir of Lamennais [by Mazzini], London, 1891, Preface p. 7.

honesty of purpose, great in his literary gift.'[1] But, continued Marzials, the English reader needed something more than Mazzini's vague rhetoric in order to understand Lamennais's position.[2]

At this time, when Lamennais was chiefly regarded as a visionary concerned with the problems of shifting beliefs, there was one attempt to rehabilitate him as a traditional apologist, and to apply his defence of Christianity to the current religious situation. It was made by Lord Stanley of Alderley, who published in 1895 a translation of the first volume of the *Essai*.[3] In the very inaccurate preface he declared that its arguments were more needed in England then than they had been seventy-five years earlier, in order to combat the rationalistic tendency of some of the Oxford Essays and the spirit of infidelity generated by the works of Voltaire and Rousseau. *Lux Mundi*, the Oxford Essays referred to, had appeared in 1889, and, although they had aroused a furore at the time, the spirit of a liberal catholicism which they breathed was fast gaining a hold on influential theologians. Conservatives like Liddon were horrified, and Lord Stanley hoped that the *Essai* would remind Christians of the traditional, firm outlines of the Church and of the dangers of making any assault whatever on her faith or structure. It was with this in mind that he hoped that the *Essai* would combat those who were contending for the disendowment of the Church of Wales. Stanley, who was deeply involved in the discussion,[4] held that disendowment was being pressed so that money which would otherwise have been used for building and maintaining churches could be employed in a more utilitarian way:

I would hazard the expression of the opinion that there is little in the Abbé Lamennais's Essay to hurt the feelings of members of the Anglican Church, and that they would repudiate as strongly as he has done the writings of various philosophical writers, both English and French; and that the Protestants whom the Abbé attacks are not the clergy of

[1] *The Academy*, 3 October 1891, p. 279; similar sentiments were expressed at about the same time in the English translation of Leroy-Beaulieu's *Papacy, Socialism and Democracy*, London, 1892: 'La Mennais, the man whose influence has been the most important of the century' (p. 11).

[2] *The Academy*, 3 October 1891, p. 280.

[3] *Essay on Indifference in Matters of Religion*, by the Abbé F. de Lamennais, translated by Lord Stanley of Alderley, London, 1895.

[4] *Nineteenth Century*, xxx, November 1891, pp. 777–82.

the Church of England, but rather those persons who consider baths and wash-houses religious purposes, and objects of endowment to be preferred to parish churches for public worship.[1]

The extent of Lord Stanley's failure can be judged from this solitary comment, from the *Athenaeum*:

Lord Stanley of Alderley has published a translation (which he executed more than thirty years ago) of the first volume of Lamennais's famous 'Essay on Indifference in Matters of Religion' (Macqueen) and has added a complacent preface in which he tells us he has never troubled himself to read the other volumes of the ' Essai', and that he 'found M. Renan an uninteresting person and not one of much learning'.[2]

In contrast to this translation was a book by the Hon. W. Gibson, which was published towards the end of the following year, 1896. This was called *The Abbé de Lamennais and the Liberal Catholic movement in France*. In spite of its title, which took advantage of the intellectual climate of the day, it was a full-length biography, the only book in English to be devoted entirely to Lamennais until Dr. Vidler's *Prophecy and Papacy*. The circumstances of its appearance and its author's background will be dealt with later.[3] Here it is sufficient to say that it was a well-written, tolerably accurate, and very sympathetic account of Lamennais's life.

Since it was more concerned with his life than with his beliefs, especially his early beliefs, it had a greater public than the translation of the *Essai* and it was widely noticed by Roman Catholics and the general press alike.[4]

This book and, perhaps even more, the reviews to which it gave rise,[5] had the effect of fixing English opinions of Lamennais. He was not a great exponent of influential ideas; he was not a

[1] *Essay on Indifference in Matters of Religion*, Preface, p. xii.

[2] *Athenaeum*, 8 February 1896, p. 180.

[3] Below, pp. 145 f.

[4] Roman Catholics: *The Tablet*, 9 January 1897, p. 52; *The Month*, lxxxix, 1897, pp. 19–27 (G. Tyrrell). Others: *Spectator*, 5 December 1896, p. 818; *Guardian*, 10 February 1897, pp. 229 f.; *Quarterly*, clxxxv, April 1897, pp. 447–76; *Athenaeum*, 17 July 1897, p. 94; *Fortnightly*, lxxii, 1899, p. 73 (W. S. Lilly).

[5] We might also add 'reviews of reviews': Dr. Barry's *Quarterly* article, which had drawn attention to Lamennais's life rather than his opinions, was itself more or less favourably noticed by the *Saturday Review* (1 May 1897, p. 481), the *Guardian* (5 May 1897, p. 694) and the *Church Times* (21 May 1897, p. 607).

thinker whose works would be returned to time and time again; he was not a leader who commanded a large following of men acknowledging their debt to his thought. But in the words of later writers, he was 'one of the most remarkable figures of his time,'[1] 'one of the most striking personalities in the history of the last century',[2] a 'fascinating and harrowing figure',[3] 'a deeply unhappy genius',[4] and a 'great and tragic figure'.[5] Even if we allow for the element of exaggeration which always tinges descriptions of this sort, it is still clear that this country preferred the man to his works.

[1] M. V. Woodgate, *Père Lacordaire, Leader of Youth*, London, 1939, p. 47.

[2] W. S. Lilly, *Studies in Religion and Literature*, 1904, p. 178.

[3] H. G. Schenk in *The Month*, June 1954, p. 338.

[4] ibid. [5] ibid., p. 332.

III

LAMENNAIS AND THE ENGLISH

If it is true, as we have suggested, that the interest shown in Lamennais was aroused more by his character than by his ideas, then we must pause for a moment to see what personal contact he had with England and the English. While no one would claim that it was extensive by modern standards, nor that it was as important as it was in the lives of Chateaubriand and Montalembert, yet it is worth more notice than it has hitherto received. In the course of his life Lamennais made a number of English friends and acquaintances. Some of them played influential parts in his life. None of them would have denied that he made an impression on theirs.

His visit to England in 1815 had a decisive effect on his career, for it was here that he made a retreat under the direction of the abbé Carron, during which he determined to offer himself for the priesthood. Believing himself to be in danger of arrest for the anti-Napoleonic nature of some passages in the *Tradition*, he had suddenly decided to leave France for the Colonies.[1] In the event he never went further than England. He arrived some time in mid-April[2] and went straight to the house of the abbé Carron at 21 Kensington Gore,[3] a five-storey terrace house overlooking the place in Kensington Gardens where the Albert Memorial now stands.

The abbé Carron's influence changed the whole of Lamennais's life, and it was probably he who persuaded him to remain in England. This decision brought its embarrassments, for Lamennais was without means and therefore forced to find a job. The biographer of the abbé Carron tells us that Lamennais came to

[1] *O.I.* i, pp. 205 f.

[2] On 5 April he wrote (under the name of Patrick Robertson) to Blaize from Guernsey (*O.I.* i, pp. 207 f.). On 25 April he wrote to Bruté from London (*L. à Bruté*, p. 94).

[3] Not 'Kensington Road' as Maréchal says (*La Jeunesse de La Mennais*, Paris, 1913, p. 496) quoting a letter of Lamennais (*L. à Bruté*, pp. 96 f.). The correct address is given in a letter to Jean (12 September 1815, *O.I.* i, p. 224).

Carron to ask his help in obtaining a post, but 'non sans beaucoup de détours pour ménager son amour-propre'.[1] Carron was well acquainted with the important Roman Catholic families in London and undertook to search among the more celebrated ladies of this society.

Among these was Mrs. Jerningham, who was seeking a tutor for her children. The Jerninghams were a staunchly Roman Catholic family, and had taken a prominent part in caring for French émigré priests at the time of the Revolution, a work which extended well into the nineteenth century.[2] The Mrs. Jerningham to whom Lamennais applied is vaguely and nearly always inaccurately described in the many versions of the story.[3] She was in fact Emily, wife of Edward, the youngest son of Lady Jerningham, and sister-in-law to the future Lord Stafford. This Mrs. Jerningham received the unfortunate Frenchman, gave him a cursory glance, and then dismissed him on the grounds that he looked so much like a fool. Although this story became well known in England when Lamennais attained fame, and Forgues maintained that it was true,[4] it is not easy to reconcile with what is known of Mrs. Jerningham's character. A convert to Rome, more given to the traditional virtues than many of those who had been nurtured in the faith,[5] she was a model of docility and humility who was regarded by her family as something of a saint.[6] If the story is not apocryphal, the incident seems to have had little effect upon Lamennais's later relations with the Jerninghams. A few months after the appearance of the first volume of the *Essai*, he sent a copy to Mr. Edward Jerningham,[7] and after Mrs. Jerningham's death in 1822 he wrote affectionate words of condolence to Mlle de Tremereuc, an acquaintance who had known the Jerninghams in London.[8] His friendship with the family did

[1] *Vie de l'abbé Carron, par un Bénédictin de la Congrégation de France*, 2 vols., 1866, ii, p. 251.

[2] *The Jerningham Letters* 1780–1843, 2 vols. ed. by E. Castle, London, 1896, *passim.*

[3] e.g. 'Lady Jerningham, sister of Lord Stafford' (1848 translation of the *Paroles*); 'Lady Jerningham, sister-in-law of Lord Stafford' (1891 translation of the *Paroles*); 'Mrs. Jerningham, the sister of Lord Stafford' (Dr. Smiles in *Howitt's Journal*, ii, 1847, p. 19).

[4] *O.P.* i, p. x.

[5] *Jerningham Letters*, i, p. 242.

[6] ibid., pp. 245–51.

[7] A. Feugère, *Lamennais avant l'Essai sur l'indifférence*, Paris, 1906, p. 276.

[8] *O.P.* i, p. 101.

not, however, survive the crisis of his breach with Rome, for in 1848 Charles Edward Jerningham, one of the children whom he might have taught had his appearance been more prepossessing, wrote:

The real estimation in which religion was held by the Parisians, appeared from the results of their elections for the National Assembly, to which they sent, amongst their other representatives men of avowedly atheistical and impious principles, and the ex-abbé De La Mennais, a more obnoxious individual perhaps than the most declared infidel—grown hoary in foul and unnatural rebellion against the mother Church that had once numbered him among her most favoured children![1]

After a short while he found a job.[2] In a letter to his brother Jean on 6th May he reported that he had moved out of the centre of London into a boarding-house kept by an Irishman.[3] Here not only was the air better than at Kensington Gore; he also found the work of teaching about thirty children very pleasant. He stayed at Mr. Morton's school[4] for at least a month[5] and then returned to the abbé Carron.

Lamennais's letters say very little about Mr. Morton. All we know is that he was an Irishman who kept a small school and that M. Armand Carron, the abbé's nephew, was staying with him.[6] There is no evidence at all that he was an Anglican, as M. Maréchal suggests.[7] Indeed, since he was an Irishman and in view of Lamennais's silence on the subject, it is more than probable that he was a Roman Catholic. M. Maréchal bases his claim solely on the assertion that the *Lettres à un Anglais sur le protestantisme*[8] were not written to his young friend, Henry Moorman, as had been previously supposed, but to someone more capable of appreciating Lamennais's arguments. This

[1] C. E. Jerningham, 'France in 1848' in *Dolman's Magazine*, viii, 1848, p. 92.

[2] On another occasion it was reported that he had appeared on the doorstep of a house belonging to a family of quality, with whom he had been invited to dine, only to be told that nothing was being given to callers that day (Boutard, i, p. 100).

[3] *O.I.* i, p. 209 (6 May 1815).

[4] The Irishman's name is known only through a chance reference to his address in a letter to Jean, 31 December 1815 (*O.I.* i, p. 246).

[5] *O.I.* i, p. 211.

[6] *O.I.* i, pp. 210 f.

[7] C. Maréchal, *La Jeunesse de La Mennais*, p. 497. Dr. Vidler mistakenly follows Maréchal at this point (Vidler, p. 63).

[8] *O.I.* ii, pp. 271–286.

plausible suggestion does not fit the facts because, as Dr. Ahrens has shown, Lamennais wrote to Senfft in December 1819, referring to the possible publication of the 'deux lettres adressées à ce cher enfant que j'ai perdu'.[1] There can be no doubt that this refers to Moorman and not to Morton.

Lamennais returned as a teacher to M. Carron's institution in Kensington and there he remained until he left London in November. As far as we know, his acquaintances during this time were few,[2] but he made one friendship during his stay which biographers have found difficult to explain. M. Maréchal, in a volume of over 700 pages, which takes Lamennais's life only to 1817, overlooks it almost entirely, and mentions Henry Moorman once in his detailed account.[3] Other biographers have been more frank in admitting the important role which Moorman played in Lamennais's life, without being able satisfactorily to account for it. M. Forgues says: 'On cherche, dans les souvenirs que la vie a pu laisser, quelque chose qui rappelle une amitié aussi peu commune. Rien de comparable, rien d'analogue ne vient à la mémoire.'[4]

Moorman was a young man who became a chemist's apprentice. How he met Lamennais is unknown, for Lamennais does not seem to have made any effort to go out and meet Englishmen who did not immediately concern him. Certainly, their friendship was not approved by Moorman's stepfather, Mr. Jefferies, who must have perceived that his stepson's relations with a French priest were unsettling him.

[1] L. Ahrens, *Lamennais und Deutschland*, 1930, p. 139.

[2] The only connection with an English (or at least British) person of which we can be certain at this time, is his acquaintance with Miss Moore, a teacher (*Lettres de Lamennais à la Baronne Cottu*, ed. le Comte d'Haussonville, 1910, p. 201 and *passim; Revue hebdomadaire*, iv, 1909, pp. 288 and 292, letters to Baron Cottu). He may also have known Miss Trelawny, headmistress of the school for English and French girls run by the abbé Carron (he mentions the Trelawny family at *L. à M.*, p. 366). *Notes and Queries* (8 November 1884, p. 368) mentions a letter from a Lady E. Sheldon, Boulogne, 1828. There was a Mrs. Sheldon in the same circle of Catholic ladies as Mrs. Jerningham (*Vie de l'abbé Carron*, ii, p. 64) but I have not succeeded in discovering the connection, if any, between them. The same note refers to letters from James Rosse, Esq., Chapel House, Moorfields, London (perhaps a distant relative through Lamennais's grandmother's family?), and from Thomas Griffiths Jun., Brentford (the same who later became Vicar Apostolic to the London District?).

[3] Maréchal, *La Jeunesse de La Mennais*, p. 497.

[4] *O.P.* i, p. xiv.

In the course of their friendship Moorman determined to become a Roman Catholic, and to add to the atmosphere of mystery which enlivened a probably rather dull life, he took to himself a secret director, a Mr. Hunt.[1] It would, however, be wrong to suppose that his sole motive for friendship with Lamennais was excitement. He clearly had a deep affection for Lamennais, whom he called Féli, and his religious faith seems to have been equally sincere. In 1816 he escaped from his parents to France, but the abbé Carron advised him to obey them and to return home, on the condition that they gave an assurance that he would be free to practise his religion.[2] He returned to England without seeing his beloved Féli. His actions and his language became even more extravagant. Although he actually lived at 94 Smithfield Bars, he asked Lamennais to address letters to him care of Mr. Thomas Bodenham, the Anti-Gallican Coffee House, Threadneedle Street, and to give them the appearance of *billets doux* in order that Mr. Bodenham might show them proper respect.[3]

It was not long before he started to make further plans for a visit to La Chênaie, and he would have made the crossing in the summer of 1818 had it not been for his parents and his health.[4] He fell ill and died at the end of the year. Lamennais was heartbroken.[5] All his letters of this period tell of his grief, and even many years later he re-read the letters written to him by his 'pauvre Henry' and remembered him with regret.[6]

The fact that Lamennais *did* write his *Lettres sur le protestantisme* to Moorman throws more light on their friendship. His relationship with the boy was more than a curiosity of his early life, a symptom perhaps of religious immaturity: it was a relationship both emotional and intellectual. It was not intellectual in the sense that there was mutual stimulation of the intellect: Lamennais was the teacher and Moorman was the most willing pupil he ever had. At this stage in Lamennais's life the way to

[1] *O.P.* i, p. xv.
[2] *O.P.* i, p. xvi.
[3] *O.P.* i, pp. xvii f.
[4] *O.I.* i, pp. 341, 351 f., 357; *O.P.* i, p. xix.
[5] On 2 February 1819 Lamennais told Jean of Moorman's death as soon as he received a letter from Jefferies to the effect that Moorman had died of an abscess on the brain on 19 November 1818 (*O.I.* i, p. 385; *O.P.* i, p. xx).
[6] *Revue des deux mondes*, li, 1909, p. 579 (Letters to Mme Cottu).

friendship with him lay through conversion. Intellectual sympathy was a prerequisite for the warmth of true affection, and this remained the case until Lamennais left the control of the visible Church.[1]

If this is true, then we can suggest an explanation which accords well with what we know of Lamennais's character. Moorman came to him, perhaps through an acquaintance or friend who was a pupil at the school, seeking instruction. Lamennais, who was shy of approaching strangers, was filled with gratitude that one should approach him, and said so. At the same time he set forth his arguments in an intellectual and not an emotional way, giving his references, not merely in order to convince his friend, but also in order to satisfy himself. Thus Moorman was provided with a document which he could show to his guide in spiritual matters, possibly his vicar. The arguments which Lamennais countered in his second letter were those which would naturally have occurred to an ecclesiastic. Once Moorman had submitted to Lamennais's reasoning by deciding to become a Roman Catholic, Lamennais's interest in him grew. It grew in proportion to the boy's dependence upon him. Lamennais acted towards him as a spiritual father and made increasing demands of affection on him. This Moorman was able to give, for various reasons: he did not feel secure at home, his mother being widowed and remarried[2]; he was trying to profess against the wishes of his parents a religion which was discriminated against both officially and unofficially by the English[3]; and he was in ill health and longed for a wider and freer life. Lamennais loved him as his own son. The fact that his intellect could not in any way be compared with Lamennais's was of no account. His paternal interest in his 'pauvre petit Moorman'[4] was apparent even to Mr. Jefferies, who after his stepson's death wrote to him assuring him that he and his wife had done nothing to hinder the presence of a priest at their son's passing and offering him mementoes, including a lock of his hair.[5]

To ignore the part which Moorman played in Lamennais's life is to ignore an essential element in his character, his spiritualized urge for paternity.[6]

[1] Compare J. B. Robertson, *Lectures on Modern History and Biography*, Dublin, 1864, p. xiv.
[2] *O.P.* i, p. xiv.
[3] *O.P.* i, p. xv.
[4] *O.I.* i, p. 351.
[5] *O.P.* i, p. xxi.
[6] We have said nothing of homosexuality. This is dealt with in an article by M. Mourre (*La Parisienne*, July 1955, pp. 752–8), the main

It is not easy to make a clear-cut judgement on the results of his visit to England. Although he complained bitterly about the cost of books, it brought him into closer touch with English literature[1] and opened up to him fields of scholarship which were to prove useful in the *Essai*.

On the other hand, he was not favourably impressed by English government and institutions, and his criticisms of England from this time onwards were almost invariably harsh. Shortly after his return he wrote, with considerable vehemence:

Il existe en Europe un pays où les opinions religieuses ont consacré le principe de la souveraineté du peuple. Depuis lors le Gouvernement demi-populaire de cette nation, plus célèbre par son orgueil que par la pureté de ses moeurs, semble n'avoir connu d'autre règle de conduite ni d'autre justice politique que l'intérêt. Ainsi que les Romains, elle a étendu, par la force et la ruse, sa pesante domination sur les contrées lointaines, qu'elle opprime avec une impitoyable sagesse, et une savante barbarie: elle règne comme eux, et par les mêmes maximes; elle finira comme eux.[2]

English society was, he believed from his experience, an offence against truth:

J'ai vu, en Angleterre, l'effet de ces conspirations générales contre la vérité. À l'aide d'un système d'impostures suivi, on parvient à vicier l'intelligence de tout un peuple, à l'abuser sur les faits les mieux connus et les plus palpables, à le séparer totalement de la raison humaine sur certains points, et je ne serais nullement surpris qu'on en vînt là dans le royaume constitutionnel du Roi Très-Chrétien.[3]

and against liberty:

Dans cette *terre classique de la liberté*, cent mille personnes encombrent habituellement les prisons; le reste, contenus par des lois de fer, vit

concern of which is to repudiate the suggestion that Lamennais was homosexual not only by inclination but also by act. Nineteenth-century friendships were more intense than modern ones because they were judged by different standards (compare the analysis of Newman from this point of view in G. Faber, *Oxford Apostles*, Penguin, 1954, pp. 211–13). Without doubt there was a strong homosexual tendency in Lamennais's affections.

[1] He read English fluently and was well acquainted with Shakespeare and Milton. Of other poets he knew Dryden, Pope, Thomas Moore, and Byron. One of his favourite quotations, 'Man wants but little here below, nor wants that little long' is from Oliver Goldsmith (*The Vicar of Wakefield*, ch. 8, Ballad, st. 8).

[2] *Essai*, i, pp. 356 f.

[3] *O.P.* i, p. 144 (18 November 1825).

ou meurt au gré des maîtres, dont la classe qui ne possède rien dépend pour son travail et le prix de son travail.[1]

Throughout his life he was convinced of England's inherent immorality and impending dissolution.[2] He deplored her internal policies and abhorred Whigs and Tories alike.[3] Her foreign policy was no better.[4] Nor did his attitude change greatly in later life, despite the extent of the change in his other opinions.[5]

This harshness of judgement was, not unnaturally, extended to the Church of England. The motives which made him an ultramontane in his early years made him oppose Gallicanism and its more extreme relative, Anglicanism, throughout his life.[6] For him Anglicanism was the first and most deadly stage of Protestanism, and it was impossible for him to view it with an unbiased eye. Any sign on the part of the Irish or English Roman Catholic clergy of being even slightly Gallican in tendency earned swift condemnation on the ground that it meant a compromise with the Establishment, and therefore betrayed true religion.[7] He regarded Anglicanism as the source of the multiplicity of sects in England and especially of the 'folles rêveries' of the millenarianist Irving.[8] For him there was no question of Anglican orders being valid.[9] This opinion may have been the result of direct observation of the ways of Anglican ministers. He claimed that Protestantism failed to arouse the priestly virtues in Anglican ministers[10] and that, although English Protestantism was not as bad as that of Geneva,[11] the

[1] *O.C.* ix, p. 24 (*Des progrès*).

[2] *Revue des deux mondes*, xviii, 1923, pp. 403 f. (9 July 1822); *O.P.* ii, pp. 292 f. (22 June 1833); *Nouvelle Revue*, xx, 1883, p. 349 (17 October 1850).

[3] See the article 'État intérieur de l'Angleterre' in *Politique à l'usage du peuple*, 1839, i, pp. 160–4.

[4] 'Que cette Angleterre est abominable! Quel fléau pour l'Europe' (11 February 1823) (*Revue des deux mondes*, xviii, 1923, p. 424).

[5] *Revue hebdomadaire*, x, 1909, p. 39 (8 January 1854).

[6] *O.P.* i, pp. 175 f. (24 April 1826); *Nouvelle Revue*, xx, 1883, p. 349 (17 October 1850).

[7] *O.P.* i, pp. 181, 185, 221; *O.I.* i, p. 312; compare *Avenir*, 19 April 1831, where he accuses the French Church of 'le pur anglicanisme' (*O.C.* x, p. 288; *A.A.* iv, p. 4).

[8] *O.P.* ii, p. 293 (22 June 1833). He possibly had first-hand information from Ch. de Coux and Ch. MacCarthy, who arranged on 4 June to attend one of Irving's meetings together (letter by de Coux, Houghton MSS., Trinity College, Cambridge).

[9] *Cottu*, pp. 207, 210, 211 (10 August–19 November 1829).

[10] ibid., pp. 216 f.

[11] ibid., p. 157 (9 April 1824, from Geneva).

difference between the two was only the difference between coldness and hatred. Anglicanism deprived the English of the ability to understand any one but themselves.[1] The effects of Protestantism on English character, politics and society, which Lamennais had observed, became for him representative of the effect of Protestantism everywhere; there can be little doubt that much of his harsh treatment of Protestantism is directly attributable to his stay in England.[2]

That this, however, was largely an *emotional* response to his experience in England is shown in his detailed treatment of the Church of England. In writing the *Essai*, for example, he had been deeply indebted to the works of apologetics published by Anglicans in the seventeenth, eighteenth and early nineteenth centuries.[3] Most of the books on oriental studies from which he drew so many of his conclusions were by Anglicans.[4] His attacks on the Church of England were supported by unreliable and unrepresentative evidence,[5] while he showed almost complete ignorance of the official formularies of the Church, the Thirty-Nine Articles of Religion and the Book of Common Prayer, which could have

[1] *O.P.* i, p. 313 (7 December 1827).

[2] *O.P.* ii, p. 21 (12 March 1829): 'Je me suis trop hâté de conclure de l'Angleterre aux autres pays.'

[3] He especially appreciated Stillingfleet (whose latitudinarianism, however, he failed to note), George Stanley Faber, author of *Horae Mosaïcae*, and Bishop Warburton, author of *The Divine Legation of Moses*. Both Faber and Warburton provided Lamennais with valuable aids to the proof of the theory of the *sensus communis*.

[4] These included Edward Pococke and Thomas Hyde, both of whom had been successively Laudian Professor of Arabic and Regius Professor of Hebrew at Oxford, Thomas Maurice, an Anglican clergyman and author of *Indian Antiquities* (7 vols., 1792–1800) and the *History of Hindoostan* (1795), and the most considerable of them all, Sir William Jones.

[5] As butts he chose Cranmer (which would have been fair had he accused him of schism and heresy—*Essai*, i, p. 241), Chillingworth (a convert to Rome, reconverted to the Church of England and hot in controversy with a Jesuit—*Essai*, i, pp. 185 f., 200, 228; ii, pp. 250 f.), Gilbert Burnet (a latitudinarian among 'high' churchmen—*Essai*, i, p. 191), Bishop Hoadly (another latitudinarian in a more latitudinarian age, but still by no means representative—*Essai*, i, pp. 223, 225), Conyers Middleton (whose theories on miracles were more unorthodox than Lamennais mentioned—and treated as such by the rest of the Church—*Essai*, i, p. 232) and Dr. Watson, Bishop of Llandaff (who alone among the writers Lamennais cites had any claim to represent the general teaching of the Church of his day—*Essai*, i, pp. 223 f.; ii, préface, p. lxix and p. 259).

provided him with some deadly ammunition.[1] However, he was quite prepared to support his arguments about the *sensus communis* by references to Anglican works which he represented as glimmers of light in the prevailing Protestant gloom.[2] Far from proving his point, these testimonies were just as inconclusive as those in the opposite sense. They left the strong impression that things were not as clear-cut as Lamennais believed. On the one hand his limited experience of England told him that some of the clergy were lax and indifferent; his reading revealed tendencies to latitudinarianism amongst Anglicans; but on the other hand he knew that Anglicans were responsible for much fine scholarship and not a little teaching which he would recognize as soundly Catholic. His theory demanded that the Church of England should be condemned, and it seems that such opportunity as he had had to observe the life of Anglicans had not encouraged him to take any other course. Nevertheless he was honest enough to acknowledge his debt to many individual Anglicans. Although he never ceased to regard them as anything but Protestant and therefore wrong-headed, he was always ready to respect them as persons.

Similarly, although he abominated English politics and society, he did not dislike English people, whom he called 'drôles et plus drôles'[3] and 'fort curieux'.[4] He was always puzzled by the English: he found them cold in their manner, but not given to hatred[5]; polite but in a rather insolent way[6]; outwardly ungrateful but inwardly well-intentioned.[7] They had sense enough to develop

[1] Lamennais quotes the Thirty-Nine Articles twice, once favourably in the course of a longer quotation from the Reverend S. Wix (*Essai*, ii, préface, p. lx) and once unfavourably, on the Royal Supremacy (*Des progrès*, pp. 262 f.). He does not quote from the Book of Common Prayer at all.

[2] Hooker (*Essai*, ii, préface, p. lxiv), Field (*Essai*, ii, préface, p. lxv), Wix, whose book *Reflections concerning the Expediency of a Council of the Church of England and the Church of Rome being holden*, was published in 1818, after the appearance of the *Essai*'s first volume (*Essai*, ii, préface, pp. xlviii and lxii f.), the Reverend E. Robson, whose *Sermons* were likewise published in 1818 (*Essai*, ii, préface, p. lxvii), and Dr. Thomas Balguy, Archdeacon of Winchester, whose works, curious to say, impressed Lamennais greatly (*Essai*, ii, p. 253).

[3] *O.P.* i, p. 335.

[4] *Revue d'histoire littéraire de la France*, 12e année, 1905, p. 302 (6 September 1837).

[5] *Cottu*, p. 157 (9 April 1824).

[6] ibid., p. 97 (18 August 1820).

[7] *O.I.* i, p. 316 (9 January 1818).

a university system which was superior to the French one.[1] They were conservative, preferring the past to the future[2] and clinging fanatically to their ideas.[3]

Although Lamennais was as comfortable and content as he could be in his surroundings at Kensington,[4] yet the atmosphere of England was inimical to him. The climate did not suit him and the country made him unhappy.[5] In later years he said that six months in France was worth twenty years in any other country.[6] He saw religion and politics only through the eyes of a passionate French Catholic, and his enthusiasm for good order made him force what he saw into categories which would not fit it. The abbé Boutard was probably right in pointing out that this attitude of his was also inspired by repugnance for that utilitarianism, explicit or implicit, which is a characteristic of the English.[7] Boutard might also have added that this repugnance was increased by the fact that the core of Lamennais's teaching lay closer to utilitarianism than he himself would ever have admitted.

Lamennais returned to Paris on 18th November 1815. In the years which followed his return he made several important friendships with Englishmen. The first was with Mr. Thomas Weld of Lulworth Castle, Dorset, a member of one of the most faithful English Roman Catholic families.[8] On his return to France Lamennais spent much of his time at the Paris *pensionnat* of the abbé Carron at 12 Carrefour des Feuillantines, Rue Saint Jacques, a teaching establishment of the same foundation as those in the Tottenham Court Road and at Somers Town in London. It was here that he met Weld, who, after the death of his wife, had

[1] *Des progrès*, pp. 116 f.

[2] *O.P.* ii, p. 116 (10 February 1830).

[3] *Revue des deux mondes*, xxix, 1905, p. 776 (28 October 1819).

[4] *O.P.* ii, pp. 422, 446.

[5] *O.I.* i, p. 209 (6 May 1815) and p. 210 (1 August 1815).

[6] *Cottu*, p. 249 (29 September 1833).

[7] C. Boutard, *Lamennais: sa vie et ses doctrines*, i, p. 103. As early as 1836, Fortoul, closely acquainted with Lamennais and later to become a Minister of Napoleon III, wrote that during his stay in England Lamennais had seen how the sovereignty of the reason had degenerated into 'un égoïsme de marchands et d'entrepreneurs de chemins de fer' (*Grande Revue*, cxv, 1924, p. 267).

[8] For Weld, see J. Gillow, *A Literary and Biographical History . . . of English Catholics*, *ad loc.;* N. Wiseman, *Funeral Oration on His Eminence Cardinal Weld*, &c., London, 1837; *Recollections of the Last Four Popes*, London, 1858, pp. 382–90.

decided to offer himself for the priesthood and to put himself under the direction of the abbé Carron. The two became acquainted and Lamennais came to trust Weld, although they were never on terms of intimate friendship and even had periods of disagreement.[1] They were, however, on sufficiently friendly terms for Lamennais to show Weld his *Lettres sur le protestantisme*. Weld was so much impressed that he wanted to have them translated into English; he received Lamennais's permission to make what alterations he thought necessary to suit the English public.[2] These plans seem to have come to nothing, for the *Lettres* never appeared.

In writing to the inmates of the Feuillantines, Lamennais often asked to be remembered to Weld, even after he had returned to England to serve in his first parish.[3] In August 1826 Weld was consecrated Bishop of Amycla, and less than four years later Pius VIII made him a Cardinal, an appointment, Lamennais said, which would certainly have a good effect in England.[4] From Lamennais's point of view Weld's summons to Rome could scarcely have been more timely. In 1831 the editors of the *Avenir* decided to submit their doctrines to be examined by the Holy See. It was essential that their intermediary in Rome should be someone who was not only in sympathy with their ideas, but who was personally acquainted with them and would be able to appreciate their motives. The person whom Lamennais chose was Cardinal Weld.[5] The Cardinal was not a discerning critic of theological questions, but he was a personal friend, and as far as the prevailing diplomatic and ecclesiastical atmosphere would allow, he was helpful. Lamennais was a frequent visitor at his luxuriously appointed apartments and was much pleased with all that Weld did and said on his behalf. 'Il a été excellent pour moi', he told Mlle de Lucinière. 'He is really a plain dealer man without politics and ceremonies.'[6] Weld made no secret of associating himself with Lamennais,[7] and even after the announcement of

[1] *O.P.* i, p. 101 (7 July 1822), p. 102 (15 October 1822), and p. 107 (13 February 1823).

[2] L. Ahrens, *Lamennais und Deutschland*, pp. 139 f. (17–18 December 1819).

[3] *O.P.* i, p. 98 (10 May 1822).

[4] *O.P.* ii, p. 118 (19 February 1830).

[5] *O.P.* ii, p. 197 (27 February 1831).

[6] *O.P.* ii, p. 230 (12 January 1832).

[7] L. Ahrens, *Lamennais und Deutschland*, p. 241.

Lamennais's failure, Weld kept his regard for him and had full confidence in his ability to render further service to the Church. He gave no sign of suspecting all the intrigues[1] and interior struggles which preceded Lamennais's unconditional submission of 12th December 1833. He saw nothing dishonest or insincere in the submission and thought that it did its author very great credit.[2] According to the young student Charles MacCarthy,[3] whose information is not always to be relied upon, he wanted Lamennais to come to Rome, even in January 1834. He wanted to procure a prelacy and a librarianship of the Vatican for him.[4] The Cardinal remained in Rome, where he died on 19th April 1837, but as far as we know, his friendship with Lamennais ended with *Singulari nos*.

For other friendships with Britons made during the years before 1833 we move back to the time of Lamennais's first visit to Rome in 1824. During his stay there he was a frequent visitor at the English College, where Dr. Robert Gradwell was the Rector and Nicholas Patrick Stephen Wiseman was a brilliant young pupil. The eccentric Dr. Gradwell never liked Lamennais,[5] but it was otherwise with his pupil. The famous author of the *Essai* was present when Wiseman defended his doctoral theses. Dr. Gradwell, describing the scintillating company, said: 'Monsieur Mennais was to have objected, but he excused himself, and said

[1] Taking part in these intrigues was Weld's son-in-law, Lord Clifford. What his contribution was is unknown, except that he later wanted to publish items of news about Lamennais in a periodical which he directed. Lamennais believed that the Pope had refused permission because in his opinion the *Paroles* had been provoked by what had been already published in *L'Ami de la religion* and to publish more would make matters worse (*L. à M.*, p. 314, 3 August 1834, and *O.P.* i, p. xcii, 24 December 1833).

[2] T. Wemyss Reid, *Life, Letters, and Friendships of Richard Monckton Milnes*, 1890, i, p. 151.

[3] On MacCarthy see below, pp. 77-88.

[4] *Le Portefeuille de Lamennais*, ed. G. Goyau, 1930, p. 125 (16 January 1834). Probably referring to this letter, Lamennais wrote to Marion (31 January 1834): 'On a noué à Rome des intrigues pour m'y attirer, et m'y clore la bouche avec je ne sais quoi' (A. du B. de la Villérabel, *Confidences de La Mennais*, Nantes-Paris, 1886, p. 100).

[5] Partly because of his opinions (see his views on the cardinalate controversy below, p. 127), but partly also because he was French: 'Monsr. L'Abbé Mennais has asked me about the English Colleges in France. I gave him what information I possessed, and told him that France behaved shabbily and ungratefully in the business' (letter to Dr. Poynter, 26 August 1824, in the Westminster diocesan archives).

that in such an assembly he could not say four words. . . .'[1] Wiseman and Lamennais became friendly. Wiseman took a letter from the abbé to Mlle de Lucinière, which included a request to put the young Doctor in touch with a society of mission priests in whom he was interested.[2] His acquaintance with Lamennais made such a profound impression on him that over thirty years later he maintained the unpopular view that the abbé had been made a Cardinal *in petto* by Leo XII.[3] Wiseman worked in England until he returned to Rome in 1828 to succeed Dr. Gradwell. He was still there when Lamennais came on his second visit. They renewed their friendship and he set down his impressions of Lamennais in words which have now become almost the standard picture of him:

How he did so mightily prevail on others it is hard to say. He was truly in look and presence almost contemptible; small, weakly, without pride of countenance or mastery of eye, without any external grace; his tongue seemed to be the organ by which, unaided, he gave marvellous utterance to thoughts clear, deep, and strong. Several times have I held long conversations with him, at various intervals, and he was always the same. With his head hung down, his hands clasped before him, or gently moving in one another, in answer to a question he poured out a stream of thought, flowing spontaneous and unrippled as a stream through a summer meadow. He at once seized the whole subject, divided it into its heads, as symmetrically as Fléchier or Massillon; then took them one by one, enucleated each, and drew his conclusions. All this went on in a monotonous but soft tone, and was so unbroken, so unhesitating, and yet so polished and elegant, that, if you had closed your eyes, you might have easily fancied that you were listening to the reading of a finished and elaborately corrected volume.[4]

Wiseman went on to tell how he used to listen spellbound to the abbé's flood of talk about historical fulfilment of scriptural prophecies and to his impassioned words about the conversion of England. Wiseman's cousin, Charles MacCarthy, who was also at the College, became an intimate of Lamennais's and kept the two in touch after Lamennais's departure. At the beginning of 1834, after Lamennais's submission to *Mirari vos*, Wiseman sent

[1] Letter from Gradwell to Poynter, 10 July 1824, in the Westminster Diocesan Archives.

[2] *O.P.* i, p. 114 (13 July 1824).

[3] Below, pp. 127-30.

[4] N. Wiseman, *Recollections of the Last Four Popes*, &c., 1858, pp. 337 f.

'mille choses' to his friend.[1] In May of the same year, MacCarthy wrote an enthusiastic and laudatory letter to Lamennais about the *Paroles*, saying that Wiseman completely shared his opinion of the book.[2] In June he wrote to say that his cousin wished to be remembered to Lamennais and was taking a lively interest in all he was doing. Some days later, Wiseman, through MacCarthy,[3] expressed his sympathy with Lamennais and his sorrow at the promulgation of *Singulari nos*.[4] MacCarthy, who was never a temperate informant, probably made the best of Wiseman's interest in Lamennais; yet there is no reason to suppose that any of these expressions of sympathy was insincere. Wiseman's moving passage about Lamennais in his article on the Oxford controversy[5] and his later firm belief that Lamennais had been made a Cardinal show that, if he disapproved of Lamennais's action, he still retained some affection for him and was deeply aware of the impression the abbé had made upon him. But Wiseman was a loyal member of the Church. After the publication of *Affaires de Rome*, or even earlier, the two had no further communication with each other.[6] In the lectures which he delivered in St. Mary's, Moorfields, London, during Lent of 1836, Wiseman expressed what must have been his final feelings on the matter:

> She [the Church] exacts such implicit obedience, that if any member, however valuable, however he may have devoted his early talents to the illustration of her doctrines, fall away from his belief in any one point, he is cut off without reserve; and we have, in our own times, seen striking and awful instances of this fact.[7]

Wiseman had met Lamennais in 1824, and it was in the same year that Lamennais made another important and valuable contact with England. Among the many Englishmen[8] he met

[1] *Portefeuille*, p. 127.
[2] *O.P.* i, p. cii.
[3] *Portefeuille*, p. 155 (21 June 1834).
[4] ibid., p. 160 (1 July 1834).
[5] Below, p. 108.
[6] *Cornhill Magazine*, xi, 1865, p. 507 (from Lord Houghton's reminiscences of Cardinal Wiseman).
[7] *Lectures on the Principal Doctrines and Practices of the Catholic Church*, 1836, i, p. 77.
[8] These included Charles Audley, an English boy whose education he had undertaken from the age of 13 and with whom he remained in touch for many years (he later became editor of the *Ami de la religion*), English priests who were attracted by the vigour of La Chênaie (*O.I.* ii, p. 18—9 July 1824; *O.P.* i, p. 391—9 September 1828), and at least one Member of Parliament, The Hon. James Talbot, who visited him in 1833 (*O.P.* ii, p. 338—27 December 1833).

in the years before the publication of the *Paroles*, it was James Burton Robertson who was later to be in the best position to see that his countrymen treated Lamennais fairly. Robertson was about twenty-four when he first made Lamennais's acquaintance.[1] He had been born in London of a Presbyterian family, but his mother had insisted that he should be brought up a Roman Catholic, and from 1810 to 1815 he attended Old Hall, Ware[2]. When he first met Lamennais he was a young man of literary ability without any settled occupation. From 1824 to 1829 they kept in touch by correspondence and through the de Senffts.[3] Robertson stayed at La Chênaie from September 1829 to July 1830. About this stay we know only what Robertson recorded in later years. So influenced was he by Lamennais that as late as 1864, in the preface to his *Lectures on Modern History and Biography*, he paid his former friend a touching and surprising tribute. The lectures were delivered before the Catholic University of Ireland, at which Robertson held the Chair of Geography and Modern History, which was subsequently united with that of English Literature. The sympathy with Lamennais which they express may well have angered the strictly orthodox among his audience. He acknowledges that Lamennais, with whom he was afterwards 'united in the bonds of closest friendship', had 'exerted the greatest fascination' over him.[4]

> As I have introduced him as one of the authorities from which I derived information on the ecclesiastical, political and literary affairs of the Restoration, I must here record my lasting gratitude to him for his many proofs of friendship as well as for examples of piety, and for lessons in religion, philosophy and literature, which have been of invaluable service to me through life.[5]

Lamennais's deep influence upon Robertson during these ten months of study and discussion[6] is evident from his estimate of

[1] J. B. Robertson, *Lectures on Modern History and Biography*, 1864, pp. xiii f.; Feugère, *Lamennais avant l'Essai sur l'indifférence*, p. 299.

[2] For biographical details see Gillow, *Bibliographical Dictionary of the English Catholics*, &c., *ad loc.*

[3] *Notes and Queries*, 8 November 1884, p. 368 refers to letters from Robertson to Lamennais, but I have been unable to trace them. See *O.P.* i, p. 179 (10 May 1826); *O.P.* ii, pp. 58 f. (5 July 1829), pp. 149 f. (13 July 1830) and p. 152 (23 July 1830).

[4] Robertson, op. cit., preface, p. xii.

[5] ibid., p. xiv.

[6] cf. J. Marie Peigné, *Lamennais, sa vie intime à La Chênaie*, Paris, 1864.

Lamennais's importance. He lists five benefits bestowed upon the Church by Lamennais: the early writings, which he maintained, in spite of contemporary disfavour, would always be esteemed in the Church; the fact that he had made more conversions from Protestantism and Deism than any other writer of his time; his co-operation with J. de Maistre in the banishment of Gallicanism; his works of piety; and his fight for the freedom of the Church and freedom of education.[1]

In the *Lectures* themselves Robertson analysed the nature of Lamennais's genius as he knew it, by comparing it at length with that of Chateaubriand. In the end, the passionately intellectual priest gets the better of the comparison with the graceful littérateur[2]—a striking tribute to the firmness of Robertson's affection for his teacher. This affection remained even through the later parts of Lamennais's life, although they had no direct contact with each other after about 1834.[3] In 1852, two years before Lamennais's death, Robertson wrote in the *Dublin Review* an account of him which stood out in contrast to the vilifications of his name usual at the time.[4] Three years later, at Newman's request, Robertson accepted the Chair of Geography and Modern History in the newly founded Catholic University of Ireland at Dublin. In 1869 Queen Victoria, on Mr. Gladstone's recommendation, awarded him an annual pension of £90 for his service to letters.[5] In 1873 Pope Pius IX made him a Doctor of Philosophy. He died in Dublin in 1877. His generosity to Lamennais in his published work prepared the way for the more understanding treatment of him by Roman Catholics in England at the end of the century.

While Lamennais was in Rome between 30th December 1831 and 10th July 1832 he had passports into two types of English society and he used both freely.

The first was his old connection with the English College and its Rector, Dr. Wiseman, whom he visited often. It was here

[1] Robertson, op. cit., pp. xiv f.
[2] ibid., pp. 290, 355, and 403. [3] ibid., p. xiv.
[4] *Dublin*, December 1852, 'Joseph de Maistre', pp. 423 f.
[5] He was touchingly grateful to Gladstone for this service and sent him copies of his works as a mark of his thanks (B.M. Add. MSS. 44404, fo. 198 and 335). He was careful to acknowledge that the award of his pension in no way implied recognition by the Government of the Catholic University.

that he met Wiseman's cousin, Charles Justin MacCarthy of Cork,[1] who had entered the college in 1828 with the intention of being prepared for the priesthood.[2] The friendship which sprang up between them was one of the most significant in Lamennais's life.

Lamennais was immediately so attracted to MacCarthy that he tried to persuade him to go back with him to Paris:

I see a great deal of Montalembert and Lamennais [MacCarthy wrote to his friend Monckton Milnes].[3] The latter has been pressing me most earnestly to accompany him to Paris, plunge myself with him into politicks and the 'Avenir', and prepare for running the same career in England which he has run in France; a proposal which I most respectfully decline.[4]

MacCarthy was not yet ready to go as far as Lamennais wanted to press him. Nevertheless, when Lamennais left for France, they kept in close touch and exchanged letters frequently, Lamennais's most earnest and priestly, MacCarthy's flippant and light-hearted. 'I have had two or three most affectionate and magnificent letters from Lamennais, and one from Montalembert',[5] MacCarthy wrote to Milnes in August 1832, but he went on to talk of *Mirari vos* in terms which fell short of Lamennais's seriousness:

When you come back you will be amused with reading a document which has lately been published here, to wit the Pope's encyclical letter to all the Bishops in Christendom. The only productions of a similar nature to which it can be compared are the proclamations of the [Tsar] Nicholas to the Poles, and the Orange manifestoes in Ireland. I should [like] to watch the countenance of Montalembert as he reads it for the first time. [I] think it would be a fine subject for a painting.[6]

[1] The only account of MacCarthy hitherto has been Dom L. Gougaud's article 'Un disciple de La Mennais, gouverneur de Ceylan, Charles MacCarthy' in *Revue des facultés catholiques*, April 1914, reprinted Angers, 1914. The following pages provide much additional information.
[2] *The Times*, 19 August 1864, p. 10. He was born not in 1820, as *The Times* said, nor 'vers 1810' as Gougaud said (op. cit., p. 1), but in 1812 (*Who's Who*, 1863, p. 165).
[3] Milnes, who later became Lord Houghton, also knew Lamennais. See below, pp. 88 f.
[4] Unpublished letter of Thursday 14 June 1832, in the Houghton papers, bundle labelled 'Sir C. J. MacCarthy', Trinity College, Cambridge. All extracts are reproduced by permission of the Master and Fellows.
[5] T. Wemyss Reid, *Life, Letters, and Friendships of R. M. Milnes*, 2 vols., 1890, i, p. 141.
[6] Same letter, letter 5, MacCarthy-Milnes, 30 August 1832.

Lamennais continued to urge him to come to France,[1] but in the autumn something else happened to disturb their relationship. MacCarthy, ever unstable, had a recurrence of a hereditary mental disease. The doctors thought it was epilepsy and MacCarthy feared for his sanity, but slowly he recovered.[2] Lamennais was upset by the news, which only served to increase his affection for the young man: 'Ce jeune homme m'intéresse toujours plus. Avec un esprit très élevé, il a une âme aimante qui attire l'amour.'[3]

MacCarthy's illness had cast a gloom over his own view of the situation, which he described to Milnes in these words:

I suppose you in your Ionian deserts have heard nothing of the Pope's Russo-Austrian encyclick letter, and of the condemnation and retraction of poor Lamennais who has retired with a furled banner and a broken heart to his seclusion in Brittany where I apprehend he will not long survive the ruin of his hopes. He writes to me the most beautiful and touching letters, and seems still to cling to the idea that he may be able at some future time to effect that reconciliation between the past and the future to the furtherance of which his life has been hitherto dedicated. But I fear that if such a union ever does take place, he is not destined to work, or even to witness it. May he rest in peace; let another generation write his epitaph.[4]

In the meantime Lamennais continued to write to MacCarthy. Hitherto none of these letters has been known, but one has now turned up among Lord Houghton's papers.[5] It enables us to judge more accurately what Lamennais's attitude to MacCarthy was. He starts by advising him to bear his illness with patience, resignation, and love, and to regard it as the cross which has to be carried by all Christ's true disciples. He then moves into one of his most highly developed apocalyptic passages, where he reviews the state of the world in general and highly coloured terms and concludes that the changes in it are the result

[1] *L. à M.*, p. 20 (14 October 1832).

[2] Letter 6, MacCarthy-Milnes, 8 December 1832.

[3] *L. à M.*, pp. 25 f. (26 November 1832). Lamennais asked Montalembert to keep in touch with MacCarthy (*M. à L.*, p. 26—4 December 1832).

[4] Letter 6, MacCarthy-Milnes, 8 December 1832. The rest of the letter is interesting. He compares Lamennais's position with that of Galileo, tells Milnes about Lamennais's progress in converting Schelling to Roman Catholicism, and says much of Wiseman, de la Ferronays, &c.

[5] Bundle 'Sir C. J. MacCarthy', 9 December 1832, see Appendix A, pp. 196-8.

of something instinctive, something organic in humanity. In these circumstances, he says, it is impossible for him to be very much interested in what is going on in Rome in connection with his recent visit. He affects a complete lack of concern for such little matters. But—and here his natural curiosity and very considerable self-consciousness get the better of him—all the same he is eager for any news of Rome which MacCarthy can give him. He asks the young man to write to him in as great detail as possible.

This letter sums up the state of his mind at this crucial period of his life. Lamennais could see the world changing around him; he could vaguely see the way his thought was tending; but he did not want to relinquish Rome. MacCarthy was one of his contacts with the city which had treated him so badly. Lamennais was trying desperately to persuade him into his circle of co-operators, which included, in December, Görres, Baader, and their German friends, but without success. 'I may', MacCarthy wrote to Milnes, 'perhaps co-operate with him where I am, but have no present intention of uniting myself more closely with him.'[1]

MacCarthy's health continued to cause Lamennais much concern[2] and in mid-March he left Rome[3] to return to England for a while. During the journey he kept Lamennais and Montalembert well informed so that Lamennais should be reassured of his health. By the end of March MacCarthy had reached Florence and wrote to Lamennais, suggesting that he should write to him care of Lady Harriet Jones[4] at Passy, near Chamonix.[5] He was still not well, which made Lamennais worry greatly.[6] After a wearisome journey he arrived in Passy on 4th April, where he received news of the death of his father.[7] Although conversation was hampered by the presence of Lady Harriet Jones, he saw Montalembert briefly and gave him several letters for Lamennais

[1] Letter 7, MacCarthy-Milnes, 18 December 1832.

[2] *L. à M.*, p. 82 (1 March 1833).

[3] ibid., p. 83 (18 March) and p. 99 (29 March 1833).

[4] Lady Harriet Jones, the only daughter of the 8th Earl of Fingal, was married to John Jones, Esq., of Llanarth Court, whose sister Apollonia married another friend of Lamennais's, A.-F. Rio (see below, p. 88) in the following year.

[5] *L. à M.*, p. 112 (22 April 1833). [6] ibid., p. 120 (1 May 1833).

[7] Letter 11, MacCarthy-Milnes, 5 April 1833.

which he had brought from Rome. These included letters from the Abbate de Luca, secretary to Cardinal Weld,[1] and Padre Ventura.[2] By the time he reached London, on 17th or 18th April, he was very weak and wrote to Montalembert giving him details of the journey.[3]

It took, however, only a few days for him to recover considerably, and when he wrote to Lamennais towards the end of April he said that he was feeling very much better.[4] He remained in England for three months and returned to France at the end of July. After a short stay in Boulogne with Lady Harriet,[5] he arrived at La Chênaie to spend from 26th August to 13th September with Lamennais.

Of his stay in Brittany Lamennais has written little,[6] but MacCarthy's record deserves to be included with some of the most vivid descriptions of the atmosphere of that household:

I have been here a week in the heart of Brittany, and shall stay at least a week longer. Shut out completely from the world by the druidical oaks from which my present abode takes its name, and at the distance of several leagues from the nearest town, I have nothing to do but to listen to the low soft voice of my host which is for ever in my ear, and to the noise of the wind among the trees not more solemn and expressive. Here indeed he seems to be in his right place, in the midst of these paternal oaks, the sole relicks of a ruined fortune, which have in turn shaded his childhood, and protected his maturity, and must now offer an asylum to his old age. Every thing around me here harmonizes perfectly with that sort of emotions of which I am just now most susceptible, that grave, quiet, somewhat melancholy cast of feeling, not unaccompanied by a certain gentle excitation and low enthusiasm of thought, which fits the mind to learn and to reflect, to bear with patience, and to hope with tranquillity. The house itself is a spacious, venerable mansion, embowered, almost embedded in trees, with bright oaken floors, and high embowéd windows, like some of our old monastick dwellings in England, only still more antique and cloister-like. The country around is like any thing but France. Dinan in particular, the nearest town to us, is one of the most picturesque spots I have seen

[1] *M. à L.*, pp. 74 f. (5 April 1833); Wiseman, *Recollections*, p. 388.
[2] *Portefeuille*, p. 118 (13 March 1833).
[3] *M. à L.*, pp. 84 f. (26 April 1833).
[4] *L. à M.*, p. 128 (5 May 1833, quoting a letter of 29 April 1833).
[5] Letter 14, MacCarthy-Milnes, 5 July 1833.
[6] *L. à M.*, p. 163 (26 August 1833); *Annales de Bretagne*, xxviii, 1912–13, p. 185 (letter to Rio, 20 August 1833).

in any country. The environs of St. Malo, they tell me, are still finer. I am going to row up the river next week as far as that town, which is only five leagues off, and if the Abbé consents to come with me, may perhaps go on in the steamboat to Jersey which, I believe, is worth seeing.

There follows this perceptive description of Lamennais:

As for my host himself, I shall be able to tell you more about him when we meet. Certainly the admiration which I have long felt for him has not been diminished by the opportunity which I now possess of reading his thoughts as they impress themselves on his mind, and by all the intimate revelations of his being, the thousand 'little, nameless, unremembered acts of kindness and of love', which come daily under my observation. What I admire most, and what I think distinguishes him most completely from the other master-spirits of our age, is the firmness, the perfection of his *will*, the voluntary concentration of all his high faculties towards one point, the highest certainly at which human thoughts and human efforts can aim. I think it is Novalis who says: 'Ein Charakter ist eine vollkommen gebildete Wille' [*sic*], and I believe it is precisely the want of this particular species of *Bildung* which makes the men of our days, with all their multifarious knowledge and fine-drawn judgment, such a puny, milk-and-water race of pygmies as they are.

The extent of Lamennais's influence upon his guest at this time can best be judged from this passage:

Since I have been here I have read almost the whole of his unpublished work on philosophy which he intends not to print for two or three years. It is certainly superior to all that he has yet published, and will create a great sensation when it appears. It is a vast, all-embracing synthesis, based upon Faith, and applied to all branches of Divine and human thought and action. With many of these applications I cannot at all agree, particularly with those peculiar views of the philosophy of history which lead to his judgments on the present state of society, politically considered. Nevertheless, such is the influence of a superior mind over an inferior one that I find myself daily backsliding into some or other of the opinions which startled me at first. But we shall be able to talk about all these things better when we meet.[1]

In spite of the reservations which he here expresses, Lamennais's influence over his mind was increasing. MacCarthy was becoming less and less in sympathy with his friend Kenelm Digby,

[1] Letter 16, MacCarthy-Milnes, 'La Chesnaye, August 31st' (1833).

the author of *Mores Catholici*, a Roman Catholic with strong medieval leanings, and more and more aware of the need for vigour in the future.[1]

From La Chênaie he went to Berne to visit Milnes,[2] who was staying there with his father after having spent a period of convalescence with Walter Savage Landor.[3] This visit greatly deepened his attachment to Milnes.[4] After a stop in Venice he spent a week in Florence with the Senffts,[5] and was in Rome by the end of November. Throughout the whole of this journey, which took place during part of the most important period in Lamennais's life, Lamennais showed the deepest affection and concern for his friend. He was eager to receive news from him and passed news back to him through Montalembert.

Once back in Rome, MacCarthy continued his correspondence with Lamennais. It is worth noting that during his journey and before his visit to La Chênaie he had written first and more fully to Montalembert, who had passed the news on to his master. But after the visit to Brittany there is a perceptible cooling of the friendship between the two young men and a corresponding increase of warmth between Lamennais and MacCarthy. For this short period Lamennais's mind dominated MacCarthy's.

In December MacCarthy wrote a spirited letter from Rome about the corruption of the city and its intrigues,[6] and in January 1834 he reported that Cardinal Lambruschini and the Jesuits were in general opposed to Lamennais's doctrines, although there were many who were for him.[7] MacCarthy did not feel easy about these latter because he feared that they believed that Lamennais was more attached than he actually was to Rome, 'cet amas de ruines'.[8] Here speaks not a deluded well-wisher but a true disciple of Lamennais. He had already given up the idea of being ordained, and Wiseman had given him permission to return to England when he wished.[9] In another letter he told

[1] Letter 17, MacCarthy-Milnes, 30 September 1833.

[2] *L. à M.*, p. 179 (21 September 1833).

[3] J. Pope-Hennessy, *Monckton Milnes, the Years of Promise*, 1949, p. 67.

[4] MacCarthy's letters to Milnes after this date are marked by greater sensitivity about little things. He often gives expression to his need for someone to love.

[5] *O.P.* ii, p. 313 (6 September) and p. 316 (27 September 1833).

[6] *O.P.* i, p. xcii (24 December 1833).

[7] *L. à M.*, p. 244 (2 February 1834).

[8] *Portefeuille*, p. 125 (16 January 1834).

[9] ibid., pp. 127 f.

Lamennais something of the pain which this caused him.[1] On 4th March 1834 he urged Lamennais to publish a statement of the full development of his ideas because, he said, he saw them fermenting on the horizon of Europe. He added, although it is doubtful if the source of his information was very reliable, that Lamennais's philosophy had had great influence on all the works of philosophy recently published in Germany.[2]

After the publication of the *Paroles* on 30th April 1834 MacCarthy started what amounted to a campaign to encourage Lamennais in the course he was already pursuing. His motives for doing so can be judged from the following extract from a letter to Milnes:

The Abbé's book is making a great stir here. 'The red eyes of strained authority' pounced upon it immediately, and are ready to start all crimson from their sockets at ye sight. It is strictly forbidden by ye police, and as ye ambassadors are complaining loudly,[3] will probably be condemned. The most charitable judges presume that ye author must be mad. As for me, I only see in it another manifestation of ye power of that democratick spirit wh. I foresee must soon stretch its sceptre over ye minds and thoughts of us all. Of course, I mean not to use ye word *democracy* in its vulgar, English, political acceptation; nothing could be farther from my meaning than such an electioneering interpretation of it. But I am so firmly convinced that all other inquiries and speculations, whether in philosophy, in politicks, in morals or in government, are rapidly melting into ye one great engrossing question —'how are ye forms and shapes of evil wh. hover over ye mass of human kind to be driven away or destroyed?'—that I cannot conceive any high mind, or any lover of men, occupying himself long with any other speculation. This I take to be ye secret of ye enigma, for such certainly was ye publication of ye book to me at first.[4]

He himself had become dominated, almost against his will, by the idea of democracy. The *Paroles*, for him, was an expression of the prevailing spirit of the times. He wrote[5] to tell Lamennais that the book had been banned in Rome. After another attack of

[1] *L. à M.*, pp. 249 f. (19 February 1834).
[2] ibid., pp. 251 f. (19 March, quoting MacCarthy's letter of 4 March).
[3] The British Consul in Rome, who, in his despatches, confined himself to commerce, politics, and haggling about his personal emoluments, made no allusion to it (F.O. 43/25).
[4] Letter 25, MacCarthy-Milnes, Rome, 31 May 1834.
[5] *L. à M.*, p. 288 (25 June 1834, quoting MacCarthy's letter of 24 May).

his nervous complaint, brought on by family troubles and tensions in the ecclesiastical world,[1] events followed each other quickly. MacCarthy and his friend Emmanuel d'Alzon kept Lamennais informed about their impressions of Rome's reactions to the latest developments.[2] They told him that Lacordaire's attack on his former master was regarded with derision at Rome.[3] They gave him the impression that English translations of the *Paroles* were being made by ardent Catholics.[4] They sent their sympathy and that of other notabilities at the news of Lamennais's condemnation by *Singulari nos*.[5] They even explained that the encyclical was not regarded as an infallible pronouncement of the Pope, and that it was a condemnation not of Lamennais but of his politics.[6] MacCarthy suggested that the time had come for Lamennais to make an open declaration of his mission, which would encourage the multitudes outside the Church who were witnessing a growth in religious fervour.[7]

All this Lamennais communicated to Montalembert, who made no comment until he heard the last piece of advice. He replied: 'N'allez pas, comme vous le conseille follement MacCarthy, faire une déclaration sur ce que vous entendez faire désormais, ni, comme l'annoncent les journaux, publier une réfutation de l'encyclique.'[8] It seems that Montalembert's mistrust of MacCarthy's wisdom had been growing for some time. In a letter of

[1] *L. à M.*, p. 294 (5 July 1834: Il 'souffre en outre de ce dont nous souffrons tous'. Emmanuel d'Alzon had observed this malady in MacCarthy for some time and had written to Lamennais about it. In reply, Lamennais expressed concern, advised plenty of exercise and gave this warning, which applies as much to himself as to his friend: 'il ne faut pas qu'il se laisse aller aux impressions tristes qui abondent aujourd'hui de tous côtés.' (*Revue bleue*, ix, January-June 1898, p. 489—8 May 1834).

[2] On 19 June MacCarthy was enthusiastic and slightly surprised at the welcome the *Paroles* had had both in France and in Germany (letter 26, MacCarthy-Milnes).

[3] *L. à M.*, pp. 298 f. (9 July 1834).

[4] ibid., p. 299, and *Portefeuille*, pp. 152 f. (21 June 1834).

[5] *Portefeuille*, p. 160 (1 July); *L. à M.*, p. 304 (15 July 1834). 'The very air that one breathes here is an atmosphere of ambient malediction. Every zephyr-sigh whispers "anathema-maranatha"' (letter 27, MacCarthy-Milnes, Rome, 31 July).

[6] *L. à M.*, pp. 307 f. (26 July 1834, referring to a letter from d'Alzon 5 July 1834).

[7] *L. à M.*, p. 314 (3 August 1834, quoting a letter of 15 July 1834 from MacCarthy).

[8] *M. à L.*, p. 241 (Innsbruck, 14 August 1834).

a few days later his tone was cool towards the abbé and condescending towards MacCarthy and d'Alzon, 'ces deux bons jeunes gens':

Il suffit que M[acCarthy], ce même M. qui vous écrivait que bien certainement Rome ne parlerait pas, au moment même où l'Encyclique était déjà signée et en route; il suffit qu'il vous dise aujourd'hui *que l'on a pris la résolution de garder un silence absolu*, pour que vous enregistriez sur-le-champ *le silence futur de Rome* parmi les bases de votre conduite future et les preuves de ce que vous appelez *l'affranchissement de l'avenir*.[1]

Montalembert was right. The enthusiastic MacCarthy seems to have picked up the more dubious rumours in Rome and to have reported them as facts. Lamennais, in his turn, drew unwarranted and deceptive conclusions from them. By now, however, the damage had been done. MacCarthy told Lamennais about the election of MacHale as Archbishop of Tuam.[2] Another letter told Lamennais that he was returning to England in the spring.[3] Then the correspondence flagged. At the end of October MacCarthy wrote:

It is now some time since I heard from ye Abbé. I fear his letters must be stopt for he is a very regular correspondent. He seems to be in a state of fearful isolation, all his friends having separated from him. Montalembert and I are I believe ye only two of his former acquaintance who have not been brutal enough to kick him now that he is down. I have not heard again from Montalembert.[4]

Montalembert, whose unwillingness to write to MacCarthy is easily understood, did, however, tell Lamennais about MacCarthy's anxiety.[5] Lamennais immediately wrote to MacCarthy (who calls him simply 'Savonarola') telling him about the forthcoming publication of his *Mélanges*.[6] And here the friendship ended. D'Alzon was already ordained and MacCarthy was preparing to return to England.[7]

His subsequent career is quickly told. Already before the ending of his relationship with Lamennais, plans had been made for MacCarthy to become a lecturer at Bishop Baines's projected

[1] *L. à M.*, pp. 246 f. (Munich, 29 August 1834).
[2] *L. à M.*, p. 330 (10 September, quoting MacCarthy, 11 August 1834).
[3] ibid., p. 334.
[4] Letter 29, MacCarthy-Milnes, Monte Porzio, 25 October 1834.
[5] *M. à L.*, p. 269 (6 January 1835).
[6] Letter 32, MacCarthy-Milnes (17 January 1835).
[7] *M. à L.*, p. 269 (6 January 1835).

Catholic university at Prior Park.[1] Although MacCarthy discussed Bishop Baines, whose position in England he believed to be analogous with Lamennais's in France,[2] he seems not to have told his friend of his plans to return to England as a lecturer. There was, however, some feeling that, gifted though MacCarthy was, he might be too immature for such a position. One of the students of theology at Prior Park wrote to Wiseman: 'Mr. McCarthy I do not know but from all I have heard feel convinced he will be an important and valuable acquisition—he is however very young and at present without weight.'[3] By the end of 1834 MacCarthy's doubts about his vocation were apparent and the matter was dropped.[4]

After a time as tutor to an Irish household,[5] he spent the next eight years in wandering about Europe, making literary acquaintances, leading an aimless life and incurring betting debts. Between 1840 and 1842 Milnes lent MacCarthy £1,000 to pay off these debts, and then found him a job as a collector of customs on Turk's Island in the Bahamas.[6] This he disliked intensely, and he eventually prevailed upon Milnes to have him transferred to Ceylon as general auditor early in 1847.[7] In the following year he married Sophia Brunel, eldest daughter of Sir Benjamin Hawes. He received rapid advancement in the Ceylon Civil Service,[8]

[1] E. I. Watkin, *Roman Catholicism in England*, London, 1957, p. 171.

[2] *L. à M.*, pp. 319 f. (5 August 1834).

[3] Letter from the Reverend H. C. Logan, an Anglican convert, at Prior Park, 1830–8, in the archives of the Venerable English College, Rome, BAI. 24 (11 November 1834).

[4] On 30 September 1834, he wrote to Milnes: 'A conviction has been growing on me during ye last year, wh. latest events and meditations have only contributed to strengthen, that my life hitherto has been a great mistake' (letter 28). There may be a veiled reference in a letter from Bp. Baines to Wiseman (28 December 1834): 'With respt to Mr. McCarthy I said nothing, thinking it better for him and you to manage that affair, as you know best ' (V.E.C., BAI. 27).

[5] W. Fischer, *Die Briefe Richard Monckton Milnes' ersten Barons Houghton an Varnhagen von Ense (1844–54)*, Heidelberg, 1922, pp. 147 f. Fischer's account is based on a Milnes-MacCarthy correspondence kept at that time in the Handschriftenabteilung der Koeniglichen Bibliothek zu Berlin.

[6] Fischer, op. cit., p. 148; Pope-Hennessy, op. cit., pp. 45 f.

[7] Fischer, op. cit., p. 148.

[8] Authorities differ on details because of the multiplicity of titles; e.g. Fischer (p. 148): Secretary 1849; General Secretary 1851; chosen as Governor end of 1859. *Gentleman's Magazine* (October 1864, p. 529): Colonial Secretary 1856; Governor 1860.

was knighted in 1857, was appointed Governor on 4th August 1860,[1] and assumed office on the 22nd of the same month. After a short and uneventful rule, chiefly remembered for his cheese-paring attitude to expenditure on roads,[2] he died on 14th August 1864 at Spa, Belgium.[3]

Parsimonious as well as prodigal, unreliable and yet a loyal friend, a brilliant writer who wrote nothing, by turns depressed and elated, lovable and yet infuriating, MacCarthy remains an enigma. Pope-Hennessy calls him 'gentle and unworldly'.[4] It is not easy to assess his importance in Lamennais's life. Too much can be made of the misleading information which he and d'Alzon passed on from Rome. But there can be little doubt that Lamennais had a great affection for him and was almost childlike in the way he trusted him. Had he not known him it is just possible that his course would have been different. By raising false hopes MacCarthy made the blows more painful to bear. He was certainly an agent in creating that bitterness which was so apparent in

[1] *Ferguson's Ceylon Directory and Hand Book of Useful Information*, 1863, p. 10.

[2] L. A. Mills, *Ceylon under British Rule, 1795–1932*, Oxford and London, 1933, pp. 114 f.

[3] Many years after the MacCarthy-Lamennais friendship was ended Richard Simpson was intrigued by a reference in the *Westminster* (N.S. xv, 1869, p. 531) to a relative of Dr. Wiseman who had known Lamennais and passed on to him the Doctor's approval of the *Paroles*. After making enquiries he received this reply from Burke, Wiseman's nephew. The relative, he said, was probably 'M'Carthy, a first cousin of the Cardinal, whom though only in minor orders, he left to supply his place as President at the English Coll. in Rome in 1836 (I think) while he was preaching his lectures in Moorfields. This M'Carthy left the College during the Cardinal's absence to try his vocation among the Capuchins, but left them in 6 months, married a daughter of Sir Benj. Hawes, received an appointment at Ceylon, was knighted, and became a Protestant' (letter in Archives of the Oratory, Birmingham, dated 11 April 1859). Newman, to whom Simpson had sent this information, replied: 'I saw at once, Mr. or Sir—McCarthy was meant. I saw him at Rome in 1833. He was then a student of the English College—and dissatisfied with his position—so much so that in 1836, when the Cardinal preached his Moorfield Lectures [*sic*], it was said in Oxford, that perhaps, as I was doing what I could to prevent men turning Romanists, Dr. Wiseman was exerting an equal force to keep his friends from turning Protestants. I should not think he ever could have been an organ of the Cardinal's sentiments, or his representative in the English College—though certainly he was close about him in 1833. I had not heard he had protestantized, and I hope it is not quite true' (letter in the Archives of the Oratory, Birmingham, dated 14 April 1859).

[4] Pope-Hennessy, op. cit., p. 97.

Lamennais's later attitude to the Church. But that he actually precipitated the break with Rome is most unlikely.

In such a cosmopolitan society as the Rome of 1832 and with such friends as Alexis-François Rio[1] and Charles de Montalembert[2] it was inevitable that Lamennais should make further acquaintances from Britain.[3] MacCarthy's friend, Monckton Milnes was among them.[4] He and Lamennais met at the English College in Rome where, according to Milnes, the conversation was as bright and coloured as that of the gayest Paris drawing room.[5] Milnes was not a Roman Catholic, but he had much sympathy with Catholicism and, as a poet, he was attracted by the colour and solemnity of Catholic customs. He became a lifelong friend of Lamennais.[6] Many years later he described a visit he had made to the lonely Frenchman in 1848. Approaching

[1] The author of *L'Art chrétien* came to Britain for the first time at the end of 1832, but he already had English friends and was to make many more. He married Miss Apollonia Jones of Llanarth. For his English acquaintanceship of later years, see L. Gougaud, 'La société lettrée de Londres observée par un écrivain français en 1839. Journal inédit de François Rio' (*Revue d'histoire ecclésiastique*, xxx, 1934, pp. 297–333, 559–86).

[2] Montalembert had been brought up in England and was well known in diplomatic and political circles (see P. de Lallemand, *Montalembert et ses relations littéraires avec l'étranger jusqu'en 1840*, Paris, 1927, *passim*).

[3] These included Sir John Malcolm, whose *History of Persia* Lamennais had cited extensively in the third and fourth volumes of the *Essai* (iii, pp. 75, 81, 91, 169, 173 and 174, iv, pp. 31 and 254), Lady Malcolm and their two daughters. The younger daughter, Olympia (who later became Baroness Usedom), received a signed copy of the *Paroles* from Lamennais (*M. à L.*, pp. 252, 275; *L. à M.*, p. 332).

[4] T. Wemyss Reid, *Richard Monckton Milnes*, i, p. 124.

[5] *Cornhill*, xi, 1865, p. 507.

[6] Whether they ever corresponded seems to be unknown. The Houghton papers at Trinity College, Cambridge, contain only this note from Lamennais, referring to the famous George Sand dinner of 3 May 1848 (on which see J. Pope-Hennessy, *Monckton Milnes: The Years of Promise*, London, 1949, p. 284):

Monsieur Richd. Ch. Milnes [*sic*]
Hotel Meurice, rue de Rivoli.

Je regrette, mon cher Milnes, de ne pouvoir accepter votre invitation. J'espère vous revoir avant votre départ.

votre ami,
Lamennais

The tone of this note and the fact that Lamennais rarely mentioned Milnes in his letters suggests that Milnes set more store by the friendship than Lamennais did. Milnes certainly made no secret of it in society (Edith J. Morley, *Henry Crabb Robinson on Books and their Writers*, London, 1938, ii, p. 545).

the house, he inquired of a workman exactly where M. Lamennais now lived. He received the reply: 'Dans cette maison-là—très-haut—tout près du ciel.'[1]

It was in Rome too that Lamennais met an Irish Bishop who had been much in sympathy with his early views. This was the turbulent Dr. MacHale, Bishop of Killala and one of the grateful recipients of money collected by the *Avenir* for the sufferers in the Irish famine of 1831.[2] He had been Professor of Dogmatic Theology at Maynooth from 1820 to 1825, when he had left without the customary vote of thanks.[3] His writings have more than a touch of Lamennais's fire in them[4]: he hit out fiercely and uncompromisingly against his opponents; in apologetics he dealt more with the Catholic doctrine of the Church as the basis of faith than with any other topic; many of his arguments bore the stamp of that utilitarianism we have observed in Lamennais.

In 1832 he met Lamennais at the Irish College and left his impression of the encounter:

> On the first of July a convivial party, possessing no small interest, met together at the Irish College, including Count Montalembert, Monsieur de Lamennais, and Monsieur Lacordaire. Fortunately for Monsieur de Lamennais, he was thus accompanied by two young friends, who loved him much, but loved truth and religion more. Though not sinking under the weight of years, Monsieur de Lamennais appeared to be sinking under the pressure of far more crushing influences; but his companions appeared the very impersonations of Catholicity and freedom; and I am much mistaken if France will not have to acknowledge a deep debt of gratitude to the one and the other.[5]

This inspired (or retrospective?) pessimism about Lamennais's position reveals nothing of MacHale's debt, which he elsewhere

[1] *Cornhill*, xi, 1865, p. 507.

[2] *Avenir*, 11 November 1831 (*A.A.* vii, p. 93).

[3] J. Healy, *Maynooth College 1795–1895*, Dublin, 1895, p. 327.

[4] This was noticed by his opponents, e.g. the Reverend Edward Nangle, A.B., *The Reverend Dr. M'Hale's Letter to the Bishop of Exeter, dissected, and the Established Church vindicated, in seven Letters*, 3rd ed., Dublin, 1834. Against MacHale's opposition to the connection between Church and State, Nangle quoted *Mirari vos* (pp. 18 f., 78, 80). MacHale's *Evidences and Doctrines of the Catholic Church*, 2nd ed., London, 1842, dealt with the problem of indifference, as did his 'Letter to the Rt. Hon. George Canning', Maynooth, 1823' (J. MacHale, *Letters*, &c., Dublin, 1888, i, pp. 160–6) in terms very reminiscent of Lamennais.

[5] J. MacHale, *Letters*, &c., Dublin, 1888, i, p. 418 (20 August 1832).

acknowledged, to Lamennais's writings, and the generosity of feeling which he preserved towards him.[1] For their part Lamennais and Montalembert were impressed by him and followed closely the progress of his career.[2] In September 1834 Lamennais heard from MacCarthy about MacHale's appointment to the Archbishopric of Tuam and the storm this had caused in high places. 'Mais le Pape,' MacCarthy wrote, 'pour cette fois, tint ferme et, malgré les accusations de libéralisme qui pleuvaient de toutes parts, confirma la nomination'.[3] MacHale, an ultramontane of Lamennais's type, is confirmed in one of the most powerful Roman Catholic positions in Ireland at the very time when Lamennais has put himself outside the communion of the Church.

These relations with Britons may well have had a significant effect on Lamennais, and certainly did something to make the author of the *Essai* and the *Paroles* and the inspirer of the *Avenir* better known in England. After his break with the Church, however, he was less ready to make friendships. Despite his eminence (or perhaps because of it) he was lonely. There was no lack of people eager to make his acquaintance, and to them all he was courteous and kind. This led many to believe that they could count themselves among his friends. His influence over them was considerable, but to him friendships meant less than they had done in earlier years.

His visitors from England included politicians, Chartists, churchmen and people with literary interests. Richard Cobden tried to interest him in his advocacy of the policy of Free Trade.[4] Lord Brougham (who was alleged to have said in 1834 that the

[1] MacHale, *Evidences* (2nd ed., 1842). Beside quoting Lamennais with approval many times (pp. 4, 5, 171, 202, 373) he adds his appreciation: 'In this enquiry, the errors of the philosophers taught me not to exalt too much the powers of human reason: yet I should not wish to follow the theories of those who labour to depreciate its advantages. Such has been the fate of a modern writer of great eminence, the Abbé de la Mennais, to whom I am indebted for some valuable reflections in the preceding pages; and though I dissent from some of his philosophical speculations, no one is more ready to acknowledge and applaud the ingenuity and eloquence with which he has combated infidelity' (p. 39).

[2] *Portefeuille*, p. 109 (12 October 1832); *L. à M.*, p. 58 (5 February 1833); *M. à L.*, p. 71 (21 March 1833).

[3] *L. à M.*, p. 330 (10 September 1834, quoting MacCarthy's letter of 11 August 1834).

[4] *The People's Journal*, iv, 1847, p. 208.

Paroles had done more harm to the Whigs than all the speeches of the Tories)[1] dined with him in 1839.[2] The prominent Chartists E. Jones, P. M'Grath, Julian Harney, and W. J. Linton, accompanied by Mazzini, went to Paris in 1848 to express their sympathy with the rising of the French Republicans.[3] It was Linton who was deputed to present a copy of their address to Lamennais and who met him many times afterwards.[4] He interested Lamennais in his journalistic enterprises, which were even more numerous than Lamennais's own. Not the least considerable of these was *The Leader*, which in the course of its ten years of life (1850–60) printed articles by many famous men, including F. W. Newman and Charles Kingsley. Lamennais took an interest in this paper, and even, it is said, made suggestions for its conduct which were adopted by the editor.[5] Linton frequently referred to his old friend the 'venerable' Lamennais, and regarded it as one of the greatest privileges of his life to have known him.

William Palmer, a Fellow of Magdalen College, Oxford, and one of the more eccentric of the Tractarians, found Lamennais 'more wrong-headed and less interesting' than any other person he had ever met.[6] Dr. Christopher Wordsworth, who later became Bishop of Lincoln, was similarly disappointed. After he had visited him in 1844, he came away from his interview saddened at the sight of the man who had been the most important and influential person of his order in France, fallen into the hands of what he called 'sceptical Philosophists, who, under the pretence of advocating universal charity and toleration, undermine the foundations of that Religion upon which charity rests for its guidance and support'.[7]

Of the literary people who met him, Mrs. Frances Trollope found him attractive, although she was not uncritical.[8] For his

[1] *L. à M.*, pp. 299 f. (9 July 1834).

[2] *Revue de Paris*, 15 March 1909, p. 327 (letter to Mme Clément, 10 April 1839).

[3] Julius West, *A History of the Chartist Movement*, London, 1920, p. 239.

[4] W. J. Linton, *European Republicans*, London, 1893, p. 193.

[5] *The Reasoner*, Sunday 12 March 1854, p. 182.

[6] Roundell Palmer, *Memorials, Family and Personal, 1766–1865*, London, 1896, i, pp. 256 f.

[7] Christopher Wordsworth, *Diary in France mainly on Topics concerning Education and the Church*, London, 1845, p. 194.

[8] Frances Trollope, *Paris and the Parisians in 1835*, London, 1836, pp. 381 f.

part, he, who already knew something of her work, was impressed by her.[1] The Irish historian and champion of the under-privileged, R. R. Madden,[2] claimed his friendship,[3] although this may have been much slighter than his frequent references to the French priest suggest.[4] There may also have been others, like the business-man of literary and artistic interests, J. Oswald Murray, who claimed that Lamennais's relationship with him was like that of a father with his son, but about whom Lamennais is completely silent.[5]

This all goes to show that Lamennais's circle of acquaintance was sufficiently wide—and in some cases, influential—to add a personal edge to the consideration of his ideas in England. How these ideas were received, even among those who, like J. H. Newman, had never seen him, remains to be described.

[1] *O.P.* ii, pp. 320 f. (6 October 1833), p. 424 (24 May 1835).

[2] On Madden see Leon O'Broin, 'Dr. R. R. Madden, Historian and Public Servant', *The Month*, October 1958, pp. 224–32.

[3] T. M. Madden, *The Memoirs of R. R. Madden, M.D., F.R.C.S.*, London, 1891, pp. 119, 202 f. (a letter from Lamennais, in which he mentions his Irish origins), p. 256; *Memoirs and Correspondence of the Countess of Blessington*, ed. R. R. Madden, London, 1855, i, p. 360; and R. R. Madden, *Irish Periodical Literature*, London, 1867, ii, p. 482.

[4] Mr. Leon O'Broin, who has access to Madden's papers, assures me that there is no other evidence that Madden had any important contacts with Lamennais. 'Madden loved to record the names of the great he met, but frequently he knew them very slightly indeed.'

[5] Varnhagen von Ense, *Tagebücher*, x, p. 277 (Monday 26 September 1853).

IV

LAMENNAIS AND THE OXFORD MOVEMENT

WHEN Dr. Wordsworth visited him in 1844 Lamennais made many enquiries from him about the character and aim of the Oxford movement, and gave his opinion that the Tractarians 'dealt with these questions too *theologically* in England; that they ought to be treated upon *wider*, by which he meant *rational*, principles'.[1] Even if due allowance is made for the fact that this was said at a time when Lamennais's sympathies had passed beyond movements of this sort, nevertheless the comment draws attention to an important difference between the aims and methods of the Tractarians and those of the author of the *Essai* and his followers.

This difference of climate has doubtless been responsible for a tendency to minimize any possible connection between movements in the Church in France, led by Lamennais, and the Oxford movement in England,[2] or to confine it to that vague 'spirit afloat' of which Newman wrote,[3] or to attribute any affinity between the two movements to the prevailing spirit of Romanticism.[4] At first sight, the 'theological' approach to the question of the authority of the Church made by the Tractarians is far

[1] Christopher Wordsworth, *Diary in France mainly on Topics concerning Education and the Church*, London, 1845, pp. 195 f.

[2] See W. H. Hutton in *Cambridge History of English Literature*, xii, p. 254, B. Newman, *Cardinal Newman*, London, 1925, p. 53; on Newman see, e.g., F. L. Cross, *John Henry Newman*, London, 1933, p. 49; and H. Tristram, 'In the Lists with the Abbé Jager' in *John Henry Newman: Centenary Essays*, London, 1945, p. 201.

[3] *Apologia pro Vita Sua*, Oxford, 1913, p. 196; for a similar view, see F. Oakeley, *Historical Notes on the Tractarian Movement, 1833–1845*, London, 1865, p. 2.

[4] G. H. Harper, *Cardinal Newman and William Froude*, Baltimore, 1933, p. 30; Y. Brilioth, *The Anglican Revival*, London, 1925, p. 57; W. Ward, *The Oxford Movement*, London, n.d., pp. 1 f.; see also 'On some German affinities with the Oxford Movement' by L. A. Willoughby, in *Modern Language Review*, xxix, No. 1, January 1934, p. 52.

removed from the apparently 'political' methods of their French brethren.

It is true also that some of the participants in the movement were possessed of an almost overpowering insularity, not to say parochialism, in their outlook. Even Newman, whose sensitivity made him acutely aware of the thoughts of others, often gave the impression in his correspondence that the world extended no further than London, and Keble, who exercised such great influence over others, remained to the end of his life largely self-contained. The *Tracts for the Times* dealt almost exclusively with matters of doctrine and practice relevant only to English churchmen. Indications in them that there were any problems other than theological problems in any countries beyond England were rare.

Yet to conclude that the Oxford movement was therefore an isolated phenomenon would be mistaken.[1] No one taught by Dr. Charles Lloyd, Regius Professor of Divinity (as many of the Tractarians were taught),[2] could for long remain ignorant of the questions agitating the Church of France. Dr. Lloyd did not share in the insularity which is usually attributed to his contemporaries. He had had dealings with the French émigré clergy and claimed that he was tolerably well acquainted with the Gallican Church.[3] He once took *Du Pape* away on holiday with him together with the *Ami de la religion et du roi*,[4] for which Lamennais had written in earlier days. It would be surprising if he had not communicated something of this breadth of outlook and interest in Continental affairs to his pupils. Even the *British Critic*, in its early days very insular, had invited its readers, in a circuitous way, to sympathize with Lamennais when he was at the height of his influence as an ultramontane. In an article on Sismondi's *Review of the Progress of Religious Opinions during the Nineteenth Century*, Sismondi's censorious remarks about Lamennais's lack of charity were criticized for their latitudinarian tendency.[5]

At about the same time as Lloyd was removed from his sphere of influence as a lecturer to the Bishopric of Oxford, another

[1] Both E. A. Knox, *The Tractarian Movement*, London, 1933, and Christopher Dawson, *The Spirit of the Oxford Movement*, London, 1933, set the movement in its European context.

[2] Mozley, i, pp. 109–13.

[3] Ed. Edward Churton, *Memoir of Joshua Watson*, Oxford, 1861, i, p. 285.

[4] ibid., pp. 284 f. (11 December 1825).

[5] *British Critic*, ii, 1827, p. 204.

influential person entered the circle of those whose ideas were preparing for the Oxford movement. This was Richard Hurrell Froude, whom Newman called 'one of the acutest and clearest and deepest men in the memory of man',[1] and who, for the rest of his short life, exercised a deep influence over Newman.[2]

Although Froude seems to be the first attested point of contact between the ideas of Lamennais and the Oxford movement, the way was in part already prepared. However dissimilar in outlook the Newman and the Lamennais of the late 1820's seemed, yet they were concerned with the same problems. In 1829 Newman wrote to his sister:

> You know I have no opinion about the Catholic Question, and now it is settled I shall perhaps never have one; but still, its passing is one of the signs of the times, of the encroachment of Philosophism and Indifferentism in the Church.[3]

and just over a month later:

> Now, without meaning of course that Christianity is in itself opposed to free inquiry, still I think it *in fact* at the present time opposed to the particular form which that liberty of thought has now assumed. Christianity is of faith, modesty, lowliness, subordination; but the spirit at work against it is one of latitudinarianism, indifferentism, and schism, a spirit which tends to overthrow doctrine, as if the fruit of bigotry and discipline—as if the instrument of priestcraft.[4]

The attitude of this letter is somewhere between that of the *Essai* and of *Des progrès*.[5] Newman fully recognizes the dangers of doctrinal indifferentism (not merely carelessness in religious observance) and he sees that it imperils the relations between Church and State (something which Lamennais did not make explicit in the *Essai*). He continues:

> All parties seem to acknowledge that the stream of opinion is setting against the Church. I do believe it will ultimately be separated from the State, and at this prospect I look with apprehension.[6]

[1] Mozley, i, p. 131 (31 March 1826).
[2] *Apologia* (Everyman, 1955), p. 47: 'His opinions arrested and influenced me, even when they did not gain my assent.'
[3] Mozley, i, p. 199 (8 February 1829).
[4] ibid., p. 204 (13 March 1829).
[5] *Des progrès* was published in February 1829.
[6] Mozley, i, p. 204.

This 'apprehension' marks a clear difference of character between Newman and the more ruthless Lamennais. The similarity of their views, however, about the function and duty of the Church in those troubled times led Newman to put forward a theory which bore marked resemblances to that of the *Essai:*

> Listen to my theory. As each individual has certain instincts of right and wrong antecedently to reasoning, on which he acts—and rightly so—which perverse reasoning may supplant, which then can hardly be regained, but, if regained, will be regained from a different source—from reasoning, not from nature—so, I think, has the world of men collectively. God gave them truths in His miraculous revelations, and other truths in the unsophisticated infancy of nations, scarcely less necessary and divine. These are transmitted as 'the wisdom of our ancestors', through men—many of whom cannot enter into them, or receive them themselves—still on, on, from age to age, not the less truths because many of the generations through which they are transmitted are unable to prove them, but hold them, either from pious and honest feeling (it may be), or from bigotry or from prejudice.[1]

The whole conflict of Church and State had caused Lamennais to consider the philosophical basis for belief and to find it in tradition as expressed by the *sensus communis*. In this passage Newman is led to the same conclusion. Although he does not actually deny the validity of reason, he sees it as the prevailing spirit opposed to faith. Newman's equivalent of the *sensus communis* is an idea very similar to it, the world conscience as preserved and transmitted by tradition.

In the autumn of 1832, shortly after Lamennais's departure and condemnation, Froude and Newman went to Rome. There they met Wiseman, Rector of the English College, as Lamennais had done. It is ironical that less than a year after Lamennais had charged Wiseman with the conversion of England[2] two Anglican divines, who by reason of their connection with Oxford seemed to foreigners more exalted in the English hierarchy than they actually were, should make enquiries about Rome's attitude to the Church of England. In these circumstances it is unlikely that Newman and Froude did not hear some account of Lamennais's work in connection with his recent visit to Rome.

[1] Mozley, i, pp. 205 f.
[2] N. Wiseman, *Recollections of the Last Four Popes*, pp. 339 f.

For the return journey Newman and Froude split up. Newman returned home via Sicily. Although the last lap of his journey was through France, it was accomplished very quickly. Froude, however, returned home in a more leisurely fashion. In a letter from Rome on 16th March 1833 he had written to Keble:

The same process which is going on in England and France is taking its course everywhere else; and the clergy in these Catholic countries seem as completely to have lost their influence, and to submit as tamely to the State, as ever we can do in England.[1]

This was a pessimistic view of the French scene which betrayed no knowledge of the results of Lamennais's efforts. But the letters written on the return journey were quite different. On 22nd April he wrote of his chagrin at not being able to speak French properly,[2] and on 23rd May he wrote a letter to his brother, expressing the 'keenest intuitive understanding' of the French.[3] There followed a passage which referred to Lamennais:

There is now in France a High Church Party, who are Republicans, and wish for universal suffrage, on the ground that in proportion as the franchise falls lower, the influence of the Church makes itself more felt; at present its limits about coincide with those of the infidel faction. Don't be surprised if one of these days you find us turning Radicals on similar grounds.[4]

It is not, however, quite accurate to say that Froude's song, 'If the State would but kick us off!' was 'caught from Lamennais, and the great democrat-Ultramontane agitation in France'.[5] Froude wrote these words from Rome in March, when, as we have seen, he seemed to know nothing of Lamennais. In Lamennais he recognized another lover of the 'theocratic church'[6] and although he certainly learned some valuable lessons from Lamennais's methods, he did not catch the desire for disestablishment from him.

When Froude returned to England affairs moved quickly. It is just possible that Dawson is right in thinking that the idea for the *Tracts* came from the *Avenir*. In view of the fate of its editor,

[1] R. H. Froude, *His Remains*, pt. 1, i, London, 1838, p. 296 (Y 41).
[2] ibid., p. 311.
[3] L. I. Guiney, *Hurrell Froude: Memoranda and Comments*, London, 1904, p. 104.
[4] *Remains*, pt. 1, i, p. 312.
[5] L. I. Guiney, op. cit., p. 114.
[6] *Apologia* (Everyman, 1955), p. 48.

any reference to this fact would necessarily be omitted from contemporary accounts of the decision to publish the *Tracts*. On the other hand, the *Tracts* did not resemble the *Avenir* very closely. Dawson may be nearer the truth when he says that Froude hoped to make the *British Magazine* into a sort of *Avenir*.[1]

While Newman was still prostrate with fever in Sicily in May 1833 an article appeared in the *British Magazine* on Schelling's lectures on Christianity. This contained an allusion to a conversation between Schelling and Lamennais on the reunion of Christendom, and spoke of Lamennais in terms of respect: 'At all events the publication of a conference on such a subject, maintained by two men of such distinguished abilities and such high reputation, would be matter of great interest.'[2]

This was closely followed in July by Froude's own opinions on State interference in the affairs of the Church, which quoted the *Avenir* at an early stage.[3] Froude started from the point that the situation in both England and France was essentially the same: the Church was under the thumb of a civil authority which, however religious it might have been in times past, was now largely infidel; the Bishops in both countries were appointed by a civil authority interested more in docile submission than in religious zeal. Following the example of the *Avenir*, Froude called upon the episcopate to abandon all money which it received from the State.[4] He showed his agreement with Lamennais by quoting Hooker on the opinion that the general consent of all gives laws their form and vigour,[5] and by showing that Churches bound to a

[1] C. Dawson, *The Spirit of the Oxford Movement* (4th impression, 1945), p. 61.

[2] *British Magazine*, iii, May 1833, pp. 521 f. This article is of exceptional importance because it revealed the substance of a conversation which was otherwise to remain unknown until A.-F. Rio published *Épilogue à l'art chrétien* (2 vols., 1870). If the signature 'R' denotes that Hugh James Rose was the author (other articles are signed with the initial letter of the author's surname), and if his informant (whom he identifies in the article as a Roman Catholic who was present at the conversation and who possessed minutes of the discussion, which he was to publish) was A.-F. Rio himself, then it is probable that Rio gave his account during his visit to Britain in the winter of 1832–3, when his itinerary included Cambridge, London, and Ely. Rose, therefore, provides another personal link between the movement (in its early days) and the circle of Lamennais.

[3] *Remains*, pt. 2, i, p. 193 (*British Magazine*, July 1833).

[4] ibid., p. 195.

[5] ibid., p. 197; he cites Hooker, *Ecclesiastical Polity*, Book 8, vi, 11.

latitudinarian government more as an instrument of State than as a spiritual force, as the Churches of England and France were, were governed not by the general consent of believers but by a civil government which had ceased to be truly representative of the faithful.

There is, however, an important difference of outlook between Froude and Lamennais, which Froude does not stress, although he mentions elsewhere that there are some views in the *Avenir* of which he in no way approves.[1] This is that Lamennais's purpose is social and therefore missionary: he envisages a mass revival of religion if his reforms are carried out. Froude, on the other hand, is a conservative,[2] who is concerned primarily with preserving the purity of the Church of England. In this he is at one with the other Tractarians. They looked principally to the primitive Church and to the Fathers, and the social implications of their work were not uppermost in their thoughts.[3] In view of this, the indebtedness of Froude to Lamennais should not be overestimated.

In addition to this series of articles which had dealt at length with the English manner of appointing Bishops, Froude wrote an account of the present state of the French Church. He distinguished three schools of thought: the Royalists, whose hopes for the Church lay in the return of Charles X to the throne; the Conservatives, who were concerned above all with preserving the connection between Church and State, however constituted; and

> a third party of persons, perhaps rather speculative than practical, . . . whose views seem to have been founded more upon an extended knowledge of Church History than an habitual attachment to the system under which they had themselves lived.
> It seemed to them . . . that the supposed identity of monarchical and catholic principles . . . was . . . no part of its theory.[4]

Of the practical results of this theory Froude approved strongly:

> The duty of the Clergy seemed clear and simple; to detach themselves from all parties, to dissolve their connection with the State altogether, to reject its pay and to resist its interference, and quietly devoting themselves to spiritual concerns, gradually to undeceive a misguided

[1] *Remains*, pt. 2, i, p. 405.
[2] ibid., p. 195.
[3] Although they were drawn out later, see the references below, p. 188.
[4] *Remains*, pt. 2, i, pp. 403 f.

people, who had been taught to regard the Church as a mere instrument of Regal oppression.[1]

He concluded:

The knowledge they possess of the actual state of France, and the talent which they display in exhibiting their opinions, as well as the indirect, though certainly very partial bearing of their observations on the situation which too probably awaits ourselves have appeared to the writer of this article not wholly unworthy of our attention.[2]

Newman was interested, and on 22nd August he wrote to Froude about a proposed series of articles for the *British Magazine* called 'Home Thoughts Abroad'. In his plans for the subject matter of this series he wrote: 'I want you to write a chapter on France, or at least to supply an account of Lamennais' system.'[3] Although by temperament Newman was no democrat (he regarded the 1830 Revolution as the triumph of irreligion,[4] and refused even to look at the tricolour),[5] under the influence of Froude his opinions began to change. In August 1833 he told Rogers that historically and theoretically he was a Tory, but that he was beginning to be a Radical practically.[6] This is reminiscent of the comment Froude had made a few months before.[7] Further, Newman writes as if he is reluctant to admit it, but 'I cannot deny the plain fact that in most ages the latter [aristocratical power] has been based on a popular power.'[8] A few days later he writes even more clearly: 'If we look into history . . . the people were the fulcrum of the Church's power. So they may be again.'[9] The background of this idea is clarified in a letter to Froude:

Of late months the idea has broken on me, as it did a little before on yourself, that the Church is essentially a popular institution, and the past English union of it with the State has been a happy anomaly.[10]

[1] *Remains*, pt. 2, i, p. 405.
[2] ibid., pp. 405 f.
[3] Mozley, i, p. 444. This chapter never appeared. Only the first article (by Newman) was published and reprinted in *Discussions and Arguments*, London, 1872, as 'How to accomplish it' (Mozley, i, p. 445).
[4] Mozley, i, p. 233 (to Froude, 28 July 1830).
[5] *Apologia* (Everyman), p. 54; cf. Mozley, i, p. 242.
[6] Mozley, i, p. 450 (to F. Rogers, 31 August 1833).
[7] See above, p. 97.
[8] Mozley, i, p. 450.
[9] ibid., p. 454 (to Wilson, 8 September 1833).
[10] ibid., p. 458 (18 September 1833).

The idea, here clearly expressed, that the power of the Church rests upon the power of the people, is foreign to the later development of the movement and is not to be connected too closely with the sub-Tractarian enthusiasm for socialism. We notice that Newman, in September 1833, describes the idea as having broken on him 'in late months' and on Froude 'a little before'. This seems to be a reference to Froude's experience in France, which was followed, on his return to England, by his passing on the information enthusiastically to Newman. There is therefore a clear case for concluding that Lamennais influenced Newman for a short period and in one particular matter.

But he soon abandoned the idea. In November he said that he had 'left off being anti-aristocratical',[1] and by the end of the month he had returned to his old preoccupation with opposition to 'the liberalisers in and out of Parliament'.[2] But he never entirely abandoned the ideas which had been consolidated by Froude and Lamennais. In 1871 he wrote to Matthew Arnold:

> ... As to your questions, I agree with what you say about the Anglican and Catholic Churches relatively to democratic ideas. It was one of Hurrell Froude's main views that the Church must alter her position in the political world—and when he heard of la Mennais, he took up his views with great eagerness. I have said the same in the beginning of the *Church of the Fathers*—'I shall offend many men when I say, we must look to the people,' &c., &c. I said this apropos of St. Ambrose, and based my view upon the Fathers. Froude had seized upon it from the intuitive apprehension he had of what was coming, and of what was fitting. We both hated the notion of rebellion and thought that the Church must bide her time. This idea is expressed several times in the Lyra Apostolica. It often happens that those who will not bide their time fail, not because they are not substantially right, but because they are thus impatient. I used to say that Montanus, Tertullian, Novatian, &c. were instances in point; their ideas were eventually carried out. Perhaps la Mennais will be a true prophet after all. It is curious to see the minute tokens which are showing themselves of the drawings of the Papal policy just now in the direction of the democracy. Of course the present Papacy is (humanly speaking) quite unequal to such a line of action—but it was the policy of Gregory VII—and, though we may have a season of depression, as there was a hideous degradation before Gregory, yet it may be in the counsels of

[1] Mozley, i, p. 476 (to Froude, 7 November 1833).
[2] ibid., p. 490 (to S. Rickards, 22 November 1833).

Providence that the Catholic Church may at length come out unexpectedly as a popular power. Of course, the existence of the Communists makes the state of things now vastly different from what it was in the Middle Ages.[1]

This letter reveals what otherwise would have been difficult to detect, that Newman's ideas on democracy came consciously near to Lamennais's, especially in his later years,[2] and that the principal difference between them lay in Lamennais's tendency to rebellion.

Froude died on 28th February 1836, before the Oxford movement became fully developed, and the Tractarians were not as convinced as he had been that disestablishment would be wholly good. By 1836 they had become engaged in the Roman controversy and from then on they were concerned to vindicate their claim, not to the nation, as had been the original intention, but to the Roman Catholics, that the Church of England was the Catholic Church of the realm. In this attempt many, including Newman, were strangled by their own logic and went over to Rome. At any rate, Froude's vision of a pure and independent Catholic Church in England faded, and the question of disestablishment did not arise again in its original form.

The years 1833–6 were momentous not only for Lamennais but also for the Oxford reformers. While Lamennais was passing through the crises of the *Avenir* and the *Paroles*, the *Tracts* were having an impressive effect on the Church of England. Lamennais had by this time proved that his course was far removed from the aims of the Oxford men, and the *British Critic*, now more closely identified with Tractarian principles, although not yet the movement's official organ, rejoiced that the *Avenir*'s attempts to march with the century had failed,[3] and expressed itself unequivocally against the *Paroles*.[4] It is significant that Bulwer's description of Lamennais in the office of the *Avenir* was quoted in full, together with Bulwer's explanation that he had dwelt on this description because of the interest which attached to Lamennais as a Christian innovator:

[1] *Times Literary Supplement*, 10 March 1921, p. 160 (letter of 3 December 1871), quoted T. Kenny, *The Political Thought of John Henry Newman*, London, 1957, p. 183.

[2] Kenny, op. cit., p. 178.

[3] *British Critic*, xvii, 1835, p. 374.

[4] *British Critic*, xix, 1836, p. 305.

. . . if I have paused thus long on the portrait of M. de la Mennais, it is not because this person was the former champion of the pope but because, within a few months from the period at which I am writing, he has endeavoured to give Christianity new doctrines, to breathe into Catholicism a new spirit, to fashion it, according to the idea of his epoch, into a new form, to raise up a democratic religion, full of energy and life and passion, in face of the spectral majesty of mitred Rome.[1]

The early *Tracts for the Times* catch exactly the spirit of the first days of the movement. They are concerned with the 'practical revival of doctrines',[2] and very few of them bear the faintest resemblance in form or content to the *Avenir*. Even Tracts 58 and 59, on Disestablishment, are far removed from the fire and eloquence of Lamennais.[3] In view of what has been said already, however, it would be surprising if there were no similarities between *Tracts* and the French movement from the *Essai* to the *Avenir*. Tract 31, for example, sets the Oxford movement in a European context. The tone of its generalizations is reminiscent of Lamennais:

Turn to the restored Christian Church, and reflect upon the perplexed question concerning the union of Church and State, to which the politics of the last three centuries have given rise: the tyrannical encroachments of the civil power at various eras; . . . [here follows an example] . . . ; the deliberate impiety of the French Revolution; and the present apparent breaking up of Ecclesiastical Polity everywhere, the innumerable schisms, the mixture of men of different creeds and sects, and the contempt poured upon any show of Apostolical zeal.[4]

An earlier Tract, on the visible Church, draws its reader's attention to a neglected aspect of the revival, religion as a social and political principle:

He [Christ] has actually set up a society, which exists even this day all over the world, and which (as a general rule) Christians are bound to join; so that to believe in CHRIST is not a mere opinion or a secret conviction, but a social and even a political principle, forcing one into what is often stigmatized as party strife, and quite inconsistent with the supercilious mood of those professed Christians

[1] *British Critic*, xix, 1836, p. 306.
[2] *Tracts for the Times*, 'Advertisement' (dated All Saints' Day 1834).
[3] Tract 58 was by Bowden, 59 by Froude.
[4] Tract 31, 1834, Ad Clerum, 'On the Reformed Church' (J. H. Newman), p. 2.

of the day, who stand aloof, and designate their indifference as philosophy.[1]

This involves, as it did with Lamennais, a theory of certitude which goes further than reliance on individual reason. Here is a faint indication of the idea of the *sensus communis*:

The common answer which we hear made every day to persons who engage in any novel undertaking is, 'You will get no one to join you; . . . you are singular in your opinion; you do not take practical views. . . .' How cheering it is to a person so circumstanced, to be able to point to others elsewhere, who actually hold the same opinions as himself, and exert themselves for the same objects! Why? because it is an appeal to a fact, which no one can deny; it is an evidence that the view which influences him is something external to his own mind, and not a dream. What two persons see, cannot be an ideal apparition. . . . In order then to supply this need of our minds, to satisfy the imagination, and so to help our faith, for this among other reasons CHRIST set up a visible Society, His Church. . . . It is a witness of the unseen world.[2]

Lamennais's strongly apocalyptic sense also has its parallel in the *Tracts*. It is a characteristic of religious reformers to see a marked falling away from established religious observance as a prelude to the day of the Lord. Lamennais was less restrained in this respect than the Tractarians. Yet there are the 'Advent Sermons on Anti-Christ', in a note on which the desertion is described thus:

This desertion will begin in a professed indifference to any particular form of Christianity, under the pretence of universal toleration; which toleration will proceed from no true spirit of charity and forbearance, but from a design to undermine Christianity, by multiplying and encouraging sectaries. The pretended toleration will go far beyond a just toleration, even as it regards the different sects of Christians. For governments will pretend an indifference to all, and will give a protection in preference to none. All establishments will be laid aside. From the toleration of the most pestilent heresies, they will proceed to the toleration of Mahometanism, Atheism, and at last to a positive persecution of the truth of Christianity.[3]

[1] Tract 11, 1833, Ad Scholas, 'The Visible Church' (J. H. Newman), p. 5.

[2] Tract 20, 1833, Ad Scholas, 'The Visible Church' (J. H. Newman), p. 2.

[3] Tract 83, 1838, 'Advent Sermons on Anti-Christ', p. 53.

We have only to compare this passage with the words of the *Essai sur l'indifférence* to see the similarity:

Partout l'indifférence pour la vérité conduit au système de la *liberté* et de l'*égalité* religieuses. Ce système se développe même, en plusieurs pays, plus rapidement qu'en Angleterre, parce qu'il n'a pas à surmonter la barrière des lois et de la constitution politique. On avoue, il est vrai, qu'une Religion est nécessaire au peuple, mais une Religion quelconque; peu importe laquelle, on lui en laisse le choix; et pour qu'il se décide plus *librement*, on les lui présente toutes avec un égal respect, ou plutôt un égal mépris. Les Gouvernemens, s'il en est qui attachent encore de l'importance aux doctrines, au lieu de chercher à s'en aider, prennent à tâche de les neutraliser réciproquement par un habile mélange.[1]

Lamennais has already asked on what principles the British have thought it right to 'garantir, par un traité solennel, aux habitans de l'île de Ceylan, la liberté de l'idolâtrie; assister, par ambassadeurs, aux cérémonies religieuses de ces peuples, et offrir à leurs divinités des dons sacrilèges?'[2] If these words from the Tract had not been a quotation from Bishop Horsley, who wrote at the end of the eighteenth century, it would have been tempting to claim that in one respect at least the *Tracts* show distinct evidence of being influenced by the *Essai*. As it is, the most that can be claimed is that there is some evidence of a similarity of purpose and approach. The significant fact is that of all the *Tracts* quoted, the only ones to have any recognizable similarity with the aims of Lamennais were written by J. H. Newman. Amongst the galaxy of learned men at Oxford, Newman and Froude alone had that broadness of sweep to their minds which enabled them, sometimes consciously, sometimes unconsciously, to embrace the ideas not only of antiquity but of their own day. Newman retained this quality throughout his life. His attitude to reason, his concept of development, the temper of his later liberal Catholicism and his philosophy of history all invited comparison with Lamennais.[3] In

[1] *Essai*, i, p. 75.
[2] ibid., p. 73.
[3] REASON: A. M. Fairbairn, *Catholicism: Roman and Anglican*, London, 1899, p. 128; J. Guitton, *La Philosophie de Newman*, Paris, 1933, p. xxv. DEVELOPMENT: W. A. Butler, *Letters on the Development of Christian Doctrine*, Dublin, 1850, p. 4 note d; J. Guitton, op. cit., p. 34; compare O. Chadwick, *From Bossuet to Newman*, p. 228 (which understates the case) and Lord Acton, who had at first believed that Newman's theory was derived from Lamennais (A. MacDougall, *The Acton-Newman Relations*,

no case (apart from his brief interest in Froude's ideas) can any direct influence be proved, but his theology, both as an Anglican and as a Roman Catholic, did much to create a climate in which the consideration of wider issues was possible.

Some time between 1836 and 1840, the movement began to broaden its theological base. Those who were able to read French and German consolidated their outlook by reading the works of some of the theologians of the Continental revival. R. W. Church, himself a Tractarian and a valued friend of Newman, wrote in his book on the first twelve years of the Oxford movement that the works of J. de Maistre, Lamennais, Lacordaire, and Montalembert did something to correct the former insularity of the Anglican revival, and that it was their ideas, amongst other things, which played an important part in W. G. Ward's attraction to the Church of Rome.[1] Wilfrid Ward, in his biography of his father, supported this claim when he wrote that J. de Maistre and Lamennais were favourite authors with the second school of Tractarians.[2]

Evidence of a more definite kind is provided in a contemporary account of the Oxford movement: *A Narrative of Events connected with the Publication of the Tracts for the Times* (1843) by the Reverend W. Palmer of Worcester College, Oxford, known as 'Palmer of Worcester' in order to distinguish him from his contemporary, the Reverend W. Palmer of Magdalen (the one who had himself met Lamennais a few years before). Writing of the period from about 1840 onwards, he says:

Romish controversialists are applauded and complimented; their works are eagerly purchased and studied; and contrasts are drawn between them and the defenders of the truth, to the disadvantage of the latter. The theory of development advocated in the writings of De Maistre and Möhler (Roman Catholic controversialists), according to which the

New York, 1962, p. 154), in *English Historical Review*, 1895, pp. 108–13, reprinted in *History of Freedom and other Essays*, London, 1907, p. 593: '. . . it is a mistake to connect Lamennais with Möhler and Newman . . .'. LIBERAL CATHOLICISM: T. Kenny, *The Political Thought of John Henry Newman*, London, 1957, p. 18; T. S. Gregory, 'Newman and Liberalism' in *A Tribute to Newman*, Dublin, 1945, p. 108. PHILOSOPHY OF HISTORY: W. Ward, *Life of John Henry, Cardinal Newman*, London, 1912, i, p. 308.

[1] R. W. Church, *The Oxford Movement, Twelve Years 1833–45*, London, 1891, p. 295.

[2] W. Ward, *W. G. Ward and the Catholic Revival*, London, 1893, p. 82.

latest form of Christianity is the most perfect . . . is openly sanctioned, advocated, avowed.[1]

He gives a list of references to the *British Critic*, which are alleged to exhibit the Roman doctrine of development as expounded by Möhler and J. de Maistre, who, he says, '*are* favourite authors with this periodical'.[2]

Palmer here makes no reference to Lamennais, but in a work published the year before (1842) there is ample evidence that he had read him. In the *Treatise on the Church of Christ* Lamennais is cited abundantly.[3] Palmer combats Lamennais's charge that the Church of England is based upon religious indifference.[4] He uses Lamennais's own methods by considering how far the notes of the Church, unity, sanctity, catholicity and apostolicity, could be applied to existing Christian communions, and by applying the twin proofs of Scripture and general consent.[5] Palmer's theory of the Church of England as a 'branch' of the Catholic church owed nothing to Lamennais, but that the Frenchman's early works were read in Oxford there can be no doubt.

It is understandable that some of the Tractarians should have read Möhler (whose appeal to the early Fathers and originality of approach are still attractive to Anglicans) and that others of a more authoritarian turn of mind should have read J. de Maistre. But why did they return to Lamennais, whose later career had done much to obscure his early services to the Church? One reason certainly was that Lamennais had a wider general reputation in England than the other writers. Another is that they were reminded of him by an interesting episode which involved Newman and Cardinal Wiseman.[6]

In 1836 Tractarians were at the height of their influence, and among the many disputes in which they engaged, the Hampden

[1] W. Palmer, op. cit., p. 45.

[2] ibid., p. 63. In later years, Lamennais's friend, J. B. Robertson, lamented the fact that, while the Oxford converts (as they then were) made not even a passing allusion to M. de Bonald, the Count de Maistre was a firm favourite with them (*Dublin*, December 1852, p. 421). This ultramontanism among High Church clergy was regarded as sufficiently dangerous to receive the condemnation of the Bishop of St. Davids, Connop Thirlwall, in his charge to his clergy, 1845, p. 14, and of the Bishop of London, C. J. Blomfield, in his charge, 1846, pp. 24, 27, 29.

[3] Palmer, op. cit., i, pp. 202 (*Réflexions*, *Essai*, *Affaires de Rome*), 223, 225, 265 (*Affaires*), 266 (*Essai*); ii, pp. 13, 19, 65, 210.

[4] ibid., i, pp. 207 ff.

[5] ibid., i, p. 7.

[6] See E. A. Knox, *The Tractarian Movement*, London, 1933, pp. 176 f.

controversy loomed the largest. Dr. Hampden, whose Bampton Lectures[1] had dealt several telling blows against the Tractarian position, and whom Newman had accused, not of heresy, but of doctrine which tended towards heresy in its effects, had been appointed by the Crown to the Regius Professorship of Divinity. This created a national uproar, and Convocation of the University of Oxford, which consisted almost entirely of clergymen of the Church of England, condemned him. But the Crown prevailed, and the Tractarians were once more faced with the problem of authority. Wiseman observed this situation and, in an article in the *Dublin Review*, contrasted the position of Hampden, who had retained his Chair in the face of widespread belief in the heretical tendencies of his doctrine, with the position of Lamennais, whose heresy had cut him off from the body of the Church. The one flourished, the body to which he belonged being unable to cut him off; the other languished, effectively severed from the Church:

It is not long since a bold and mighty genius after having fought and conquered the rampant infidelity of the last age, and indifference, its baneful progeny in this, had gathered around him a band of fresh and youthful minds, free from either taint, panting after what is pure and holy, and eager to be led, under his banner, to the sacred war. In an ill-fated hour, he swerved, like Tertullian, from the very principles by which he had so often confuted error, and suffered the suggestions of an enthusiastic imagination to prevail over the former convictions of his mind. The Head of the Church pronounced his award of disapprobation—he yielded not; but he has ever since stood like a scathed and shattered oak, which the lightning hath touched, the energies of his mind exhausted, the intellectual sap dried up; and of all those whom he trained and cherished, not one has followed him in his disobedience; they have all wept and mourned over his fall, but their principles have been stronger than their affections, and they have remained banded together, but under the best and only sure guide—the Church itself which they defend.[2]

Wiseman's shaft struck home. In July of the following year (1837) Newman wrote to Rogers: 'I am going to review Lamennais' work in October. It is *most curious*.'[3] The work referred to was *Affaires de Rome*, and the review turned out to be no mere

[1] R. D. Hampden, *The Scholastic Philosophy, considered in its relations to Christian Theology*, London, 1832.

[2] *Dublin*, May 1836, p. 260, 'The Oxford Controversy'.

[3] Mozley, ii, p. 238 (5 July 1837).

objective account of an interesting and topical book.[1] It was a phase in the working out of the doctrine of authority as it was taught by the Tractarians. Wiseman had taunted Anglicans with lacking any effective authority. Newman replied that from Lamennais's evidence the Church of France was more subject to the secular power than was the Church of England, and that she had less control over matters of faith and order than Anglicans had. But more than this: Newman's article revealed his current attitude to Lamennais. It revealed that he considered Lamennais's worst sin to be, not his dangerously democratic ideas, but rebellion. From his attitude to the Gallicanism which Lamennais attacked we can assume that Newman was substantially in agreement with him on this issue. But by 1836 his earlier sympathy for Lamennais's methods had disappeared, and he was coming more and more to realize the value of submission. The atmosphere of restless, penetrating, self-assertive logic which pervades Lamennais's work was repugnant to him, and so he concludes his article with words which have been often quoted[2]: he admits that there is much that is excellent in the doctrine, but that it has an ill flavour which reminds one that it is drugged and unwholesome. The same spirit which led its author to reject the civil authority may also lead him to reject the authority of religion. In this conclusion we may perhaps see why Newman never followed Lamennais far down the path of disestablishment. It involved conflict, and conflict meant violence, which was not a characteristic of Newman's. After his initial desire for disestablishment,

[1] *British Critic*, October 1837, xxii, pp. 261–83, reprinted in *Essays Critical and Historical*, London, 2nd ed., 1872, i, pp. 102–42, 'The Fall of De La Mennais'. Knox (*The Tractarian Movement*, p. 176) alleges that this reply was framed with reference to Lamennais's *Des progrès*, which Newman does not mention. Otherwise Knox's outline of the episode is accurate.

[2] Although not always accurately, e.g. P. Devine, *Life of Fr. Dominic*, London, 1898, p. 44, quotes them with Fr. Dominic's condemnation of the philosophical basis of the *Essai*, to show that both Newman and Fr. Dominic were thinking along the same lines at the same time: 'Curious that this poor Passionist and Newman should have been of the same opinion, at that very moment when La Mennais was in the ascendant.' In fact Fr. Dominic's criticisms had been made eleven years earlier when Lamennais's views had quite a different appearance from those of *Affaires de Rome*. The mistake is repeated in Urban Young, *Life and Letters of the Venerable Dominic*, London, 1926, p. 40, and in *American Essays for the Newman Centennial*, ed. J. K. Ryan and E. D. Benard, Washington, 1947, p. 195.

he took up an attitude of obedience to established authority, an attitude which, subject only to the urgent demands of his conscience, he retained to the end of his life.

The other significant point about Newman's analysis of Lamennais is that he regarded him as being essentially political.[1] This, too, has personal overtones. Newman himself had been political in his attitude to the Church question early in the history of the movement.[2] But he soon ceased to be so and by the time of his article he had moved to a personal and doctrinal position rather than a political one.[3]

In all this there is little mention of Lamennais's doctrines themselves, which contained, Newman said, much that was excellent. He condemned the spirit in which they were propagated, but we are justified in concluding from his silence on general matters of doctrine and from his exposure of Gallican abuses that he did not disapprove of the principles of the *Avenir*.

Of Oxford's attitude to Lamennais the article tells us little, unless one short passage is not just an oversimplification of Lamennais's words. Describing the links between the *Avenir* wing of the French Church and Catholics in other countries Lamennais had written in *Affaires de Rome:*

Des liens semblables se formèrent avec les catholiques d'Irlande et d'Angleterre, et une union plus étroite encore s'établit avec la Belgique. . . . Ses paroles trouvèrent de l'écho jusque dans le Nouveau-Monde, d'où lui parvinrent de nombreuses marques d'adhésions, depuis la Nouvelle-Orléans jusqu'à Boston.[4]

This Newman paraphrased as ' "Its words found an echo" in England, Belgium and the New World, from New Orleans to Boston,'[5] thus abolishing Lamennais's distinction between those countries which had formal links with the *Avenir*, and those in

[1] 'He is thoroughly political in his views and feelings' (*British Critic*, October 1837, p. 276).

[2] A glance at his letters for 1833 and 1834 shows a preoccupation with ideas of Church and State, political schemes (e.g. the Irish Bill) and the niceties of party allegiance. Uppermost in Newman's mind is the need for preserving the influence of the Church in the political sphere.

[3] See Newman on the principles of the Oxford Movement in *Apologia*, part IV (Everyman), pp. 67–74. His published correspondence for 1835–6 is largely concerned with doctrinal aspects of the *Tracts* and discussions of the Fathers.

[4] *Affaires*, 1836–7, p. 73.

[5] *British Critic*, October 1837, p. 278.

which its teaching was simply greeted with approval. Was there at the back of his mind Froude's enthusiasm for the *Avenir*, an enthusiasm perhaps shared by some of his contemporaries?[1]

One young man who had his attention drawn to Lamennais at this time was W. E. Gladstone. The first edition of his *The State in its Relations with the Church* (1838) had made no reference to Lamennais, but the fourth expanded edition (1841) was furnished with indications that he had become aware of Lamennais's treatment of the subject in the meanwhile.[2] Other of his writings bear witness to a sympathetic understanding of Lamennais's purpose.[3] Indeed, Lamennais so interested him that he spent some of his spare time in Oxford in 1853 dipping into his works.[4]

Among the Romanizers of the movement there was a strong anti-Gallican feeling. Thomas William Allies, J. D. Dalgairns, and F. W. Faber, all of whom later entered the Church of Rome, travelled the Continent to observe the state of religion there.[5] Faber may not have been one of the most representative of Tractarians, but he spoke for all who held strong views when he wrote (in 1841), 'Were I a French priest (I) should belong to the school of De Maistre.'[6] And in 1842, after he had travelled in France, he noted with approval the decline of Gallicanism and the increase of ultramontanism as a result of Lamennais's teaching.

[1] For example, the two sub-Tractarians, T. T. Carter and Charles Woodcock were in Paris for the crucial period 1831–2, and would certainly have known about the *Avenir* (*Life and Letters of T. T. Carter*, ed. W. H. Hutchings, London, 1904, 2nd ed., p. 10).

[2] Gladstone, *The State in its Relations with the Church*, 4th ed., 1841, p. 33, which cites 'Les Maux de l'église et de la société' from *Affaires de Rome*, and p. 243, where Lamennais is called a writer 'of abundant ability'.

[3] Gladstone, *Church Principles considered in their Results*, London, 1840, p. 367; see also his articles in the *Quarterly*, December 1844, p. 169 (reprinted in *Gleanings of Past Years*, 1879, v, p. 116), January 1875, p. 298 (reprinted in *Rome and the Newest Fashions in Religion*, 1875, p. 182); in the *Edinburgh*, April 1852, p. 361 (reprinted in *Gleanings*, iv, p. 145); and in the *Contemporary Review*, October 1878, p. 447 (*Gleanings*, iii, p. 255), where he calls Lamennais 'the greatest genius of the French clergy of his day'.

[4] J. Morley, *Life of Gladstone*, London, 1903, i, p. 457.

[5] Allies: T. W. Allies, *Journal in France*, London, 1848; Dalgairns: W. Ward, *The Oxford Movement*, p. 40; Faber: F. W. Faber, *Sights and Thoughts in Foreign Churches and among Foreign Peoples*, London, 1842.

[6] *Life and Letters of F. W. Faber*, London, 1869, p. 83.

He forebore to go into the details of Lamennais's fall, but concentrated only on his triumph over Gallicanism.[1]

Perhaps, however, the most significant pointers to the Oxford attitude to Lamennais were to be found in the *Ecclesiastic*, a magazine already referred to.[2] While other periodicals of Tractarian sympathies practically ignored him,[3] the *Ecclesiastic*, edited by the Vicar of St. Thomas's, Oxford, and numbering among its contributors many distinguished theologians and writers,[4] showed an appreciation of his character and some of his views which was at least as perceptive as anything published about him during the century. It condemned him principally for his disobedience and lack of discipline:

> We have dwelt thus at length upon the career of Lamennais because it is a great warning to Catholic Christians not to leave the safe path of obedience to the powers that be, and follow the wandering lights of revolutionary doctrines.
>
> He who breaks laws and simply follows an *idea*
>
> is in imminent danger of losing the faith which those alone can keep, who submit themselves to authority, and suffer, rather than do, wrong. What has happened in the case of one highly-gifted man is as likely to happen in the case of a great number.[5]

The *Ecclesiastic* believed firmly that his principles were good but that the pressing of these principles to extreme conclusions in defiance of authority brought about his downfall. In this article, and elsewhere,[6] it expressed an unusually deep and personal feeling for Lamennais:

[1] F. W. Faber, *Sights and Thoughts in Foreign Churches*, pp. 113–16. He calls Lamennais 'a kind of theological O'Connell'.

[2] Above, p. 44.

[3] Both the *British Critic* and the *English Review* were vague about his current opinions. The former thought in 1842 that he had been seduced by the popular French idea that the prevailing opinion of the age was the standard of truth (*British Critic*, 1842, xxxii, p. 262), and the latter continued to mention him as an orthodox upholder of the faith (*English Review*, 1847, viii, p. 112, and 1848, ix, p. 100).

[4] The editor was for most of the time the Revd. Thomas Chamberlain. Contributors included J. Baines, Lord Campden, J. G. Cazenove, H. J. Coleridge, B. J. S. Coleridge, W. Denton, A. P. Forbes (later Bishop of Brechin), E. A. Freeman, Beresford Hope, W. J. Irons, Dr. R. F. Littledale, Lord John Manners, Dr. J. M. Neale, H. Newland, H. N. Oxenham, T. W. Perry, N. Pollock, and Robert Wilberforce.

[5] *Ecclesiastic*, January-June 1848, v, p. 276.

[6] See especially *Ecclesiastic*, v, 1848, pp. 267–89; vii, 1849, pp. 365–72; xix, 1857, pp. 260–9.

Alas! the history of M. de Lamennais shows that, the 'Blessed vision of Peace', its infallible guidance, and living authority, are no safeguard against the subtle trials of faith. The great man of whom we speak may pass through the danger in the strength of his eminent sanctity, but who will answer for those many sensitive hearts, and restless intellects, whom his example and writings have set philosophizing in religion, and launched upon a sea of doubts?[1]

It was finally this attitude, rather than opinions about his anti-Gallicanism, or his teaching about Church and State in the *Avenir*, which prevailed. It was reflected in the writings of R. W. Church, who lived with the movement from its early days to the last decade of the century, in his sensitive reviews of Lamennais's correspondence,[2] and in other comments on the history of the Church in the nineteenth century.[3] In an address to the Junior Clergy Society in St. Paul's Cathedral in 1880, he warned his youthful hearers against lack of self-discipline by referring them to the example of Lamennais and Lacordaire. After outlining the position in which they had found themselves when opposition to the policy of the *Avenir* began to rise, he went on:

Then began the trial of temper—the trial of seeing brilliant theories more and more in disaccord with realities, of seeing authority making short work of logic, of meeting distrust and disapproval of what it had cost them so much to offer, of being reminded at each turn and in all sorts of indirect ways that they were practically wrong. Lamennais was not a character which could stand such a trial. From the first, passion —eager, headlong, scornful passion—had been as strong with him as his powerful and ambitious intellect. And when with his acknowledged successes he still found that he could not move the world as he would, that the latent necessities of a system and its intangible powers of resistance were too much for him, a fierce bitterness of temper, increasing by perpetual indulgence took possession of his soul. Not Rome only, for which he had invented new arguments, nor the Pope, whom he would have made absolute over the modern world, but Christianity, but religion itself, were at last enveloped in his disgust and despair.[4]

[1] *Ecclesiastic*, v, 1848, p. 276.

[2] See above, pp. 54 f.

[3] *Guardian*, 18 July 1883 (reprinted in R. W. Church, *Occasional Papers*, London, 1897, ii, p. 237), *Christian Remembrancer*, July 1848 (reprinted in R. W. Church, *Essays and Reviews*, London, 1854, pp. 345, 354, 382, 387).

[4] R. W. Church, *Cathedral and University Sermons*, London, 1892. Address on 'Temper and Self-discipline', p. 199.

With Lamennais he contrasted Lacordaire's, at least outward, obedience. And yet it was Lamennais—Church knew it well—who had had the greater influence, both for good and for ill:

One man's temper, it is impossible not to see it, was the leading influence to intellectual change, and had much, if not all, to do in breaking up his position; it drove him from his moorings, and sent him adrift into the 'wild and wandering sea' of doubt. . . . Perhaps to us here the stormy career calls forth the keener interest. In view of the Master's judgment-seat, who commissioned both, it is a different matter.[1]

[1] R. W. Church, *Cathedral and University Sermons*, London, 1892. Address on 'Temper and Self-discipline', p. 200.

V

LAMENNAIS AND ENGLISH ROMAN CATHOLICISM

In April 1829, the month when the Catholic Relief Bill received the royal assent, the author of an article on foreign views of the Catholic question wrote in the *Foreign Quarterly Review*:

> Those who support the view of papal dangers press into their service the spirit and declarations of another writer . . . the Abbé De la Mennais. The principles of this vigorous, unflinching and intrepid champion of the Holy See, would be dangerous enough, if, like the preaching of Peter the Hermit, they found the world prepared for a crusade.[1]

Fortunately for the Roman Catholics who had so long worked for emancipation, little use had been made of the writings of a Frenchman whose major works to this date had paid great attention to England. If more play had been made with them, the anti-emancipationists would certainly have been more alarmed than they were at the dangers of allowing some of the King's subjects to acknowledge the absolute authority of a foreign ruler. It was perhaps fear that this conclusion could be too clearly drawn from Lamennais's writings and a suspicion that the moderate Catholics had not been fully represented in them which prevented the emancipationists from disseminating them more widely. For in the *Essai* Lamennais took little account of the tension which existed between the old-established Roman Catholic believers, who were more Gallican in their outlook then ultramontane, and not disposed to force their claims on a potentially hostile populace, and the openly militant party, who were fierce in the expression of their allegiance to the Holy See. As Lamennais saw it, Roman Catholics everywhere were united in desiring freedom to exercise their duty of practising and propagating their faith. The atmosphere of cautious and even genteel Romanism was unknown to

[1] *F.Q.R.*, April 1829, p. 283.

him, and for examples of English Roman Catholicism he relied upon the *Orthodox Journal*[1] and the writings of the irascible Dr. Milner.[2]

This was the principal reason why restraint was exercised in the use of Lamennais's powerful apologetic—which would otherwise have been useful because there was no comparable English Roman Catholic theologian at the time. A second was a practical one. Popular though the book was in France and elsewhere in Europe, it had not been published in English, although a translation may have been made at an early date.[3] Therefore the people to whom it was accessible were comparatively few.[4]

The third reason is one of chronology. By the time the *Essai* appeared the movement for emancipation was well under way. The brunt of the journalistic campaigning was borne by W. E. Andrews, who chose to do battle with the cudgels of common sense rather than the rapiers of theological speculation. For seventeen years (1813–30) the *Orthodox Journal* fought for this cause, not infrequently clashing with its own ecclesiastical authority. It maintained that public opinion was the standard of truth; it attacked Protestantism and indifferentism in religion, and demanded religious toleration and civil and religious liberty.[5] Andrews had no need to fly to Lamennais for his arguments, even if he knew much about him,[6] because he had an abundance of material to hand in his own country. But, while Andrews was probably not influenced by Lamennais, it is not impossible that

[1] *O.I.* i, p. 222 (12 September 1815); *O.I.* i, p. 387 (9 May 1819); *Essai*, i, p. 180.

[2] Dr. Milner was an ultramontane when few of his English co-religionists were. Lamennais cites his *Letters to a Prebendary* (1801)—*Essai*, i, p. 223; ii, p. 210, and *The End of Religious Controversy* (1818)—*Essai*, ii, préface, p. lxix, and p. 206. Both these books are courteous refutations of the Anglican position.

[3] Above, p. 30; and *O.I.* i, p. 381 (8 November 1818).

[4] In a letter to Père Anfossi, Lamennais speaks of flattering comments he has received from many countries, including England (*O.I.* i, p. 410—1 December 1821).

[5] e.g. *Orthodox Journal*, viii, 1820, pp. 333–45.

[6] The only allusion to Lamennais I have found in any of Andrews's publications is in the *Truthteller*, where the Bishop of Hermopolis, speaking on the Gallican liberties, is reported to have referred to the errors of a 'man of great talent'. Andrews adds the explanatory footnote: 'M. de la Menais [*sic*] who has published what has been construed as ascribing temporal power over Princes to the Pope' (iv, 15 July 1826, p. 45).

Lamennais was influenced by Andrews. He read his publications while he was in England[1] and he certainly continued to receive them after his return to France.[2]

W. E. Andrews, however, was not the only journalist to fight for the cause of emancipation. There were other militant magazines, among them the *Catholic Spectator* (1823–6) and the *Catholic Miscellany* (1822–30). Both of these played an important part in making Roman Catholics aware of Lamennais's work. The *Spectator* tried to clarify theological ideas in their practical context, to work out the theme that religion was the first and most important element in social order. To that end it reprinted several of Lamennais's articles translated into English. The article 'On our duty at the present moment' established the principle of the invincibility of truth. It stated clearly that religion was truth, and therefore any education not firmly grounded in religion was not really education at all.[3] This article was followed shortly afterwards by a translation of a letter of congratulation from Lamennais to the *Mémorial catholique*[4] and by his first contribution to the *Mémorial*, 'On spiritual authority and its relations with political order'. That this article was of peculiar importance to the situation in England at the time was quickly noticed by the editors. Lamennais's thesis was that submission to authority by the people was the only attitude which made society possible at all. The question therefore was, to what sort of authority should they submit? Individual reason and political authority were both ruled out, and the only remaining possibility was spiritual authority. Lamennais went on to argue that it was exactly this spiritual authority which Protestants denied, and therefore it was a significant fact that those countries which were in revolt were Catholic, and those whose political affairs seemed to be quiet were Protestant. This was a symptom of the presence of anti-social doctrines in society, which Catholics took upon themselves to combat by force, but in which Protestants acquiesced through indifference. Lamennais devoted special attention to the Church of England. He censured it for trying to make the best of both worlds: for

[1] *O.I.* i, p. 222, to Jean, 12 September 1815.

[2] ibid., p. 387. He sent a copy to Jean, 9 May 1819.

[3] *Catholic Spectator*, ii, 1824, pp. 19–24, translation of 'Du devoir dans les temps actuels' (1823), reprinted in *O.C.* viii, 1836–7, pp. 378–88.

[4] ibid., p. 93, translation of 'Lettre au rédacteur du Mémorial catholique', *Mémorial catholique*, January 1824, pp. 15 f.

denying spiritual authority, when occasion demanded, and thereby condoning new anti-social and therefore anti-religious doctrines; but also for invoking, when it suited it, in its dealings with sects, the Catholic principle of authority, to which, on its own showing, it had no claim. Lamennais could see only two ends for the Church of England: either it would lose what little Christianity it retained, or it would fly to the bosom of the Church of Rome.[1] It is difficult to assess what effect an article like this would have had at the time, but Lamennais's ability to describe the issues with such deceptive clarity could not but have fortified his less coherent English brethren. In the same year (1824) two more of his articles on politico-religious subjects[2] were translated, and in 1825 yet another, which called for a nineteenth-century crusade against social and religious indifference under the leadership of the Pope.[3] How closely the *Catholic Spectator* identified itself with Lamennais's views[4] can be seen from the issue for April 1826, which printed a long and enthusiastic article by Comte O'Mahoney on *De la religion*[5] and a full account of the subsequent trial.[6] Lamennais's final appearance in its pages was in a translation of a letter which he had written to a Protestant in order to convert him to Catholicism. The argument turned upon authority, individual reason and the Real Presence.[7]

In these translations, the *Catholic Spectator* gave its readers a very fair idea of Lamennais's thought in the middle twenties, a digest which could not have been made available in any other form. Its purpose was to encourage the Catholic faithful in their demands for emancipation, and to give them clear, profoundly expressed reasons for doing so.

The *Catholic Miscellany* took another line. It did not leave

[1] *Catholic Spectator*, ii, 1824, pp. 94–8, 'De l'autorité spirituelle dans ses rapports avec l'ordre politique', *Mémorial catholique*, January 1824, pp. 16–23.

[2] ibid., pp. 327–9, 'Some Analogies between Religion and Politics'. This article is not from the *Mémorial* and is not reprinted in the *Mélanges*, *O.C.* vi, viii, or x. *Catholic Spectator*, pp. 357–61, 'On the Pride of our Age', is a translation of 'De l'orgueil dans notre siècle' (1820) (*O.C.* viii, pp. 242–9).

[3] ibid., iii, 1825, pp. 139–43, 'The Holy Alliance'.

[4] Lamennais's *Mémorial catholique* commended the *Catholic Spectator* for defending 'saines doctrines' (ii, December 1824, p. 301).

[5] *Catholic Spectator*, iv, April 1826, pp. 124–34.

[6] ibid., pp. 135–7.

[7] ibid., pp. 337–40.

Lamennais to talk for himself, but lauded him and his achievements, as some would think, a little excessively. This, for example, is an account of the *Mémorial catholique:*

But the life, the all-pervading soul of the *Mémorial Catholique* is the Abbé de la Mennais. It is now eight years since this splendid luminary first rose above the literary horizon; and the admiration which hailed its first appearance has not diminished, as it has traced its glorious orbit in the heavens. Religion, politics, philosophy, no subject is foreign to this amazing mind; and amid the most various and arduous occupations, it shrinks from no call of honour or duty.

Indeed, this great man displays in the cause of religion the same skill, energy, and indefatigable activity which Voltaire, in the last age, exerted in the cause of impiety; and as the great champion of irreligion formed his disciples with incredible art and prescribed to each his particular duties, so the Christian philosopher has formed a chosen group of writers, whose labours he directs, whom he assists by his advice, and animates by his example. It is from this school that the editors of the *Mémorial Catholique* proceed.[1]

On Lamennais's trial the *Miscellany* was non-committal.[2] Later in the year it rashly gave its unreserved approval to Lamennais's philosophic method of *sensus communis*, 'a philosophy which, we may assert with confidence, is destined to supersede every other in Catholic Europe, and which, if it could ever gain admittance into the Colleges and Universities of Protestant Europe, would effectively undermine heresy and infidelity.'[3] It went on to announce that a young clergyman of talent and piety had agreed to translate Rohrbacher's *Catéchisme du sens commun*, in which the essentials of Lamennais's ideas were contained, and promised a full account of his work in later numbers. It is a matter for both regret and speculation that this account never appeared. It is almost certain that Lamennais's method did not supersede other methods, at least in England,[4] and the ensuing silence suggests that the *Miscellany*'s confidence did not meet with official favour. This lively but not very skilful attempt to popularize Lamennais in the narrow circle of hereditary Roman Catholics was a failure.

[1] *Catholic Miscellany*, v, 1826, pp. 289 f.
[2] ibid., p. 369.
[3] ibid., vi, 1826, p. 277.
[4] Enquiries made from Ushaw College, Durham, Oscott College, Birmingham, St. Edmund's, Ware, and Downside have yielded no evidence on this point.

After this it continued to be fulsome in his praise,[1] although to the end it persisted in refraining from telling its readers what Lamennais's ideas actually were.

The extent to which he was read and admired may best be judged from a work which had great popularity at the time and made a considerable contribution, if not to the thought, at least to the atmosphere of the Catholic revival. This was Kenelm Digby's *Broad Stone of Honour*.[2] In analysing the medieval concept of chivalry, Digby concluded that it was that general spirit or state of mind which disposed men to heroic and generous actions and kept them conversant with all that was beautiful and sublime in the moral world.[3] This was a subject upon which Lamennais had little to say. He did not believe he was concerned with a revival of the modes of faith which belonged to past ages. He was more concerned with a living faith in the present and for the future. Nevertheless Digby cited his authority on such subjects as faith,[4] love,[5] revolution,[6] Catholic principles of government,[7] the spiritual independence of the Church,[8] and others besides.[9] Another work of similar intentions, produced by Digby and running to eleven books, also contained references of the same respectful nature—but only in the first two books, which were published in 1831 and 1832, before Lamennais's fall into disfavour.[10] The remaining books, the last of which was published in 1842, although alluding to his friends and co-operators, eschewed all reference to him.[11]

Once emancipation had been achieved, it was inevitable that Roman Catholics should look more to Rome. The emancipation controversy had caused them to make a close examination of the

[1] *Catholic Miscellany*, viii, 1827, p. 360; viii, 1827, pp. 188 f.; N.S. ii, 1829, p. 467.

[2] Digby (1800–80) was converted while still an undergraduate at Cambridge in 1823, and, together with Ambrose Phillipps de Lisle and Pugin, was the principal romanticizing element in nineteenth-century Roman Catholicism in England.

[3] *Broad Stone of Honour* (ed. 1877), i, p. 109 (the first volume was first published in 1822).

[4] ibid., v, pp. 200 f.

[5] ibid., p. 334.

[6] ibid., i, p. 257.

[7] ibid., p. 321.

[8] ibid., p. 329.

[9] e.g. ibid., i, pp. 43 and 338; iv, pp. 53, 89, 106; v, pp. 233 f.

[10] *Mores Catholici, or Ages of Faith*, 11 books, 9 vols., London, 1831–42, i, p. 141; ii, p. 182.

[11] De Maistre, Bonald, Chateaubriand, Montalembert, De Coux, and Ozanam are all mentioned.

relations between Church and State, and to examine the evils of the establishment in England. In these circumstances the papal theory was in a strong position to command widespread assent.

At the same time a similar process was going on within the Anglican Church. The effects of Catholic emancipation, especially as they were seen in Ireland, forced churchmen to reconsider the extent to which it was legitimate that the Church should be under the legislative control of the State. This was not the whole story of the rise of the Oxford movement, but it represents an important aspect of it. As we have seen, complete disestablishment never became an official article of Tractarian policy, but it was held by many Tractarians at one time or another. All Tractarians had to face the problem of authority. All of them denied the right of the State to make decisions in matters of doctrine, but they did not all take the same path towards a solution of the problem. Some sought refuge in the tradition of the ancient Church and justified present practice by means of history. Others could not be reconciled to this method and so betook themselves to a communion which could provide them with a living authority dependent upon tradition and yet having an immediacy of its own. It is significant that the majority of the most distinguished converts to Rome around the middle of the nineteenth century, notably W. G. Ward, Manning, and F. W. Faber, became some of the most ardent ultramontanes.

In this atmosphere, in which men were trying to define where true sovereignty and authority lay, Lamennais's personality and example played a small but telling part. He had been on both sides of the fence: he had popularized ultramontanism as a political creed, and then, having found that its centre of authority, the Pope, did not live up to his expectations, denied it as empty and futile, and enthroned the authority of the people in its stead. His change of allegiance was accompanied by a number of circumstances which seemed to his opponents to suggest that he had thereby cut himself off from divine favour: none of his closest associates followed him into apostacy; even in anti-clerical France he was not honoured but lived in misery making a pitiful living from writing; the fire of inspiration which had glowed in his early work, and even in the *Paroles*, became dim and his works became monotonous repetitions of well-worn catch phrases.

Perhaps the greatest influence on, and the most faithful reflection of, Roman Catholic opinion at this time was the *Dublin Review*, founded in 1836 by Wiseman. What it has to say about Lamennais is of special interest, because in general it does not represent the views of an idiosyncratic editor but of a responsible section of Roman Catholic opinion. It expressed views already held and yet helped to impress them on others. One of its first articles was a review of Gerbet's *Considérations sur le dogme générateur de la piété catholique* (1829).[1] This showed that the *Dublin* adhered quite closely to the ideas of the *Essai* as developed in Lamennais's course of lectures which later became known as the *Essai d'un système de philosophie catholique*. The *Dublin* apparently took no note of the disfavour into which these ideas had fallen. It quite freely quoted examples from pagan Mexican art to show the oneness of Christianity and the universality of the Christian revelation, ideas which in themselves had led to that very indifferentism condemned not only in the *Essai* but also in *Mirari vos*.[2] It speaks in laudatory terms of the pre-1830 Lamennais,

> who, in his *Essai sur l'indifférence en matière de religion*, destroys at one blow the foundations of heresy and impiety, rivals his most illustrious European contemporaries in the profundity of his philosophic views, and surpasses them all in the vigour of his ratiocination and the fervid power of his eloquence,[3]

and with dramatic regret at his tragic fall:

> alas! a dark, but let us hope a passing cloud of fanaticism, overcasts the setting hour of a once glorious luminary.[4]

This merely prepares the way for more which is to come in the same issue. This is the article by Wiseman, which has already been referred to in the account of the Tractarian controversies[5] and which set Newman reading *Affaires de Rome*. From the Roman Catholic point of view it was noteworthy because it condemned Lamennais for nothing more than disobedience. The errors in his teaching had not yet been analysed.

[1] *Dublin*, May 1836, pp. 200–21. In a letter to Milnes, written 2 January 1837, Rio says that no copies of *Dogme générateur* were to be had because Gerbet had had them all destroyed (Houghton Papers, Trinity College, Cambridge).

[2] ibid., p. 205.

[3] ibid., p. 219.

[4] ibid., p. 201.

[5] Above, p. 108.

Lamennais's subsequent career called for no comment in the *Dublin*. He was not, however, lost completely from view. *Dolman's Magazine* (1845–9), a Roman Catholic monthly, spoke of him several times, and, with the exception of Jerningham's one passionate outburst,[1] always in terms of sincere regret for his defection after such a brilliant career.[2] That the English ultramontanes looked back particularly to the example of Lamennais may be inferred from a review of F. P. Kendrick's *Primacy of the Apostolic See* (1845), which curiously refers to 'the eloquence of M. De La Mennais' splendid work *Du Pape*',[3] a mistake which may reflect a situation in which de Maistre's ideas were made popular by the turbulent history of Lamennais.

There was also the *Weekly Register*, owned by the convert Henry Wilberforce, in which Acton's first journalism appeared. This was sympathetic to Lamennais and referred to him frequently with real grief.[4] It stated its position, enigmatically, in a review of *La Vie du Père Marie Ephrem*:

> Here [the Royal College of Toulouse] our young friend, after many a hard struggle with conscience, that stern monitress, imbibed the opinions of that, alas! too mischievous school now so rife not only in France, but in England as well, a school represented with eloquence most rare, with talents of the highest order by one whose name we grieve to note down, De La Mennais.[5]

The 'mischievous school' alluded to was the ultramontanism of which Lamennais had been an extreme exponent in France, and which was increasing in influence in England through the efforts of Ward, Manning, and some of the Oxford converts. The *Weekly Register* showed some of the spirit which was later to appear in the *Rambler* and the *Home and Foreign Review*, and therefore could not be expected to sympathize with the early Lamennais.

All mention of Lamennais in the *Dublin* was avoided until 1852, when J. B. Robertson's article on J. de Maistre appeared.[6] In

[1] *Dolman's Magazine*, viii, 1848, p. 92, above, p. 62.

[2] The anonymous author of an article on the Tractarian movement refers at length to conversations with Lamennais, and to his understanding of the English and Anglican mind (*Dolman's Magazine*, i, 1845, p. 144; also iii, 1846, p. 402, and vii, 1848, p. 209).

[3] ibid., i, 1845, p. 505.

[4] e.g. *Weekly Register*, 29 September 1849, pp. 137 f.; 5 January 1850, p. 360; 26 January 1850, p. 404.

[5] ibid., i, No. 23, p. 358.

[6] Above, p. 76; *Dublin*, December 1852, pp. 418–67.

this Robertson paid tribute not only to the character of his old friend, but also to his teaching. In particular he mentioned the 'system of metaphysics'[1] which Lamennais had developed and imparted to his disciples at La Chênaie. He, like the earlier reviewer of Gerbet, approved of it wholeheartedly and believed that if it had been published while Lamennais was still within the Church, his reputation as a philosopher would have stood much higher.

The combined effect of these comments is to suggest that, at least until his death, Lamennais's method of approach to the problems of apologetics had become part of common Catholic teaching. Certainly Roman Catholic missionaries from abroad would be well aware of his general outlook. On the one side, there was the celebrated Father Dominic,[2] who was one of the first to detect the dangerous tendencies of the second volume of the *Essai.*[3] He spent much of his time teaching in England and was the monk who had the privilege of receiving Newman into the Roman Church. On the other side, however, there were people like Père Bernard Hafkenscheid, who was well instructed in the teaching of Lamennais and preached in English when he conducted missions here,[4] and Father Vladimir Pecherín, who, having been converted to Christianity by the *Paroles d'un croyant*, became a Roman Catholic priest, lived and worked in England, and always looked upon himself as the 'exilé' of the *Paroles.*[5] Also to be taken into account are the considerable numbers of British priests[6] who were trained with the Frères de l'Instruction Chrétienne at Ploërmel under the personal supervision of the abbé Jean. Although the curriculum had no connection with that of La Chênaie, it is impossible to believe that the early views of

[1] *Dublin*, December 1852, p. 423.

[2] Denis Gwynn, *Father Dominic Barberi*, London, 1947.

[3] The Reverend P. Devine, *Life of Fr. Dominic*, London, 1898, pp. 42–45, but with reservations, above, p. 109; similarly Urban Young, *Life and Letters of Fr. D. Barberi*, London, 1926, pp. 38–41.

[4] F. J. J. Vrijmoed, *Lamennais avant sa défection et la Néerlande catholique*, Paris, 1930, p. 354.

[5] *Dublin*, 1949, pp. 139–53, 'A displaced person. The strange life of Fr. Vladimir Pecherín (1807–1885)' by Victor S. Frank.

[6] Twenty-three entered upon a course with the Frères between 1848 and 1851, of whom twenty-two subsequently returned to Britain. In 1851 a school of the same order was started at Hammersmith. (For details of these priests I am indebted to the Frères de l'Instruction Chrétienne, Highlands College, Jersey.)

Lamennais, those which his brother approved so heartily, were excluded, and that the contrast between the abbé Jean's and the abbé Féli's attitude was not often meditated upon.[1]

It was only after his death that anyone in England firmly linked Lamennais's self-excommunication not simply with disobedience, but with false theology. Discussing the tendencies of modern logic in the *Dublin*, Professor Jennings wrote:

The sad end of Lammenais [*sic*], still fresh in the memory of our readers, but too strongly illustrates the danger of admitting false theories in philosophy, and the impossibility of dissociating speculative error from practice.[2]

In an evil hour he undertook to speculate upon one of the most intricate problems of metaphysics, and deviating from the right path here, he was led step by step through the many scenes of his strange life, ever receding further from the temple, till at last he cared not to look behind upon it any more, or to remember that he had ever knelt before its altar.[3]

In the following year the same author made more detailed criticism of Lamennais's theory and repudiated the whole basis upon which it rested, the first time that this had been expressly done in English since Lamennais propounded it.[4] This struck a new note in criticism of Lamennais. Hitherto, while his action had been deplored, his thought had been applauded.

But this brief denial of Lamennais's philosophy was not sustained, for his conclusions, if not his methods, were needed in the infallibilist controversy, which ended with the Vatican Council of 1870. E. S. Purcell, Manning's biographer, for example, in 1860 called the *Essai* a 'magnificent work' and numbered Lamennais among the staunchest defenders of Catholicism,[5] and in 1863 maintained that Lamennais, together with de Maistre, Bonald, Gerbet, Montalembert, and Lacordaire, had 'not only triumphantly vindicated Christian philosophy and ethics against all opponents' but had 'imparted greater depth and fixedness to the

[1] See *Weekly Register*, 29 September 1849, pp. 137 f., an account by 'Henricus' of a visit to Ploërmel.

[2] *Dublin*, June 1854, p. 435.

[3] ibid., pp. 435 f.

[4] ibid., March 1855, p. 169, 'The legitimate influence of Authority in Philosophy', especially pp. 176 f.

[5] *Dublin*, November 1860, p. 122; see also *The Pope, the Press, and Napoleon III considered in a letter to Count de Montalembert*, by an Ultramontane, London, 1860, p. 18.

modern school of Catholic thought'.[1] It is impossible not to regard this support for Lamennais's philosophic outlook (as opposed to his political outlook, which Purcell unhesitatingly repudiated)[2] as a preparation for repeated appeals to the encyclical *Mirari vos*. For *Mirari vos*, although directed against the Lamennais of 1830–2, condemned that very liberalism of thought which Lamennais had also condemned in his earlier works. In the *Dublin Review* for the years 1860–70, especially under the editorship of the extreme ultramontane W. G. Ward,[3] we therefore see persistent references to *Mirari vos*, to the necessity of a close partnership between Church and State, and to the infallibility of the Supreme Pontiff.[4]

The Month, which had started in 1864, did the same sort of thing. Until 1870, in its frequent allusions to Lamennais, the emphasis was always on his lack of a proper sense of obedience, rather than on the falsity of his theology.[5] It tried, if not to rehabilitate him, at least to see him in the best possible light and to explain his disobedience. To this end it published in 1867 a translation of Père V. Mercier's 'Lamennais: étude psychologique', under the title 'The Early Years of Lamennais'.[6] This sought to prove that his error was in his nature, that his disobedience sprang from a lack of vocation rather than from any theological weakness.

With 1870, however, this part of Lamennais's usefulness was over, and he was once more attacked for the unsoundness of his theology.[7] He was still living as an image in the eyes of Roman

[1] *Dublin*, April 1863, p. 406, in 'Modern Intellectualism and the Roman Catholic Church'.

[2] ibid., p. 397: 'It [the separation of Church and State as advocated by Lamennais] was wrong in principle and would have failed in practice.'

[3] Ward was editor from 1863 to 1878.

[4] e.g. *Dublin*, February 1862, pp. 195 f.; April 1863, pp. 391–406; July 1863, p. 66; January 1865, pp. 41–69; July 1868, pp. 77 and 245; October 1868, p. 518; January 1869, pp. 2 and 242; April 1869, pp. 363 and 482.

[5] *The Month*, v, 1866, pp. 232 f.: 'De la Mennais was, in reality, at the turning point of his life; the point at which by a thorough and hearty acceptance of the condemnation of his doctrines, he might have raised himself to a height of real greatness, such as he could never have reached in any other way. Unhappily, another path was open to him, the path of pride and littleness; he dashed into it, and shattered at once the prestige of his name and the peace of his soul.' See also vi, 1867, p. 49; and viii, 1868, pp. 211 f.

[6] ibid., vii, 1867, pp. 436–50.

[7] ibid., xii, 1870, p. 645.

Catholics, but it was an image which changed with the theological climate.

There was almost as much dispute between the several schools of Roman Catholic thought at this time as there was in the Church of England, although it was less publicized. An episode which illustrates this and in which Lamennais played a prominent part was the controversy over the alleged cardinalate of the historian Dr. Lingard, who was identified with the old school of hereditary Roman Catholics.

In 1858 Cardinal Wiseman published his *Recollections of the Last Four Popes and of Rome in their Times*, in which, in the course of a description of Leo XII's pontificate, he gave it clearly as his opinion that it was Lamennais and not Lingard who had been created a Cardinal *in petto* at the consistory of 1826.[1] The review of this work in the *Rambler* made a special point of mentioning Wiseman's opinions on this matter, and of supporting them.[2] This provoked an angry letter to the *Rambler* from the Reverend M. A. Tierney, Canon of the Roman Catholic Chapter of Westminster, demanding to know why the Cardinal preferred the 'wretched man'[3] Lamennais to the venerable Lingard. He cited much evidence against Wiseman, the chief of which was a letter from Dr. Gradwell in Rome to Tierney (1 November 1826) which said, in reference to the alleged cardinalate: 'Some bigots thought Lamennais though the last has almost surfeited Rome.'[4]

Wiseman thought this attack on him so important that he replied with a formidable privately printed letter,[5] which he distributed to his friends and to many of the Roman Catholic clergy in England. In this letter he considered the four arguments which Tierney, in his Memoir of Lingard[6], had adduced in favour of Lingard's elevation to the purple: the description of the unknown candidate in the allocution, the general opinion in Rome at the time, the conversation between Leo XII and Lingard, and

[1] Wiseman, op. cit., pp. 328–41.
[2] *Rambler*, April 1858, p. 280.
[3] Wiseman, op. cit., p. 341.
[4] *Rambler*, June 1858, p. 431.
[5] *A Letter to the Canons of the Cathedral Chapter of Westminster, in reply to one published in the Rambler for June 1858, relative to a passage in the 'Recollections of the last Four Popes'*, by H.E. Cardinal Wiseman, London, 1858. A postscript requests the recipients not to allow the letter to be published entire or in part; so successful was this request that the only copy I have been able to trace is in the library of Ushaw College, Durham.
[6] *The Metropolitan and Provincial Catholic Almanac*, 1854, pp. 3–25.

the medal given to Lingard by the Pope. The last two have little bearing on the present problem, but the first two bring some interesting facts to light.

Tierney in his reference to the papal allocution of 2nd October 1826 had been vague about its exact wording and had referred only to writings drawn 'ex authenticis fontibus'. Wiseman, however, claimed to have procured from Rome the exact words of the allocution, which seemed to refer more pointedly to Lamennais:

> Praeter hos quatuor, Cardinalem creamus Virum religione, pietate, ac doctrina archetypis, et nativis e fontibus hausta insignem, qui libris editis catholicam adversus haereticos, et schismaticos veritatem strenue non minus quam feliciter tuetur.[1]

Wiseman went on to review the nature of Lamennais's publications up to 1826, and to show how they fulfilled the requirements of the allocution. He was careful to dissociate himself strongly from Lamennais's later opinions:

> Far be it from me to become his panegyrist, or recommend his writings: for some may doubt if even then he was sincere. God alone knows it; but we, merely discussing an historical point in 1826, must not look at its unhappy subject through the total eclipse which has since covered his memory for ever, but must contemplate him as then in his splendour, even should it have been unmerited.[2]

On the second point, the opinion of Rome at the time, Wiseman produced some interesting new material. His method was to enquire of as many of Lamennais's contemporaries as possible about this point. Unfortunately the Cardinal did not give the names of his correspondents, nor have their letters survived in his papers at Westminster, but from his description of them and from their replies we can guess at the identity of at least three of them, Lacordaire, Montalembert, and Gerbet, all of whom supported the Cardinal's view. It is regrettable that Gerbet's letter has been lost, because Wiseman says that it contained matters relating to the fall of Lamennais known only to Gerbet and one other friend. To these informants, who could easily be accused of partiality, Wiseman added an array of evidence from other prelates and officials, including one who had been with him in the English College at the time.[3]

[1] *A Letter*, &c., p. 7.
[2] ibid., p. 10.
[3] ibid., p. 19.

To this letter Wiseman received many replies, all approving his reasoning. These words of Serjeant Edward Bellasis, himself one of the 'new Catholics', are typical: 'everyone . . . must be glad that your Eminence has been able to clear up an historical incident of some interest, and at the same time to show how entirely without ground or justification was the attack made upon your Eminence'.[1] If Wiseman received any letters in the contrary sense they have not been preserved.

Tierney immediately replied, also with a fully documented privately printed letter.[2] On the first point, he strongly denied that the words of the allocution were apposite to Lamennais. He argued at some length that Lamennais was already under suspicion before the papal consistory and that it would have been difficult to find any educated Catholic of the time who was ignorant of the dangerous tendency of Lamennais's works.[3] As to the general opinion in Rome, Tierney could do little more than question Wiseman's authorities and reaffirm his confidence in Dr. Gradwell.[4]

Tierney's letter was very irate and by no means as well argued as the Cardinal's. Doubtless personal relations between members of the chapter at Westminster had something to do with the extraordinarily bad feeling aroused by this incident, but we cannot help noting that it was the 'new Catholics' and their protagonist Wiseman who, while dissociating themselves from Lamennais's later opinions, supported the Lamennais who had done so much to establish the view which they now held, and the 'old Catholics' who bitterly opposed him in favour of their candidate Lingard.

The affair was brought to a diplomatic conclusion by Richard Simpson in an article in the *Rambler*. Not wanting to give offence to either contestant, he said that it seemed probable to him that Lamennais's passion and Lingard's accuracy had ensured that both of them had been awarded the Cardinal's hat.[5]

[1] Westminster Diocesan Archives, letter of 15 November 1858. There are seven others in the archives in the same vein.

[2] *A Reply to Cardinal Wiseman's Letter to his Chapter*, by the Reverend M. A. Tierney, London, 1858.

[3] ibid., pp. 17 f.

[4] ibid., pp. 19–21.

[5] *Rambler*, November 1859, pp. 75–83. See J. L. Altholz, *The Liberal Catholic Movement in England*, London, 1962, pp. 76 f.

Whatever the truth of the matter,[1] it revealed the presence of at least two conflicting interests in English Roman Catholicism.[2] The one party, Gallican in outlook, declared that the Pope could not possibly have given any sign of favour to a person who, like Lamennais, was so much opposed to the Gallican cause. The other party, leaning towards ultramontanism, declared that the Pope, in honouring Lamennais, was applauding his means of overcoming infidelity.

Both of these views took it for granted that the Pope was unlikely to err seriously. There was, however, a third party which did not accept any such presupposition. Their view was expressed in a letter from Acton to Richard Simpson:

In the volume *De vita et rebus gestis ven. servi Dei Innocentii XI Commentarius*, Romae, 1776, is related how Innocent wanted to make Arnauld a Cardinal. Can you not use this in your article, by way of justifying our Cardinal, who has not insulted the wisdom of the Holy See by believing in the intended elevation of Lamennais, since the same dignity was designed for the great Jansenist who had dedicated the second volume of his work, 'De la Perpétuité' etc. to Innocent? I

[1] The principal summaries of the evidence are to be found in M. Haile and E. Bonney, *The Life and Letters of J. Lingard, 1771–1851*, London, 1911, pp. 220–9 (fair but occasionally inaccurate, they decide in favour of Lingard); Bernard Ward, *The Eve of Catholic Emancipation, 1803–1829*, iii (1820–9), London, 1912, pp. 350–4 (biased against Wiseman, he leaves the matter open); W. J. Hegarty, 'Was Lamennais a Cardinal?', *Irish Ecclesiastical Record*, 5th series, lxxix, February 1953, pp. 81–93 (he gives no new evidence and puts the maximum weight on Lamennais's claim). If Tierney and Gradwell, who believed that fifteen Cardinals had been made on 2 October 1826 (four publicly, eleven *in petto*, of whom six were subsequently made known), were right, then both Lamennais and Lingard *could* have been made Cardinals. It is more probable, however, that Wiseman was right in believing that *eleven* Cardinals were created in all, and that therefore the name of only one remained unrevealed. J. Schmidlin (*Papstgeschichte der Neuesten Zeit*, i (1800–46), Munich, 1933–6, p. 455) knows of only ten, which means that, unless contemporary witnesses were wrong, all record of the unrevealed Cardinal has disappeared. Since Leo XII had more cause, on political grounds, to delay the announcing of Lamennais's elevation than Lingard's and since the record of the creation of a Cardinal *in petto* would be more embarrassing to the Holy See, if it were believed to refer to Lamennais rather than to Lingard, it seems probable that Lamennais, and not Lingard, was the person so designated.

[2] Newman took a characteristically independent line. Although generally in sympathy with the converts, he was dissatisfied with the tone of Simpson's article, which was pro-Lamennais. (Ward, *Life of Newman*, i, p. 635—letter to Acton, 5 July 1859).

have extracted these passages from the above work. You will be able to make something of them, with a skilful hand, if you do not too openly disclose the purpose of the quotations.[1]

The purpose of the quotations was to suggest that both factions in England were right and both were wrong. The Gallicans were right as to the falsity of Lamennais's early teaching, and the ultramontanes were right as to his fame. But both were wrong in believing that the Pope could not err. The obvious conclusion to be drawn was that the Pope did indeed select Lamennais, but that in doing so he made a mistake.

With this third group of Catholics Lamennais was also to some extent involved. His liberalism had been developed largely from political motives. The liberties he demanded were all liberties of action: freedom of the press, freedom of conscience, freedom of association, and freedom of education. They were demanded, not for their own sake, but because he believed that this was the Church's only hope of harnessing the rising power of the people. Lamennais was not a liberal by nature. He was an authoritarian, but one who believed firmly in the *sensus communis*. He spent the rest of his life fighting for that liberty which he judged to be the desire of most people, and opposing tyranny, not only by individuals but also by parties and even by the people themselves.

The liberalism which arose among Roman Catholics in England around the middle of the century had a different emphasis. The tyranny it opposed was intellectual rather than political, and the liberties it advocated were not simply practical expedients but essential to the type of Catholic belief it sought to promote.

As Lamennais's liberalism owed much to political circumstances, so English Catholic liberalism was partly shaped by ecclesiastical circumstances. The restoration of the Roman hierarchy in England had produced a rigid framework of rather self-consciously authoritarian divines, most of them more distinguished for piety than for learning. Discipline was strict, and any deviation from the papal line was not encouraged. Into this organization came many able Anglican clergymen who, because they were married, were prevented from taking new orders. Most of them were more able than their diocesan superiors. They still had the fervour of their new-found faith. The only way they

[1] Abbot Gasquet, *Lord Acton and his circle*, London, 1906, pp. 61 f. (letter of 13 February 1859).

could express it was by writing for periodicals. Thoroughly Catholic though their views were, they rarely gauged the state of Roman Catholic opinion in England and not infrequently brought to bear on their new faith that freedom of enquiry to which they had been accustomed in their Anglican days. It is not surprising therefore that they were received coolly and that their ideas met opposition which in normal circumstances would have been unwarranted.

Among these converted clergymen were Henry Wilberforce, who owned the *Weekly Register*, Frederick Capes, who founded the *Rambler*, Richard Simpson, who assisted Capes, was for a time editor of the *Rambler*, and was associated with the *Home and Foreign Review*, and Thomas Wetherell, who helped Newman when he took over the editorship of the *Rambler*, and later edited *The Chronicle* and the *North British Review*.

But the genius who towered above them all was not a convert. John Dalberg Acton had been educated abroad, largely under the guidance of Dr. Döllinger, and he started his journalistic work in 1857, when he was twenty-three years old, in the *Weekly Register*. In the next year he became joint editor of the *Rambler*.

Acton was not troubled by the practical difficulties of the converts; he did not feel, as they must have felt, that there was any anomaly in his position. By the age of twenty-three he had made prodigious studies in politics, history, and theology, and already he had come to the conclusion that the key to society was freedom, that the proper end of society was not the happiness of the greatest number, nor the security of its members, but the freedom of all.[1] This meant that for him freedom was at the very heart of true religion, not the freedom to believe as one liked, but the freedom to bring to bear on the unalterable dogmas of Christianity the full light of science, by which he meant the whole realm of cognitive knowledge.[2]

Here lies the fundamental difference between the liberalism of Acton and that of Lamennais. For Acton freedom was an unalterable principle of society and nothing could be permitted to deny this, not even the authority of the Church. For Lamennais love

[1] 'The History of Freedom in Antiquity' in *History of Freedom and other Essays*, London, 1907, pp. 1–29.

[2] Especially 'Conflicts with Rome', *Home and Foreign Review*, iv, 1864, pp. 667–90, reprinted in *History of Freedom*, &c., pp. 461–91.

was the unalterable principle, and freedom was but one of the means of obtaining the end.

Nevertheless the liberal Catholics were acutely conscious of the figure of Lamennais. This is particularly evident in the pages of *Brownson's Quarterly Review*, an American publication re-issued in England and widely read by Roman Catholics.[1] Dr. Orestes A. Brownson had been a socialist of a religious type and had done much to promote the *Paroles* and the *Livre du peuple* in the United States,[2] but had been converted to Roman Catholicism in 1844 by careful thinking about the divinity and humanity of Christ and the doctrine of the Church as the Body of Christ. Since thinking, and not the need for submission, had brought about his conversion, and since he saw no occasion to stop applying the findings of reason to his religion after his conversion, he was a valuable, if somewhat erratic, ally of Acton, who valued him highly. He was also occasionally an embarrassment to orthodoxy. Throughout his *Review* there is a double attitude to Lamennais. There is the repudiation of Lamennais's idea of the *sensus communis* as a basis of certainty, which led, according to Brownson, to the tyranny of democracy. Not unnaturally this theme is stressed.[3] But there is also frequently expressed admiration for Lamennais's adherence to the idea of liberty in the Church. This is summed up in one notable article[4] on Lamennais and Gregory XVI. This went as far as it was possible to go in defence of Lamennais, acknowledged the value of much of his teaching and even upbraided the Church for her treatment of so distinguished a son.[5] The reader is left in no doubt that Brownson is still fighting for Lamennais's famous liberties, but without forcing the Church into an alliance with political liberals and democrats.[6]

[1] Cardinal Wiseman was rather rueful about the popularity of the *Rambler* and *Brownson's* (*Dublin*, December 1856, pp. 441–70, 'The Present Catholic Dangers').

[2] Carl Wittke, *The Utopian Communist: a biography of Wilhelm Weitling*, Baton Rouge, Louisiana, 1950, p. 18; for a brief biography of Brownson see *Atlantic Monthly*, June 1896, pp. 770–80, 'Orestes A. Brownson' by George Parsons Lathrop.

[3] e.g. *Brownson's*, July 1859, p. 375: 'The gravest error of Lamennais was in identifying Christianity with the general or universal reason, and making the common consent of the race the authority for doctrine and faith'. Also: ibid., April 1853, p. 266; April 1856, p. 251; April 1859, pp. 258 f.; October 1860, p. 430.

[4] ibid., July 1859, pp. 372–95.

[5] ibid., p. 374.

[6] ibid., July 1857, p. 389; April 1859, p. 259; January 1861, p. 83.

These words sum up his rather equivocal position:

Poor Lamennais, anxious to relieve Catholicity of its apparent alliance with the despotic courts of Europe, and to ally it with the popular sentiment of the age, ran into heresy, and died a rebel to the Church of God. These instances admonish us to be on our guard.[1]

Brownson was sensitive to the element of heresy and rebellion implied in the name of Lamennais,[2] but he was still consciously and avowedly under his influence as far as liberty in the Church was concerned.

The same was true of the English liberal Catholics, except that they were a shade harder on Lamennais's heresy and less obviously insistent on his idea of liberty. It was the liberal *Rambler* which had sparked off the cardinalate controversy by choosing from Wiseman's book the two important references to Lamennais and by making much of them,[3] when other critics had not thought it necessary even to mention that the Cardinal had said anything of Lamennais.[4]

Then started a series of attacks on ultramontanism.[5] In August and December of 1858 Montalembert was criticized for his early ultramontane views.[6] In November of the following year Simpson called Lamennais's early method 'hit hard, without minding whether you hit right', and his weapons, 'irony, bitterness and contempt'.[7] A more significant attack appeared in the *Home and Foreign Review* for July 1863.[8] Acton, writing on ultramontanism, traced the history of the relations between religion and science. He showed how deep the cleavage between the two went, and how Lamennais's ideas of universal consent had grown out of it.

[1] *Brownson's*, April 1856, p. 251.

[2] ibid., January 1847, p. 43; October 1855, p. 499; July 1859, p. 327.

[3] *Rambler*, April 1858, pp. 279 and 280.

[4] e.g. Dr. C. Russell in *Dublin*, March 1858, pp. 219–43; Alessandro Gavazzi, *My Recollections of the Last Four Popes and of Rome in their Times*, London, 1858.

[5] cf. an earlier comment of Acton's on Lamennais and de Maistre: 'Because Lamennais appropriated and distorted some of his [de Maistre's] ideas, his influence has not been altogether beneficial' (*Rambler*, May 1855, p. 74).

[6] *Rambler*, August 1858, p. 142; December 1858, p. 424.

[7] ibid., November 1859, p. 82.

[8] *Home and Foreign Review*, iii, July 1863, pp. 162–206 (reprinted in *Essays on Church and State*, ed. Douglas Woodruff, London, 1952, pp. 37–85).

This cleavage led naturally to the idea of the impotence of reason, which was in itself a denial that any knowledge acquired by man was relevant to religion. Acton characterized the *Avenir* as a denial of the rights of reason and an appeal against it to the people as the source of power, an attitude to which he was whole-heartedly opposed. He saw the 'subtle influence of the theories of Lamennais'[1] as a serious obstacle to the growth of true ultramontanism, which he defined in such a way as to exclude Lamennais.[2] In October of the same year the phrase 'L'Église libre dans l'État libre' was described as an 'oracle of Lamennais' and stigmatized as an 'hallucination'.[3] The most important statement on Lamennais came in the article 'Conflicts with Rome', signed boldly 'John Dalberg Acton', which wound up the *Home and Foreign Review*.[4] He illustrated his decision to stop publishing the *Review* by appeal to the two cases of Lamennais and Dr. Frohschammer. The former, he said, had been guilty of making science submit to faith, and the latter of making faith submit to science. Both consequently foundered and fell. Lamennais had been completely bewildered by science and had sought refuge in the absolutism of Rome. His fall, while impressive as a warning, was of no great historical importance and 'one of the natural consequences of dissociating secular from religious truth'.[5] Acton's first explanation of Lamennais's failure is significant. It is that his philosophy was too narrow and made no allowance for the political and intellectual liberty which must find some place in the Church's scheme of things. Other reasons are that his faith was weak and his thought loose.

As late as 1881 Acton described Lamennais's style as 'unhealthy eloquence'[6] and in 1895 he devoted a considerable part

[1] *Home and Foreign Review*, iii, July 1863, p. 192.

[2] 'When [a man] has worked out the problem of science or politics, on purely scientific and political principles, and then controlled this process by the doctrine of the Church, and found its results to coincide with that doctrine, then he is an Ultramontane in the real meaning of the term' (ibid., p. 205).

[3] ibid., October 1863, p. 727.

[4] ibid., iv, April 1864, pp. 667–90 (reprinted in *History of Freedom*, &c., pp. 461–91, and *Essays on Freedom and Power*, ed. Gertrude Himmelfarb, London, 1956, pp. 244–74).

[5] ibid., p. 671.

[6] ed. H. Paul, *Letters of Lord Acton to Mary Gladstone*, London, 1904, p. 78 (7 March 1881).

of his review of Flint's *Historical Philosophy in France and French Belgium and Switzerland* to his comments on Lamennais.[1]

Although there seemed to be opposition to all Lamennais's ideas from the liberal Catholics, yet he seemed to be constantly before their eyes and to be given more prominence in their writings than in those of other of their co-religionists.[2] In the *Rambler* for May 1859 there was a long and penetrating article on Lamennais, whom Acton had previously called a 'very suggestive and prophetic figure',[3] by the Baron d'Eckstein, a friend of Acton's and formerly a close associate of Lamennais.[4] To this were added notes on the lives of Lamennais and his contemporaries[5] by Acton himself, who had gone to Munich specially to gather them.[6] The article was uncoloured by any party prejudice, and Acton expressed himself pleased with it.[7] For him, Lamennais was a writer of extraordinary power with an almost unprecedented ability, if not to influence, at least to stimulate the great minds of his day.[8]

While the whole spirit of Lamennais's arguments, ultramontane or liberal, was apparently foreign to Acton, the historian nevertheless felt impelled to penetrate more deeply into his thought

[1] *English Historical Review*, 1895, pp. 108–13 (reprinted in *History of Freedom*, &c., pp. 588–96). In fact, Dr. Flint's book had not given disproportionate space to Lamennais. Acton's main complaint was that this man with 'a soul of flame in which reason and passion were combined as light and heat in fire' and who 'was a greater and more interesting personality than either De Maistre or De Bonald' (Flint, p. 367) had been linked too closely with de Maistre and Bonald in Flint's account.

[2] Ryley, a contributor to the *Rambler*, believed that Acton was 'treading in the footsteps of Lamennais' (letter from Acton to Simpson, 5 December 1861, Downside MSS., quoted in J. L. Altholz, *The Liberal Catholic Movement in England*, London, 1962, p. 172).

[3] Gasquet, *Lord Acton and his circle*, p. 15 (to Simpson, May 1858).

[4] *Rambler*, May 1859, p. 41.

[5] ibid., pp. 70–77.

[6] Gasquet, op. cit., p. 64. He wrote to Simpson 1 April 1859 saying he could find neither the date of Lamennais's first article for the *Drapeau blanc* nor any account of his visit to Guernsey. As no printed mention of Lamennais's brief stay in Guernsey in April 1815 appeared before Blaize's edition of his letters (1866), Acton must have heard it from one who knew him (cf. his letter to Lady Blennerhassett, 1890, in his *Correspondence*, ed. Figgis and Laurence, London, 1917, i, pp. 63 f., about his stay in Munich).

[7] Gasquet, op. cit., pp. 69 f. (to Simpson, 21 April 1859).

[8] *The Chronicle*, ii, No. 45, Saturday 1 February 1868, p. 106. An article by Acton on 'Ozanam on the 5th Century' begins: 'Rarely has there been a school of writers so rich in literary power as that which sprang from the ruins of the party of Lamennais.'

and to try to understand there some of the motives and philosophical bases of problems of the day. Archbishop Mathew even goes so far as to say that Acton's understanding was more political than his writings would suggest and that for this reason 'he certainly understood the springs of action of the Abbé de Lamennais much more clearly than ever he did those of the Abbé Migne'.[1]

It is evident from his meticulous annotation of Eckstein's article that even in his youth Acton was much interested in Lamennais's ideas; and he continued to regard him as of great importance in the history of philosophy in the nineteenth century and to study him throughout his life. By the time he died he had assembled enough information, some of it little known, to write a thorough study of Lamennais's ideas.[2]

The plan for Acton's intended treatment of Lamennais may be outlined from the classification of his notes. They are filed under the following headings: The Future (fo. 1–34), Decline (35–73), Lamennais 1848—(74–99), *Paroles* (100–26), *Sens Commun* (127–66)—Lamennais's own words—, *Sens Commun* (167–232)—mostly extracts from other writers on the same subject—,Religion and Liberty (233–74), Belgium (275–80), Ireland (281–3), *Avenir* (284–304), Protestants (305–9), Rome (310–42). There are two points of note about this scheme: there is no section devoted to ultramontanism or absolutism, the element in Lamennais's thought which Acton so much deplored when he was writing for the *Rambler*; and the notion of *sens commun* was the aspect of Lamennais's philosophy which interested him most. Lamennais's middle period is seen almost entirely in the light of his attitude to liberty, the subject which occupied Acton more than any other.

What sort of a study of Lamennais would have emerged from these notes is difficult to say, because Acton was always scrupulous

[1] D. Mathew, *Acton: The Formative Years*, London, 1946, p. 83.

[2] The Acton MSS. in the Cambridge University Library consist of some 180 notebooks and 275 boxes and folders, all full of carefully copied extracts from works in his famous library or transcripts of inaccessible documents. One of the 275 boxes (Add. 4970 (F)) is devoted entirely to Lamennais, and another contains a thirty-page summary and critique of Lamennais's doctrines, written in Italian, by Mgr. (and from July 1834, Cardinal) Paulo Polidori (Add. 4890 (B) fos. 603–33). The Lamennais box has 342 entries on file cards of the usual size, written, with one exception (Add. 4970 (F) fo. 193), in Acton's own hand.

to study every side of a question and to try to make out a better case for his opponents' views than his opponents themselves could devise. It may be, for example, that he intended to collect every shred of evidence for Lamennais's advocacy of religious liberty, simply in order to deny that he really desired any such thing. But in the absence of evidence to show that this was the case, I shall take the straightforward view that Acton's notes were intended as documentation for a description of Lamennais's views, if indeed Acton ever intended to write such a description.[1]

In Acton's view there were several points to be made about the notion of *sens commun*. Lamennais thought that his theory was entirely novel.[2] It required the total dethronement of individual reason.[3] The only criterion of certainty was the reason of the whole human race.[4] From this it followed that the opinions of the people were often to be preferred to those of the wise.[5] It also followed that revealed religion was involved in a process of development and that paganism contained an element of true religion.[6]

From his next section, which contains extracts from other writers on the subject, it is clear that he had sufficient material to deal largely with each of these points. For example, on the claim that Lamennais's theory was novel he notes:

They [Lamennais's opponents] objected that the theory was new, and that the infallible authority ought to have known of it before. The theory was not new.[7]

Another note reads:

Lamennais's predecessors—Pellisson, Jurieu, Barrow, Stillingfleet, Butler, Reid, Bonald, Ellicott.[8]

Another:

Lamennais's theory. Barrow, Stillingfleet, Butler, Reid, Bonald—the Traditionalists. Show how he came by it. The same motive made the

[1] In Add. 4970 (F) fo. 169, the note 'Show how he came by it' may show an intention to develop this argument at greater length.

[2] fo. 153.

[3] fo. 128.

[4] fo. 134 *et passim.*

[5] fo. 147.

[6] fos. 148 and 150.

[7] fo. 231.

[8] fo. 168.

trad[itionalists] cling to Bonald. See Ferrari: who are the Traditionalists.[1]

Yet another:

Lamennais, sens commun. Descartes, Malebranche, Stillingfleet, Barrow, Butler, Reid, Ellicott.[2]

These overlappings and slight variations suggest that the notes were made at different times. Many cards are covered with extracts from these writers to support Acton's thesis, and very plausible it appears. Acton, who himself held a theory of development,[3] made a note that 'Malebranche seems to confirm Lamennais—and to carry it over to Newman'.[4] He was not content to trace the idea in thinkers who might have been Lamennais's direct predecessors in an ordered line of philosophical development: he noted a few examples of allusion to *sensus communis* in the ancient authors[5] and tracked down cases where modern writers had accepted it as a philosophical truth.[6] Perhaps Acton's final judgement on the idea of *sensus communis* is summed up in the note:

It was a familiar argument of English divines. Reid had made much more of it than they. Buddha had not yet dawned upon the West. But B. Constant exposed its weakness.[7]

In this Acton was at one with Brownson.

If, however, Acton was suspicious of Lamennais's means of apologetic, he approved, with Brownson, of his views on liberty. He collected a catena of sayings from Lamennais's correspondence, from *Des progrès*, *De la religion*, and even from *Du passé et de l'avenir du peuple* and *Le livre du peuple* to show that liberty was one of his principal aims. He also included extracts from writers who described Lamennais's views in the same way. But Acton's critical attitude to his subject is shown by his selection from the

[1] fo. 169. [2] fo. 170.

[3] G. E. Fasnacht, *Acton's Political Philosophy*, London, 1952, pp. 48–63, 'The Idea of Development'. [4] fo. 172.

[5] e.g. Cicero (fo. 197), Tertullian (fo. 195), Quintilian (fo. 196), Seneca (fo. 193).

[6] e.g. Brunetière, Rémusat, Pattison (fos. 183–5), and Jefferson (fo. 201).

[7] fo. 211. Elsewhere he says Buddha 'made the most tolerant religion the most numerous' (cited by Fasnacht, op. cit., p. 143 from *Some Hawarden Letters*, ed. March-Phillips and Christian, London, 1917, p. 187).

Avenir. Only five of the twenty-one extracts from this paper deal with the question of liberty.[1] Others deal with the rights of the people and the desirability of revolution, ideas with which Acton was not in sympathy. At least one other shows that he was determined to give Lamennais a fair hearing. This is a short note dealing with decentralization of government, a corollary of the concept of liberty held by both thinkers.[2]

On the whole it seems likely that Acton would have approved of Lamennais's general outlook on liberty in his middle period, but he would have had some reservations about an uncritical application of this policy to current politics. His selection of one of the most inflammatory remarks of the *Avenir* suggests that he would have used it to deplore its revolutionary tone.[3]

For further guidance on this matter we might expect to look in the section on the *Paroles*, but we should be disappointed, because it contains no extracts from the work at all, only references more or less relevant to its general tone.[4] The section, 'Lamennais 1848–, contains further clues, although it by no means confines itself to the post-1848 period.[5] Nearly all the extracts are concerned with the primacy of liberty in the life of man, although several talk of the spirit of progress in the sort of unscientific way of which Acton would have disapproved. Only a few are decidedly revolutionary.[6] The selection is so judicious that Acton must have been far from dismissing the later Lamennais as a disillusioned crank: 'Lamennais in the Livre du Peuple 1837, still declares his views those of Xty. Rights depend upon duties, and to discharge these we must know them. Religion therefore necessary to liberty.'[7] The extent of Acton's sympathy can be seen from this note: 'Lamennais Liberalism in 1848. Democracy had not

[1] fos. 284, 288, 290, 294, 297.

[2] fo. 296, cf. Acton's 'American Commonwealth' in *History of Freedom*, &c., pp. 575–87, for his views on federalism.

[3] fo. 292: 'Nous avons applaudi à toutes les révolutions faites, nous applaudissons à toutes les révolutions à faire.'

[4] Acton believed that democracy should be achieved by discussion rather than by election, and that all States, democratic or not, should have only limited authority (Fasnacht, op. cit., pp. 81–116, 'The State, Government, and Democracy').

[5] fos. 77, 79, 82, 88–91.

[6] fos. 81, 86, 88. Others show Lamennais in a favourable light, e.g. fo. 91 (the need for individual private property) and fo. 79 (an assurance to Laurentie that he will say nothing to affect his friend's faith).

[7] fo. 77.

made him untrue to liberty'.[1] While he deplores Lamennais's faith in democracy, Acton acknowledges the importance he places upon liberty.

The other sections of his study of Lamennais are perhaps more personal and less objective; they show more interest in Lamennais as an individual than as a philosopher. In the two sections, 'The Future' and 'Decline', Acton makes a clever selection of Lamennais's conflicting views about the future: the early premonition of impending disaster, his apocalyptic,[2] and the later optimism.[3] But, as Acton notes, the two views were not distinct in time, for in 1848 Lamennais was still able to write that he was expecting the general dissolution of society.[4] These two apparently contradictory ideas were of great interest to Acton, although he had not lived through the same times and was not of the same temperament. His idea of development and his definition of science made it inevitable that he should take a view which was closer to Lamennais's optimism than to his apocalyptic, without, however, the eccentric mysticism with which Lamennais disguised them.[5]

It is impossible not to detect a hint of bitterness in his selection of Lamennais's opinions of Rome. There is not a single extract from any passage which deals with the infallibility of the Pope, the primacy of Rome, or Rome as the focal point of Christendom. Instead Acton has collected scraps of Lamennais's disillusionment, possibly in order to use them against Rome in the Vatican controversy.[6]

Acton's method seems to have been to read works and to make a note of anything which might later be of use to him. He did not make indiscriminate notes. The consistency of his aim can be seen from the fact that in several cases he copied the same extract on two different occasions.[7] In philosophy, Lamennais's exploitation

[1] fo. 123.
[2] fo. 45.
[3] fos. 16 and 24.
[4] fo. 21.
[5] But Acton's strong sense of sin placed him well away from either extreme (e.g. *Letters of Lord Acton to Mary Gladstone*, 2nd ed., 1913, pp. 180–3, quoted Fasnacht, op. cit., pp. 26–28).
[6] e.g. fo. 317, where he quotes from Spuller's *Lamennais*, 1892, p. 198, a letter written to Gerbet in 1832: 'L'Église est complètement sacrifiée à la politique; ce sont les puissances hérétiques, schismatiques, impies, qui gouvernent à leur gré les choses du catholicisme; et malgré ces énormes prévarications, le Pape ne sauvera pas son pouvoir temporel; il se dissout de tous les côtés, et l'on doit désirer que cette dissolution soit prompte, car autrement la foi périrait.'
[7] e.g. fos. 110 and 111; fos. 153 and 154; fos. 157 and 158.

of the notion of *sensus communis* was for Acton a link in the chain of development of western thought. In politics, his emphasis on liberty was a significant phenomenon in nineteenth-century history. Had Acton written his projected *History of Freedom* it is certain that these two points would have emerged and that Lamennais, although criticized, would have appeared as a greater figure in nineteenth-century history than English historians have allowed. Acton was addicted to strings of names illustrating the development of a line of thought. It is interesting to see where Lamennais appears or does not appear in these lists. None of his books was considered by Acton to be sufficiently epoch-making to be included in a list of the hundred books which have most moved the world.[1] In this list ultramontanism is represented by *Du pape*, which forged the 'alliance of Religion with absolute Monarchy', and socialism by Fourier, 'the originator of modern socialism'. Lamennais does, however, appear in a document which Acton prepared in order to trace the idea of liberty through its many channels, philosophic, scientific, and political, down to Acton's time.[2] Lamennais is placed at the end of a long list of thinkers, classed as Continental liberals, whose principles sprang directly from the ideas of the French Revolution. These names are themselves divided into several groups: the residuum of the French Revolution, the Doctrinaires, the Saint-Simonians, the Socialists and Comte's school, and finally, in a group of his own with no descriptive tag, Lamennais.[3] It was Acton's opinion that after 1848 these separate 'schools' combined to produce a unified result, which had a powerful influence on the development of Continental political thought. In all this there is not a word about Lamennais's traditional link with de Maistre. Indeed, Acton explicitly disapproved of any such link being made.[4] Rather than seeing in Lamennais one who reacted against the ideas of the Revolution, he saw one who sprang from them. Acton's stress on Lamennais's idea of development, even though it did not coincide with his own, showed that he regarded him as essentially a liberal, and not, as many people have done, an authoritarian of shifting allegiances.

[1] ed. March-Phillips and Christian, *Some Hawarden Letters*, London, 1917, pp. 190 f.

[2] Acton MS. Add. 4955, analysed by Fasnacht, op. cit., pp. 229–40.

[3] Fasnacht, op. cit., p. 239.

[4] *History of Freedom*, &c., p. 593 (written in 1895).

Liberal Catholicism was dealt a fatal blow by the definition of papal infallibility in 1870. As a result the liberalizing influence of Lamennais's thought was temporarily forgotten in favour of his early zeal for the supremacy of the Pope, and shortly after he arose again, this time as a factor in the modernist controversy.

Maude Petre, who was in the forefront of the modernist battle which raged around George Tyrrell at the end of the last and at the beginning of this century, wrote in 1930 that although Lamennais had been almost forgotten, his oblivion was not total and he made 'periodic reappearances'.[1] At first sight there seems to be little reason why one of these reappearances should be on the modernist scene.[2]

The label 'Modernism' is usually attached to a movement within the Roman Church to secure the recognition of a critical treatment of the Bible, together with everything that would accompany such a treatment. Nothing, it seems, could be further from the spirit of Lamennais's work than this. For him criticism meant private judgement, which was abhorrent to him. Even in his later days he gave no hint of any serious critical approach to the Scriptures.

This attitude, however, led the modernists (although they were not a 'school' in the sense that they had a common programme and a unified method) to be inclined towards pragmatism in philosophy, a system of belief in which the test of the truthfulness of an idea is in its practical consequences: 'The real is not to be investigated by metaphysical speculation, but rather according to the values developed through its being known.'[3] This was one thread in Lamennais's justification of religion in the *Essai*, and it remained an important element in his thought, even into later life. He would certainly have maintained the proposition that the proof of a fact is not an act of the pure reason, since human reason is incapable of any such action, 'but rather an account of how the fact has come to be accepted as justifying itself by practical results'.[4] Thus a proof of the existence of life after death is not to be

[1] *The Modern Churchman*, xix, No. 11, 1930, p. 641.

[2] The most that Dr. Vidler will say, after having stressed the fact that modernism is not a continuation of liberal Catholicism, is that the modernists may 'have discovered precedents for some of their own ideas in the writings of Lamennais or Döllinger or Rosmini or in the *Rambler*' (*The Modernist Movement in the Roman Church*, London, 1934, p. 51).

[3] ed. F. L. Cross, *Oxford Dictionary of the Christian Church*, article 'Pragmatism', p. 1095.

[4] ibid.

found in an examination of the metaphysics of life, but in the fact that belief in the after life has had the practical effect of maintaining a system of morals by means of the expectation of future rewards and punishments.[1] The affinity between Lamennais's idea that the truth of a proposition is established by the *sensus communis* and the pragmatists' idea that the truth of a proposition is established by its good results is close. Both tend to relativism. Both feel the need of an absolute standard, but both fail to bridge the gap between absolute and relative. Lamennais in the *Essai* showed that humanity had but groped towards the absolute truth of God by means of the common reason, but he could offer no suggestion as to how this absolute truth could ever be known. The pragmatists exalted the idea of utility and abolished truth as an absolute by making it the label for those ideas which had good results. In so doing they substituted one absolute, the good, for another, the truth, and so did not further their argument.

Nor is this the modernists' only affinity with Lamennais. They took a teleological view of history. They were more concerned with its issue than its origins, a preoccupation which eventually led to their condemnation in the decree *Lamentabili* (3rd July 1907). Their error was that in their teaching they failed to put sufficient stress on, or were even careless of, the historical origins of Christianity, but were more concerned with its results. The same tendency, although not fully developed, can be seen in Lamennais. There is very little in the *Essai*, his principal work of apologetic, concerning the earthly life of Christ, or the origins of the Church. There is, on the other hand, much about the developed life and characteristics of the Church and about religion in general. With this is combined a concern for the future, for religion as the regenerative element in society. Lamennais, like the modernists, does not give a prominent place in his teaching to the orthodox doctrine of the redemptive work of the historical Jesus.[2]

[1] e.g. *Essai*, iii, ch. 27 and iv, ch. 36.

[2] But their motives were different. While Lamennais was within the Church he was not particularly concerned with, and therefore he did not question, the facts of Christian origins. To the modernists, however, it seemed that biblical and historical criticism had made damaging inroads on the faith for which they cared so greatly; much of the historical material upon which the faith was built was now at the best uncertain, and so their tendency was to emphasize those aspects of religion which *were* obviously true.

Interest in Lamennais rose during the last decade of the nineteenth century with the publication in English of several books by or about him.[1] Of these the most influential was Gibson's *Abbé de Lamennais and the Liberal Catholic Movement in France*.[2] Liberal Catholicism was still professed by men of a liberal turn of mind, not necessarily modernists. It was in the Oxford of the 1880s that William Gibson, son of the Lord Chancellor of Ireland, was converted from Anglicanism to Roman Catholicism, and in 1896, when he was still only twenty-eight, he published his book on Lamennais. It is possible that he was converted by liberal-minded Roman Catholics at Oxford, and in examining their ideas became interested in Lamennais.[3] Just before the publication of his book he married a French Protestant, whom he immediately converted. They settled in England and gathered a wide circle of friends of their own faith, but of a liberal outlook, among whom were the Wards.[4]

Gibson's book was widely read and reviewed in England in the following years[5] and may have been partly responsible for Lamennais's brief appearance in modernist company. The Jesuit reviewer of it in *The Month*[6] was none other than George Tyrrell, who shortly afterwards was to be involved in a series of clashes with authority, which led in 1906 to his suspension *a divinis*. It is significant that Tyrrell did not content himself, as others had done, with a potted account of Lamennais's career and a few comments on Gibson's work. He tried to arrive at the root of

[1] Among those for Roman Catholic readers was Maria Catherine Bishop's *Life of Mrs. Augustus Craven*, London, 1894, which did much to popularize the Catholicism of Montalembert and Lacordaire, and to bring to a wider public the sister and daughter of intimates of Lamennais and the author of the *Récit d'une sœur* (see above, p. 52). [2] Above, p. 58.

[3] W. K. Firminger, with whom he co-operated in the Society for the Study of Social Ethics at Oxford, also wrote on Lamennais, below, p. 158.

[4] For these and other details of the picturesque life of Gibson (later Lord Ashbourne) I am indebted to his nephew, Mr. W. E. H. Porter of Dublin.

[5] Apart from *The Month*, the only considerable review for Roman Catholics was in *The Tablet* (Saturday 9 January 1897, p. 52). This was both sympathetic with Lamennais and appreciative of Gibson. It condemned the error upon which the *Essai* was founded, but upbraided Gibson for saying too little about Lamennais's devotional works. It rated his influence upon the Church very highly and concluded that he had fixed the religious regeneration of France.

[6] *The Month*, lxxxix, 1897, pp. 19–27, reprinted in *Faith of the Millions*, 2nd series, London, 1901, pp. 80–95.

Lamennais's attitude to religion and the Church, and in doing so concluded that his later aberrations were to be attributed to his self-taught life and lack of discipline. He made two interesting comments on Lamennais's method. One was that it was characterized by lack of patience; and the other, that Lamennais abandoned metaphysics without replacing it with anything else.[1] This second point links Lamennais with what the modernists themselves were doing. For in a sense it is true to say that they also abandoned traditional metaphysics, although they did at least try to put something, in the shape of pragmatist philosophy, in its place. That Tyrrell was aware of the similarity between Lamennais and the pragmatists is shown by a comment in an article of May 1899,[2] after he had begun to move in the direction of modernism under the influence of Bremond. There he pointed out that Lamennais credited humanity with a certain infallibility in guarding the deposit of primitive religion. He summarized Lamennais's views with the words: 'What all religions agree in, he holds to be true',[3] which, although, not in a direct line of reasoning with the pragmatists' assertion, is analogous with it.[4] There is a more revealing comment in his preface to *Christianity at the Crossroads*, his posthumous work (1909). There he found it necessary to distinguish between Liberal Catholics, by whom he meant Lamennais, Lacordaire, Montalembert, and Newman, and Modernists. The former, he said, wished to allow Catholic doctrine to develop with the Catholic Church, but the latter were convinced that Catholic Christianity could not live much longer on the old lines.[5] In spite of the fact that he placed Lamennais first among the Liberal Catholics, his very definitions make it clear that he really regarded him as a modernist. This view is supported by an opinion which he gave later, that Lamennais's conflict with orthodoxy sprang not from historical causes but from

[1] *Faith of the Millions*, 2nd series, p. 86.

[2] *The Month*, May 1899, pp. 493–504, 'Authority and Evolution, the Life of Catholic Dogma', reprinted in *Faith of the Millions*, 1st series, pp. 136–57.

[3] *Faith of the Millions*, 1st series, pp. 139 f.

[4] Tyrrell put his own position concisely when he wrote: 'As far as I know myself I sympathise with Pragmatism a great deal, but I am not a pure Pragmatist. . . . I believe, not that truth is subordinate to action, but that they are co-equal, co-ordinate factors (or aspects) of life' (Tyrrell, *Letters*, London, 1920, p. 116—to an Italian professor, 27 April 1908).

[5] *Christianity at the Crossroads*, p. xix.

his philosophical convictions.[1] This emphasis on the underlying philosophy of Lamennais's work persists through all Tyrrell's allusions to him, and suggests that he took Lamennais more seriously than many of his contemporaries did. He could scarcely have failed to notice the similarity between their careers.[2] They were both converts—Lamennais from agnosticism, Tyrrell from Anglicanism. Both earned fame through their writings and their devotional works. Both encountered increasing episcopal hostility as their views deviated from the orthodox. Both continued to publish works of a religious nature and both maintained that the religion of the future would be a universal religion much developed from traditional Christianity, although their conceptions of this religion differed greatly. Both suffered virtual excommunication although neither was expressly excommunicated by the Pope. On their deathbeds both refused to recant and neither received Roman Catholic burial. Most observers would probably say that the main difference between them was that Lamennais suffered for his politics, while Tyrrell suffered for his theology. But Tyrrell knew better. It was he, in common with other perceptive people like Father Dominic, who saw that Lamennais's fundamental philosophy was incompatible with orthodoxy. Father Dominic saw it and remained orthodox. Father Tyrrell saw it and went the way of Lamennais.

Von Hügel, Tyrrell's friend and a leader of the modernists and ever well-disposed towards Lamennais, took a different view. He maintained that Lamennais's quarrel with Rome was simply a matter of liberalism, and that if the Bishops had been as liberal as the Holy See Lamennais would have remained within the Church.[3] In 1913 he wrote to J. M. Connell that he hoped to compile a book of devotional reading which would include, among others, some of the writings of Lamennais[4]; and in 1921 he wrote to Professor Clement Webb about the Hebrew prophets, referring to them as 'Carlyles and Lamennaises—men who could not touch a subject without lighting it up indeed, yet also not without burning up its

[1] *Christianity at the Crossroads*, p. 12.

[2] ed. M. D. Petre, *Autobiography and Life of George Tyrrell*, London, 1912, ii, pp. 73 f. (to Bremond, 20 September 1899).

[3] Maisie Ward, *The Wilfrid Wards and the Transition*, London, 1934, p. 317.

[4] ed. B. Holland, *Baron Friedrich von Hügel. Selected Letters 1896–1924*, p. 203.

substance by the perhaps necessary, but none the less most dangerous exaggerations'—an understanding comment on Lamennais's method, but which still says nothing of his matter.[1]

Closely associated with von Hügel and Tyrrell at the time of the modernist crisis was Maude Petre. It is not surprising that she too had something to say about Lamennais,[2] although she reserved it for some thirty years later, well after our period.[3] Miss Petre saw Lamennais's tragedy not in his autodidacticism but in his search for the philosopher's stone which would give access to religious certainty. But apart from chiding him for his alchemistic approach to religion, she is all sympathy. He was, she says, a man for whom the spiritual life meant everything but who found little joy or hope in it.[4] To the end of his life 'he never dissociated the life of man on earth from his life in heaven, nor loosed his hold on the banner of spiritual faith and endeavour'.[5] As a philosopher, the aspect of him which Miss Petre, like Father Tyrrell, found most interesting, he failed because he tried to confine the infinite on earth and to stretch the limitations of human life to fit the infinite.[6] This is a restatement of the old pragmatist problem of the absolute and the relative.

Further light is shed on this question by her spiritual autobiography, *My Way of Faith*, in which she says: 'My scepticism results from the twofold sense of the immensity of the universe, physical or metaphysical, and the inadequacy of the human mind'.[7] It is this very scepticism which she feels to be at the root of both her thought and Lamennais's. It is no accident, therefore, that she finds comfort in Lamennais's conception of art as the expression of the infinite in terms of the finite.[8]

All these comments show that the modernists' interest in Lamennais was more than a superficial glance at the outward similarities of his position and theirs. He had raised philosophical questions which they were to raise again, in the changed environment of the turn of the century, and they were not unmindful

[1] ed. B. Holland, *Baron Friedrich von Hügel. Selected Letters 1896–1924*, p. 326.

[2] She tells us she made 'a somewhat detailed study of the philosophy of Lamennais' (*My Way of Faith*, London, 1937, p. 183).

[3] *The Modern Churchman*, xix, Nos. 10–11, January and February 1930, pp. 592–8 and pp. 641–53.

[4] ibid., January 1930, p. 597.

[5] ibid., p. 598.

[6] ibid., February 1930, p. 653.

[7] *My Way of Faith*, p. 162.

[8] ibid., pp. xvi, 41, 136.

of his example. This was strikingly shown in a novel published in 1906, the year of Tyrrell's final break with the Jesuits.

The novel was *Out of Due Time* by Mrs. Wilfrid Ward, the wife of the cultivated and influential editor of the *Dublin Review*, who had always been well aware of Lamennais's influence on the nineteenth century.[1] This was not the first of her novels in which Lamennais figured. In an earlier one a young politician had thrilled and moved an audience with a recital of extracts from the *Paroles*.[2] But it was in *Out of Due Time* that the theme of Lamennais was fully developed.

The novel has two threads. One is the human element, the complicated progress of the love of four people: Paul, Comte d'Estranges, who loves nothing but ideas, Elizabeth, the daughter of a traditionally Roman Catholic family, George Sutcliffe, a writer with few claims to physical charms, and Marcelle, Paul's step-sister. This part of the plot however, soon becomes submerged in a more serious theme, the progress of 'The Cause', the struggle for the reconciliation of science and religion. From the literary point of view this is regrettable, as the *Times Literary Supplement* was quick to point out,[3] but from the point of view of the history of ideas it is invaluable because the novel as it stands gives an illuminating insight into contemporary thought.

The serious plot is briefly that Paul, with the assistance of Sutcliffe, is leading a movement for the regeneration of Catholicism. They found a journal called the *Catholic International*, which, for a time, is restrained in its criticism of the old theology, but which casts off its restraint after a great Catholic International

[1] His biographies of Newman, Wiseman and his father W. G. Ward reflect it: *W. G. Ward and the Catholic Revival*, London, 1893, pp. 82, 101, 103, 114, 234; *Life and Times of Cardinal Wiseman*, London, 1897, i, pp. 47, 94, 99, 137, 298 f., 305–7; ii, 214, 406; *Life of John Henry, Cardinal Newman*, London, 1912, i, pp. 175, 308, 314 f., 365, 458 ff., 506, 635; and his other published writings reiterate the theme of Lamennais's contribution to the nineteenth-century Zeitgeist (e.g. *Problems and Persons*, London, 1903, pp. 8 f.). All his judgements were based on first-hand acquaintance with Lamennais's work. 'My chapter' (probably the one on Liberal Catholicism in his *Newman*, i, pp. 458–77) 'is based on reading the actual work of the men I deal with as far as France is concerned' he wrote in an undated, unaddressed letter from Lotus, Dorking, which also contained a comparison of the *Avenir* and the *Home and Foreign Review* (Ward's papers, Sheed and Ward, London).

[2] *The Light Behind*, London, 2nd ed., 1903, pp. 25–27.

[3] *Times Literary Supplement*, 6 April 1906, p. 125.

Scientific Conference. It incurs the Bishop's condemnation, and Paul, confident in the wisdom of the Holy See, decides to appeal to Rome. The journey to Rome is accompanied by scenes of enthusiasm which are strongly contrasted with the lethargy and reticence of the Holy City itself. In this environment Sutcliffe decides that he cannot support Paul any longer and leaves abruptly. The months drag on and Paul presses for a decision. He even has an audience with the Pope, who is charming but evasive. Finally, in response to his pressing requests, Paul is condemned. He leaves the Church and travels abroad. Marcelle, his stepsister, eventually dies, and the manner of her death is the cause of his reconversion. He becomes a Dominican, and the story ends with Elizabeth and Sutcliffe, who in the meantime have married, listening to him preaching his only sermon before he retires into a monastery.

Even these bare bones of the plot are sufficient to indicate the similarity between Paul and Lamennais, a similarity which is alluded to at many points in the story.[1] Several of Paul's characteristics are exactly those of Lamennais, and Mrs. Ward herself actually admitted that Paul was modelled on him:

The story started with me from my intense interest in the history of *l'Avenir*. I had read constantly all I could find of the lives of de Lamenais [*sic*], Lacordaire and Montalembert. Paul is a lay edition of de Lamenais, though not a portrait. I have never known anyone like Paul myself. His interest in the intellectual as divorced from the devotional side of religion was essentially French, as it seems to me.[2]

Interesting though this is for Mrs. Ward's attraction to Lamennais, it is even more interesting for the way in which the Lamennais motif is woven into the story. The dispute is not political, as Lamennais's was, but doctrinal. The questions discussed at the Catholic International Scientific Conference are matters of biblical criticism, the Graf-Wellhausen hypotheses concerning the construction of the Pentateuch, and the attitude of the Church towards scientific advance. These are problems which recall not Lamennais but Acton and the liberal Catholics. The fate of

[1] op. cit., pp. 163, 192, 235, 274, 276. At the end, Paul says: 'I was attracted to them [the Dominicans] by the history of Lacordaire. It seemed to me that Lamennais and Lacordaire were typical, the one of my past, the other of what I fain would make my future, however faintly, resemble' (p. 378).

[2] Wilfrid Ward, *Last Lectures*, London, 1918: Introductory study by Mrs. J. Ward, p. xxxix n.

the *Catholic International Review* is similar to that of the *Rambler*. In this way Mrs. Ward dovetails the question of authority as it was exemplified in Lamennais's life with the question of liberalism in the Church. She links the essential elements in the character of Lamennais with those of her husband, Wilfrid Ward, the outline of whose mental position is, as she admits,[1] sketched in the character of George Sutcliffe. In thus combining into one story the controversies of three-quarters of a century, she showed quite clearly that the urgency of the problems dealt with by Lamennais had abated very little, and furthermore, that he was still acknowledged as the driving force behind many of the revolutionary trends of modern theology, modernism included. It is a novel, and no attempt is made to assess the extent of Lamennais's influence on liberal Catholicism or on modernism, but in Mrs. Ward's mind at least—and she represented an influential section of Roman Catholics[2]—the problems which he raised and for which he suffered were still the problems which agitated the Church.[3]

[1] Wilfrid Ward, *Last Lectures*, London, 1918, p. xxxix n.

[2] Henri Bremond had written a serious analysis of her novel *One Poor Scruple* for *Études*, 5 and 20 January 1900.

[3] For contemporary comments on *Out of Due Time* see Maisie Ward, *Insurrection versus Resurrection*, London, 1937, pp. 239–53. In *Modernism. Its Failure and its Fruits*, London, 1918, M. D. Petre started chapter 2 on 'Unconscious modernism' with a quotation from *Out of Due Time*, which she called 'a novel which, if not professedly, yet actually, contained a review of the modernist movement' (p. 8). George Tyrrell called the book 'interesting and actual' and said that there had been many guesses about the prototype of Paul, including Baron von Hügel and Gibson (Lamennais's biographer) (*Letters*, p. 102). In later years Fr. C. C. Martindale, S.J. wrote to Mrs. Ward (4 July 1927) that he had re-read the book and gave some reflections on it. He interpreted it as a picture of the modernist movement and Paul as a portrait of the Baron. Mrs. Ward must have replied with her own account of its genesis, for he replied (17 July) adjusting his view (Ward's papers, Sheed and Ward, London. Extracts were published in *Insurrection versus Resurrection*, pp. 239 f.).

VI

LAMENNAIS AND THE LEFT

It is difficult to find a name which will adequately describe all those who were tinged with differing shades of red during the last century. On the one wing were the 'red revolutionaries' pursuing a career of destruction and hatred in order to achieve their ends; and on the other were the moderate reformers, concerned with improving, but not necessarily radically altering, the lot of the working classes. Neither extreme was strictly speaking socialist, any more than Lamennais was himself.[1] The whole century is a fascinating network of rival social theories interwoven with beliefs, religious, philosophical, and economic. Slightly anachronistic though the term is,[2] 'the Left' will have to serve to cover them all.

A socialist historian, G. D. H. Cole, wrote that Lamennais was 'the direct progenitor of much Christian Socialist doctrine and a great deal nearer to Socialism than many who later called themselves, or were called, Christian Socialists'.[3] On the face of it, the author of the *Paroles* and *Une Voix de prison* ought to have had some perceptible influence upon the early Christian Socialists in England, F. D. Maurice, Charles Kingsley, and J. M. Ludlow, and at least one later Christian Socialist, the Reverend M. Kaufmann, repeatedly pointed to such a connection.[4] But, in fact, what was called Christian Socialism in England was quite different

[1] F. Lamennais, *Question du travail*, Paris, 1848, pp. 8 f.

[2] In England it was first used in the sense of 'political or religious innovators' about 1837 (*Shorter Oxford English Dictionary*, Oxford, 1959, p. 1124).

[3] G. D. H. Cole, *Socialist Thought, the Forerunners, 1789–1850*, London, 1953, p. 199.

[4] The Reverend M. Kaufmann was an Anglican priest of some academic distinction, whose book *Christian Socialism*, London, 1888, contained a chapter entitled 'Lamennais: or Christian Socialism in France' (reprinted from *Good Words*, 1882, pp. 575–83). In this and in his *Charles Kingsley, Christian Socialist and Social Reformer*, London, 1892, he made frequent comparisons between the two reformers (see especially pp. 13, 129, 197, and 236 of *Charles Kingsley*).

from the religious sympathy with the people which Lamennais showed in his later years.[1]

Christian Socialism sprang directly from the observation by a small group of Christians of the social and industrial evils of the day. The Evangelicals and the Tractarians had by-passed these issues in their theology, and even, it might be claimed, because of their theology. The Evangelicals with their emphasis on individual conversion had found that industrial conditions only served to underline the miserable, depraved state of man, and therefore his need of salvation. The Tractarians, on the other hand, harked back to the teaching of the early Fathers, who had little to tell them about the morality of modern industry. It was not surprising, in view of these and many other circumstances, that socialism developed largely in opposition to Christianity, although it was a series of accidents which made this inevitable. There was no fundamental reason why it should be so. Maurice and his associates saw the simple truth that so much unalleviated suffering could not but be contrary to the will of God. Maurice was sure that it was God's will that all men should be enabled to benefit from life. This belief was grounded on the sound doctrine, too little recognized by Evangelicals, who tended to pietism, and by Tractarians, who tended to asceticism, that matter in itself is not evil, and that man is not merely an immortal soul housed in a corruptible and evil body. With this belief firmly accepted, Maurice and his followers turned their minds to the practical steps which could be taken to relieve the exploited workmen. It was not a question of exhorting them to recognize the divine origin of liberty and therefore of their right to it, nor even of first appealing to them to recognize the principle of brotherhood. It was a question of finding a means of improving the workman's lot which would not be contrary to Christian practice. The very fact that recognized Christians were associated with this task was to be a witness to their assertion that Christianity and social justice were not incompatible. Hence the deliberately provocative title, 'Christian Socialist'.

Their method of attaining this end was the principle of co-operative workshops originated by Louis Blanc in France. J. M. Ludlow had been educated in France, and in many ways preserved

[1] L. Brentano, *Die christlich-soziale Bewegung in England*, Leipzig, 1883, pp. 3 f.

a French outlook in his ideas.[1] It was often his frank witness to his religion and his refusal to compromise with those who supported the practical aims of the Christian Socialists without acknowledging the Christian end to which all their work was directed, which prevented Christian Socialism from becoming an imported brand of French socialism. They therefore set about forming workmen's associations in which it was intended that the men should associate for mutual benefit, not only material, but also moral and spiritual. Maurice was always careful to insist that the principle of association was a more Christian one than the principle of competition. He was not primarily concerned with artificially raising the wages of the workers. In fact, in the early days of the workers' associations, wages were comparable with average wages elsewhere. The superiority of the associations from the workers' point of view lay not in higher wages, but in more favourable conditions of work, less fear, more comfort, and, in time, the amenities of baths and libraries.

Action was backed by the printed word. At first a weekly periodical, *Politics for the People*, was an organ for Christian Socialist opinion. The prospectus declared that politics could not be separated from religion:

> The world is governed by God; this is the rich man's warning; this is the poor man's comfort; this is the real hope in the consideration of all questions, let them be as hard of solution as they may; this is the pledge that Liberty, Fraternity, Unity, under some conditions or other, are intended for every people under heaven.[2]

But the principle having been stated, the paper's purpose was to consider those questions which were agitating the workman of the time: the extension of the franchise; the relation of the capitalist to the labourer; the function of the government in finding work and pay for the poor.

When this paper came to an end the leaders of the movement devoted their energies to the founding of Working Men's Associations, based on Louis Blanc's Ateliers Nationaux,[3] and by the end of 1850 a journal had been started to provide news of them.

[1] It was his letters from Paris in the spring of 1848 which fired Maurice's imagination and inspired him to undertake the theological leadership of the Christian Socialists.

[2] *Politics for the People*, London, 1848, prospectus, p. 1.

[3] C. E. Raven, *Christian Socialism*, London, 1920, p. 140.

It was the *Christian Socialist, a Journal of Association, conducted by several of the Promoters of the London Working Men's Association.* Its general object was 'to diffuse the principles of co-operation as the practical application of Christianity to the purposes of trade and industry'.[1]

The Christian Socialist was, by modern standards, a very sober magazine. It dealt with a large number of practical problems without trying to impose on them any narrow dogmatism. Its treatment of property is typical. It did not condemn it as iniquitous, and yet it did not imagine 'that the remedy against starvation is ... the ownership of a patch of land'.[2] It was moderate in its proposals for Church reform, suggesting that only those reforms should be carried out which were necessary to ensure that the practice of the Church's teaching was consonant with its spirit. A great part of the paper was devoted to news of the Workers' Associations. When it was discovered that the journal was uneconomical to run, the items sacrificed were those other than the Gazette of the doings of the Associations, which was regarded as of primary importance. The whole paper gives the impression of being thoroughly down to earth.[3]

For many reasons which could not be foreseen the Associations did not all flourish and this aspect of the movement had to be abandoned. But Maurice and the others turned their energies to the Working Men's College, an activity which perhaps bore more fruit than any other they had undertaken. The principle of co-operation continued, although it became removed from its specifically Christian setting.

This brief sketch is sufficient to show that Christian Socialism was no vague attempt by a few well-meaning clerics to reconcile two parties which they saw drifting apart. It did not say, 'Christianity *is* Socialism'. It was an effort to encourage socialism with Christian motives and restraints; to free it from revolution, hatred and self-seeking, not by preaching but by practice. In its immediate

[1] *Christian Socialist*, i, No. 1, 2 November 1850.

[2] ibid., p. 2.

[3] There are, however, some exceptions. For example, a letter from 'A Sacred Socialist' (i, No. 12, p. 93), full of generalizations about love and brotherhood, is connected, in an editorial note, with the small socialist school of James Pierrepont Greaves, 'whose influence we ... by no means ... undervalue'. Greaves, who is often quoted in the pages of the *Christian Socialist*, was an exponent of German transcendentalism and some of the theories of J. Boehme.

aims it failed, but its more remote success was that it made each side aware of the claims of the other and stimulated further attempts at reconciliation.

Of the three principal figures in the movement, J. M. Ludlow was the most open to French influence. Brought up as he had been in France and acquainted with French socialist systems, he quoted, in the movement's heyday, frequently from Fourier, Proudhon, Pierre Leroux, and Louis Blanc, but not once, in his published writings, from Lamennais.[1] That Ludlow knew about him is indisputable: a note in his diary records the impact of the *Avenir* upon him;[2] he associated with the friends of Montalembert;[3] and he had the *Esquisse* and several other works in his library.[4] The reference to the *Avenir*, however, was not so much to its doctrines as to its effectiveness; it brought home to Ludlow the need that every movement has of a good press. He was not of the cast of mind to appreciate Lamennais's visionary social theories.

Maurice and Kingsley, less practical perhaps, seem to have known Lamennais less. Maurice mentioned in 1839 that he had been reading *Affaires de Rome*, and that he hoped that Lamennais was 'an honest man in spite of his wildness'.[5] But in later years he betrayed no knowledge of him nor any particular affinity with his thought. Kingsley, despite all Kaufmann's comparisons and assertions, never showed any interest in Lamennais either. He toured the Continent in 1851 without so much as an allusion to him. *Politics for the People* mentioned him once during the whole time of its publication, and then only incidentally in an account of a lecture on French socialism given by someone else.[6] The *Christian Socialist* did not mention him at all.

[1] Later, Ludlow wrote that the significant thing about French socialism in 1848 was that it was by no means atheistic. There was 'a passionate cry for a uniting Christ, but to that cry the churches were deaf. Among the Calvinists Philippe Boucher [*sic*] struggled for the cause, but has no helpers; Lamennais had put himself out of communion with the Church by his views' (*Atlantic Monthly*, January 1896, pp. 109 f.). Ludlow was deeply concerned that this should not be the case in England.

[2] T. Christensen, *Origin and History of Christian Socialism, 1848–1854*, Aarhus, 1962, p. 63.

[3] ibid., p. 38.

[4] *Catalogue of the Library of J. M. Ludlow, Esq., C.B.* (No. 16, 1911–12) includes 'Lamennais, Philosophie, 3 vols. 1840 and others'.

[5] *Life of F. D. Maurice*, ed. F. Maurice, London, 1884, i, p. 257, letter of 12 February 1839 to the Reverend R. C. Trench (who had been in Lamennais's circle in Rome).

[6] *Politics for the People*, p. 90.

This is not surprising when we compare the aims and methods of Lamennais with those of the Christian Socialists. Lamennais, in spite of his denials, was an impatient revolutionary inspired by a Utopian vision. He never succeeded in being both Christian and socialist. The *Livre du peuple* and his later writings were radical and religious but not Christian. The firmness, clearness, and theological soundness of the English Christian Socialists are in sufficient contrast to these. Lamennais's mind ranged freely among concepts like 'liberty', 'property' and 'family'; he could condense the course of history into generalizations occupying a few pages; he lingered little in the present but inspired his readers with apocalyptic visions of the future. The Christian Socialists were opposed to anything of this sort, believing that the solution to present difficulties was to be found not in escape but in prayerful involvement. Lamennais was not satisfied with the Christian religion but outlined his own, which, he believed, would fulfil the needs of the new society he was creating. English Christian Socialists, however, worked from a well-grounded orthodox theology; Church reform was to be a matter of organization, not of doctrine. These and many other points of contrast show that the two had little in common.

The Christian Socialists believed that man had two natures, material and spiritual, and that his end could be achieved only by the full and co-equal development of the two. Lamennais's approach, however, suggested that the two natures were really one nature and that the development of the one would inevitably bring about the development of the other; this idea led to the confusion of socialism and religion. Lamennais was deluded into accepting a powerful political force and adapting his theology to it. Maurice, on the other hand, tried to purify and correct one by means of the other. It was not simply individual piety which made the English Christian Socialists draw their inspiration from the weekly study of the Bible.

As Maurice Reckitt has shown, Christian Socialism in England between 1854 and 1884 was like the seed growing secretly.[1] It was not an organized movement, but rather an attitude of mind which manifested itself in many people in many different ways. In the last decade of the century these views were expressed most clearly in the Church of England by the Guild of St. Matthew

[1] M. Reckitt, *Maurice to Temple*, ch. 4, p. 94.

inspired by the combative Stewart Headlam, and the Christian Social Union led by Henry Scott Holland. The difference between these two cells within the Church is reflected in the characters of their leaders. Headlam was rebellious, defiant, colourful, and thirsting for action. Scott Holland was thoughtful, donnish, primarily academic. 'While Headlam strove to vindicate the outcast and to defy their oppressors, Holland sought to interpret the signs of the times and to win men to his own understanding of what that interpretation required'.[1] Their characters are reflected in their respective journals. The G.S.M. spoke through the *Church Reformer* (1882–95), one of the liveliest and best informed Church newspapers of the day. The *Reformer* concerned itself almost entirely with contemporary questions and items of news and devoted very little space to book reviews or historical articles. Its task was to quicken the Christian conscience of the time. The C.S.U., on the other hand, issued a more scholarly journal, the *Economic Review*. This was under the direction of dons and dealt largely with economic questions and with their background of philosophy and history.

It is not surprising that although there is no hint of Lamennais's influence in the *Church Reformer*, it appears distinctly in the *Economic Review*. In 1896 it published a long and penetrating article on Lamennais by a young priest fresh from the mission field, Walter K. Firminger.[2] In it he affirmed that Lamennais was a 'figure well known to most of us'.[3] He appraised him as a philosopher and insisted that his faith was a reasoned one 'based on a wide inductive historical basis'.[4] He gave a sympathetic summary of Lamennais's social ideas and concluded that only in the priest-orator was found a steady recognition of the limits within which the social thinker had to work.[5] These comments give some pointers to the attempts which the later Christian Socialists were making to formulate a consistent philosophy and theology.

The views of the G.S.M. and the C.S.U. were not the only ones calling themselves Christian Socialist at the time. There was yet another journal, the *Christian Socialist*, which was an organ of

[1] Reckitt, op. cit., p. 137.

[2] On Firminger's connection with Lamennais's biographer, Gibson, see above, p. 145.

[3] *Economic Review*, vi, 1896, p. 29.

[4] ibid.

[5] ibid., p. 31.

its own society, and which had no connection with the *Christian Socialist* of 1850–1. Unlike the G.S.M., it was less concerned with facts than theories and did not hesitate to propagate scurrilous fiction if it suited its purpose; and unlike the C.S.U., it was not primarily theological or even thoughtful (despite its subtitle—*A Journal for Thoughtful Men*). Its advertisement in the *Church Reformer* sums up its attitude:

A journal for those who work and think, which while maintaining the Christian spirit upon which the teachings of Maurice and Kingsley were based, will not hesitate to advance the principles of Socialism, with all the significance which has been added to that term by the patient economic investigations of such men as Lassalle, Karl Marx and Henry George.[1]

One of the editors was H. H. Champion, an aristocrat but leader of the unemployed. He was extreme in his socialism and yet was considered sufficiently orthodox in the faith to be invited to address the Church Congress in 1887.[2] The other was James Leigh Joynes, author of *A Socialist Catechism.*

Their journal took much of its inspiration from Lamennais. The opening article by a 'London Parson' defined what the paper meant by Christian Socialism. It was 'not connected with a new sect, like the Socialism of the sixteenth-century Anabaptists, but proceeding directly from the historical Church of each nation'.[3] The writer paid tribute to Lamennais for having called upon the Church to separate herself from kings and to join hands with the people:

Had the appeal of the great French Catholic been echoed rather than silenced by Gregory XVI, not only would the fiery zeal and gifted intellect of Lamennais have been saved from shipwreck, but the present extraordinary vehemence of French hostility to all forms of religion would never, we are convinced, have been developed.[4]

These remarks set the tone for the attitude of the paper to Lamennais in the future. In April 1885 appeared the first instalment of Alfred Tapley's lecture, 'Lamennais, the Prophet of Democracy'. When, where, and to whom this lecture was delivered we have no means of knowing, but we do know that it was thought to be so important that it was afterwards published as a pamphlet

[1] *Church Reformer*, 1884–5, *passim.* [2] Reckitt, op. cit., p. 134.
[3] *Christian Socialist*, June 1883, No. 1, p. 6. [4] ibid.

by W. Reeves of Fleet Street, was sold at 3*d.* and was still in print in 1890. Advertisements for it appeared in the *Christian Socialist* above those for a translation of Marx's *Das Kapital* and in letters just as large.[1] The lecture itself was fulsome in its praise of Lamennais and not a little careless of fact. Tapley set out to show that there was no contradiction in Lamennais's life, and that, whatever the appearances, Lamennais had always been a prophet of democracy: 'As such I long to introduce him to those who know him not, indeed I could wish his words and deeds as a religious radical reformer in the truest sense of the expression were known to all honest men, convinced, as I am, that they have only to be known to be approved, admired and adopted'.[2] The leading principle of his life was his religion, which compelled him to battle for the social and political rights of man; to fight for the salvation not only of individuals but of the whole human race.[3] The culture of the individual and the progress of the race were closely connected. Faith was of supreme importance. Progress in religion was the root of all progress. Humanity progressed in proportion to the advance it made in its conception of God.[4] These were the ideas for which Lamennais was praised and by which he was thought to have contributed to Christian Socialism.

Following the custom of the time, the magazine filled spare spaces at the foot of a column with uplifting aphorisms from great writers. Lamennais contributed two.[5] There were also two more extended quotations, one on the Sovereignty of the People, which occupied one and a quarter columns,[6] and nearly a column of 'Society an Organized Fraternity'.[7] The equality of men, the authority of the people, the work of God shown forth in the overthrow of despotic rulers, the coming of the new dawn—these were the ideas with which Lamennais's name was connected.

In 1887 an interesting controversy blew up over one point in Lamennais's teaching. In the report of the visit of a prominent American socialist to Edinburgh, the Reverend John Glasse

[1] *Christian Socialist*, iii, February 1886, No. 33, p. 142. The advertisement appeared regularly until April 1890. There is no copy of this pamphlet in either the British Museum or the Bodleian.

[2] ibid., ii, May 1885, No. 24, p. 180.

[3] ibid., iii, August 1885, No. 27, p. 43. [4] ibid.

[5] ibid., November 1885, No. 30, p. 93; January 1886, No. 32, p. 124.

[6] ibid., ii, October 1884, No. 17, p. 77.

[7] ibid., February 1885, No. 21, p. 133.

quoted Lamennais to support a claim that property was essential to freedom.[1] This evoked a protest from the Reverend Philip Peach,[2] a faithful supporter of the *Christian Socialist*, who said that such a doctrine amounted to individualism and was therefore anti-Christian and anti-social.[3] Glasse replied that he would have thought that Lamennais's socialism was beyond suspicion and that the teaching should be understood in the context of Lamennais's own age.[4] Peach retorted that the orthodoxy of Lamennais's socialism was not the point but that it seemed to him to be a doctrine of 'All thine is mine'.[5] (The editors later quite properly took exception to this distortion of the truth.)[6] He therefore withdrew from the Society.

This exchange touches on a crucial point in Lamennais's later beliefs and shows that the tradition passed on by W. J. Linton[7] had been faithfully received. The esteem in which Lamennais was still held can be judged from Glasse's words: 'The words of Lamennais are, of course, directed against the exploitation of labour, and one must be entirely ignorant of the generous Frenchman to believe he was capable of writing anything in favour of the selfishness involved in competition'.[8] This idea was later taken up and powerfully expressed by G. K. Chesterton and the Distributists.

In 1889 appeared a series of articles on the phases of Christian Socialism.[9] The phases were theory, experiment, and scientific reconstruction, and Lamennais was assigned to the first phase. The writer, who signed his articles 'H.W.J.', recognized that Lamennais had no scheme of social reconstruction, and did not really go much beyond a belief that society would be better if, of his own free will, the rich man shared his property with the poor:

> Lamennais was not a Socialist in the sense of being an advocate of the nationalization of industry, but only because this definite and practical solution had not presented itself to his mind. All his doctrines lead

[1] *Christian Socialist*, August 1887, pp. 122–4. The quotation is taken not straight from Lamennais but from W. J. Linton's *English Republic*.
[2] Rector of Pawlett, Somerset, 1886–9.
[3] *Christian Socialist*, September 1887, p. 139.
[4] ibid.
[5] ibid., p. 149.
[6] ibid., p. 150.
[7] Below, pp. 166–71.
[8] *Christian Socialist*, September 1887, p. 139.
[9] ibid., October 1889, pp. 154–6.

inevitably to an equalization of the rewards of labour and to the ordering of society on the basis of mutual help and mutual responsibility. If F. D. Maurice and Bishop von Ketteler claim to be Christian Socialists, we have every reason for ranking Lamennais as a precursor in the same school. Indeed, his convictions were deeper and his zeal more burning, in that he sacrificed his position and all worldly prospects and advancement in raising his voice in the battle against tyranny and oppression.[1]

From these examples it is evident that some members of the Church of England, in groping for a truly Christian expression of their socialism, had not forgotten the example of Lamennais. Nor can the revival of interest in Lamennais be traced to any one Christian Socialist source; the G.S.M., C.S.U., the Christian Socialist Society, and the Reverend M. Kaufmann were very different from, and in some cases antagonistic to each other. The G.S.M. acknowledged the *Christian Socialist*,[2] which in turn expressed the strongest solidarity with the C.S.U.[3] Both the G.S.M. and the *Christian Socialist* spoke very disparagingly of Kaufmann.[4]

The interest therefore arose in several places simultaneously and may indicate a desire to broaden the basis of the movement, to release it from the narrow confines set by Kingsley and Maurice, and by placing it in a European context to give it a greater degree of intellectual respectability. More likely, however, is the possibility that the combination of Christianity and socialism was creating more problems than its early enthusiasts had anticipated. Lamennais was a good example of a Christian whose life seemed to have a thread of consistency running through it, and whose boldness in speech and action made very clear the issues which were involved. It may be that in looking to Lamennais in this way they did not understand him properly, but there is no mistaking the fact that his fearlessness served them both as a warning and as a guide.

[1] *Christian Socialist*, October 1889, pp. 155 f.
[2] By printing such detailed advertisements of it.
[3] *Christian Socialist*, November 1890, p. 141.
[4] *Church Reformer*, February 1890, p. 45; *Christian Socialist*, May 1888, p. 73, accused Kaufmann of encouraging those who thought that Christian Socialism meant nothing at all. The difference between them was that Kaufmann believed that Christian Socialism worked from the inside and the *Christian Socialist* that it worked from the outside.

In the nineteenth century much of the political agitation took place in the field of religion. The Establishment was identified with the old order, and dissenters of all sorts, Roman Catholic and Protestant, allied themselves with the Radicals to achieve their own ends. Dissenters and rationalists therefore fought for the same cause. This unusual combination was split across the middle by education. On the one hand there were those who had been led by philosophy to take a radical view of politics. Their views were expressed by the *Westminster*, the organ of the Philosophical Radicals (a term which included many shades of political opinion).

The *Westminster*'s attitude to Lamennais passed gradually from contempt and hatred to grudging admiration of him as his opinions changed. In 1825, in a two-barbed attack on both the conservatism of Montlosier and the domination of the Church, it sarcastically called him a 'meek churchman',[1] in 1827 a 'fanatic',[2] and in 1830 'the strenuous supporter of the papal power in the unmitigated violence of barbarous ages',[3] but by 1834 'that involuntary pioneer of liberty'.[4] In 1838 it noticed his edition of Estienne de la Boétie and praised its 'sonorous and statuesque Republicanism'.[5] In 1866 it called him an 'able and noble-hearted man whose works have left an indelible impress on the literature of the nineteenth century',[6] but three years later it modified this opinion by its low estimate of the *Paroles*.[7] Throughout it showed a certain admiration for Lamennais but little enthusiasm. The most eminent contributors, Bentham, James Mill, W. J. Fox, George Grote, Roebuck, and Southern, although deeply committed to radicalism, showed no particular interest in Lamennais, and so we must conclude that it was not to the intelligentsia of the Left that he appealed.[8]

[1] *Westminster*, iii, January 1825, p. 48.

[2] ibid., January 1827, p. 73, a review of Lamennais's *Réflexions* and *Mélanges* and two other works. He is taken as typical of the dominant party in the Church of France.

[3] ibid., January 1830, p. 216.

[4] ibid., April 1834, p. 437. The writer must have paid close attention to Lamennais's career, for the *Paroles* had not yet been published (30 April 1834).

[5] ibid., August 1838, p. 332.

[6] ibid., xxx, October 1866, p. 372.

[7] ibid., N.S. xv, 1869, p. 531; see above, p. 56.

[8] The *Westminster* described his later philosophical position as 'Roman Catholic ultra-Radicalism' (April 1838, p. 1).

On the other hand there was the mass of agitators of different sorts, uneducated or partly educated, who, if they were to be encouraged from abroad, needed translations to help them.

The first English translation of the *Paroles*[1] was published by B. D. Cousins of 18 Duke Street, Lincoln's Inn Fields. Cousins was known for publishing anything which would be subversive of accepted opinions without making any great positive contribution to the advancement of the people's cause.[2] He was in the midst of the war against the stamp duty on newspapers, 'the tax on knowledge' as radical papers were fond of calling it.[3] A Scandinavian contemporary, Harro Harring, gives an unflattering account of him:

> Wer sollte wohl glauben, dass die Uebersetzung in's Englische keinen Verleger erster, zweiter oder dritter Classe fand.—Ein untergeordneter Buchhändler (als Editor für's Volk bekannt) entschloss sich endlich, dieses weltberühmte Werk in die englische Litteratur einzuschmuggeln, und hat denn auch richtig wohl kaum hundert Exemplare davon abgesetzt.[4]

The authorship of the translation is uncertain, but it seems likely that it was the work either of the Reverend J. E. Smith, a heterodox Scotsman, or of Gertrude Collier, daughter of Admiral Collier and later the wife of Charles Tennant, M.P. for St. Albans.[5] The name of its publisher, however, ensured that its public would be largely left-wing and free-thinking.

The *Words*, which cost 1*s.* stitched and 1*s.* 6*d.* bound in boards,[6] got off to a slow start. Harro Harring, an admirer and

[1] *The Words of a Believer: and having thus spoken he was eternally damned by the Pope of Rome for having uttered them.* Translated from the French of l'Abbé de la Mennais, London, 1834.

[2] Among his regular publications were the *Crisis*, the *New Moral World* (Owenist, but important enough to carry articles by Engels; it was used for the dissemination of early communism of Weitling's type), and the *Pioneer*.

[3] Thomas Frost, *Forty Years' Recollections: Literary and Political*, London, 1880, p. 60 calls Cousins's shop 'one of the chief emporia of the literature of free thought'.

[4] Harro Harring, *Skizze aus London*, Strasburg, 1838, pp. 38 f.

[5] For a full discussion see Appendix B, p. 199.

[6] *Crisis*, 26 July 1834, p. 128, and thereafter weekly until 16 August, the day of publication. The *Crisis* was wound up on 23 August, and so a valuable source of information about the *Paroles* in England is denied us. By 1851 it was selling at 6*d.* (*The Reasoner*, x, 1851, p. 467).

imitator[1] of Lamennais, who was in England at this time,[2] was astonished at the coolness of the reception which it received.[3] He attributed it to the Englishman's love of facts, of which there were few in the *Paroles*, and the utter remoteness of English literature from the conditions of the people.[4] Harring never ceased to wonder at the blindness of the English in not recognizing that one chapter of the *Paroles* was worth more than all the poetic output of one of the preceding centuries.[5]

The reaction to the *Words* in traditional circles has already been considered.[6] Among radicals very little was heard at once. *Bell's New Weekly Messenger*, influential with moderate radicals,[7] gave it careful consideration but only qualified approval:

It is an extraordinary book, and we feel compelled to bear witness to the genius, the patriotism, the virtue of the writer: but, at the same time, respect for the religious feelings (prejudices, if you will) of the community occasions our regret that a man of such immense power as the Abbe de la Menais [*sic*] should have written a book which, while it contains some of the grandest moral precepts, some of the finest political principles, is nevertheless alloyed with so much extravagant imagery, that it can never be recognized in society as a guide book either in politics or virtue. Rid it of all this ridiculous imagery, and it may then become useful.[8]

As Harring noted, the Englishman wanted something practical, not a poem. The *Poor Man's Guardian*, a paper edited by Henry Hetherington, with whom Cousins was co-operating in the fight against the newspaper tax, published chapter XL of the *Words* for

[1] Harro Harring, *Worte eines Menschen—Dem Gläubigen von La Mennais gewidmet*, Strasburg, 1834.

[2] He arrived here in September 1834, just after the publication of the *Words*, and left in January 1835. He returned at the end of September of the same year and stayed for two years. Thereafter he wandered and visited England occasionally. He was found dead in London, 21 May 1870.

[3] 'Der menschliche Verstand steht uns stille, wenn wir von La Mennais Schicksal in England hören' (*Skizze aus London*, p. 39).

[4] cf. a similar judgement by Miss Mary Berry, writing to Macaulay in 1834, *Journal and Correspondence of Miss Berry*, London, 1866, 2nd ed., iii, p. 419.

[5] Harro Harring, op. cit., p. 84.

[6] Above, pp. 33–36.

[7] W. J. Linton, *James Watson, a Memoir*, Appledore Private Press, Newhaven, U.S.A., 1879, p. 47.

[8] *Bell's New Weekly Messenger* (The Reviewer, No. 154, Sunday 7 December 1834, p. 97); see also No. 153, 30 November, p. 95.

the encouragement of its readers.[1] Other radical magazines and newspapers failed to notice it at this time.

It must soon have come into general circulation, for a few years later a Scottish magazine told its readers that 'The Abbé's "Cry in the Wilderness" made a considerable sensation, even in this country, though in a comparatively small circle'.[2] There was one startling rumour that Richard Carlile had been converted to Christianity by it.[3] Although it turns out that this was not true,[4] it is some indication of how powerful the work was thought to be.

There was, however, one Englishman who was genuinely converted by the *Paroles*, not to Christianity but from Anglicanism to radical religious enthusiasm. He was W. J. Linton, one of the most intelligent of the Chartists, a writer of considerable talent and

[1] *Poor Man's Guardian*, 22 November 1834, p. 335.

[2] *Tait's*, November 1845, p. 744. The reviewer added that he believed that several English translations had appeared. This is certainly wrong but testifies to the fact that the work was not entirely ignored.

[3] *Literary Gazette and Journal of Belles Lettres*, 25 October 1834, p. 717. This article by Wm. Jerdan contains the mystifying assertion that Carlile republished the *Paroles* in England. I have discovered no justification for this statement.

[4] Carlile was an atheist. In common with other atheists he was regarded with particular hatred and suffered greatly for his beliefs (G. A. Aldred, *Richard Carlile*, London, 1923—a bitter denunciation of his opponents—; and G. D. H. Cole, *Richard Carlile*, 1943, 37 pp.). On one of these occasions when he was in gaol, around 1832, a change came over him. On his release he bought a licence to preach. This cost him 2*s*. 6*d*. and gave him the status of a dissenting minister. But it soon became apparent that he had not changed his views. In a letter to Sir Robert Peel soon afterwards he explained his position: Christ, he said, was the Logos, the rational, intellectual principle in men; the Church should therefore be a place for encouraging this principle, a school with no mystery of any sort attached to it (*Church Reform: the only means to that end. Letter to Sir R. Peel*, 1835). He developed this idea in his short-lived periodicals (e.g. *Carlile's Railroad to Heaven* and the *Christian Warrior*), until it became clear that he had changed not his principles but merely his technique; he preached atheism in Christian terms (Aldred, op. cit., pp. 159 f.). His aim was to substitute science for superstition in the education of the people, and he imagined that he had transposed his radical ranting into a religious key. This subtle move achieved for him considerable success and publicity. But there is no question of his 'conversion'. If he ever read the *Paroles* it did not change his outlook. As is shown by a letter of 24 November 1833 (printed in the preface to *Church Reform*, &c., 1835), five months before the *Paroles* was published, he had already adopted his new method. He had been converted to this by the allegorical method of interpreting the Bible used by the Reverend R. Taylor, a heterodox Anglican priest (see *The Lion*, 4 vols, 1828–9; and Cole, op. cit., p. 26).

one of the best wood-carvers of the time.[1] He readily acknowledged his debt, in one place associating the 'stirring words of Lamennais in his famous Scripture anathematized by the Pope—the *Paroles d'un croyant*'[2] with Thomas Wade (the editor of *Bell's New Weekly Messenger*), Voltaire, and Shelley, and in another place with Fox.[3] He was an indefatigable publisher of periodicals, in which he propagated the ideals he had partly learnt from Lamennais. In the *National: a Library for the People*, which appeared briefly in 1839, he reviewed the *Words*, and revealed his own attitude to its author:

> And no common believer is the Abbé: but one whose spirit has beheld the face of the far future, and who has drawn therefrom a faith not only to inspire high thoughts and fearless expression, but evidenced in his actions, as one of the staunchest of the French Republicans.[4]

He concluded that the *Words* (and the *Book of the People*, which he reviewed with it) contained a little too much mysticism for his liking, and a little too much of the Catholic creed, although true Catholicism, love, was manifest on every page.[5]

It is remarkable that although there were many imitations of Lamennais's style in French and in other languages, hitherto none has been recognized in English. But there was one. In this same paper, the *National*, Linton published a poem in biblical prose after the manner of Lamennais called 'Revelations of Truth'. It is divided into two books, with seventeen chapters in the first and eight in the second. The general pattern follows that of Lamennais's poem. Some chapters are in the form of visions and others of exhortations; others again set out a programme of reform or are frankly didactic. Linton's touch is heavier than Lamennais's. Although he was an artist, he did not have Lamennais's skill in evoking a sentimental picture. He had to rely more on slogans, persuasion, and allegory. Like the *Paroles*, *Revelations* opens with a biblical quotation: 'The voice of one crying in the wilderness, Prepare ye the way of the Lord, make straight in the desert a highway for our God' (Isaiah xl. 3). This quotation

[1] Apart from his own works, quoted later, the only biographical material is W. F. Hopson, *Side Lights on William James Linton 1812–1897* (reprinted from *Papers of the Bibliographical Society of America*, xxvii, 1933). [2] Linton, *James Watson, a Memoir*, 1879, p. 47.

[3] Linton, *Memories*, London, 1895, p. 26.

[4] *National*, 1839, p. 365. [5] ibid., p. 367.

illustrates the difference between the two poems: Lamennais quotes from the New Testament, Linton from the Old; Lamennais's 'Au nom du Père et du Fils et du Saint Esprit' has the ring of direct authority; Linton loses this effect through self-consciousness. Lamennais starts as if he is speaking under divine compulsion; Linton sounds as if he knows from the start that no one will listen to him.

The subject matter is similar in both: love, unity, the tyranny of kings, liberty, equality; but Linton's poem has not the restraint and charity which we can now see in most parts of the *Paroles*. Neither is it so specifically Christian in its clothing. With the exception of one or two passages, the *Paroles* may be read as an attempt to harness the passions of the people in the service of religion. This is not a position that Linton is prepared to take up. He prefers to denounce the evils of the Church (I, 5), of priests (I, 14), and of religion (I, 15), and to substitute for them a vague religion of the heart (II, 4). He is not steeped in the language of the Bible as Lamennais was, with the result that he makes unbiblical use of the Old Testament imagery of the serpent in the Garden (II, 4). Lamennais's use of the same story is more familiar and has more poetic force (ch. III).

There are, however, many similarities with the *Paroles*. In both works there are visions of tyrants drinking blood from skulls.[1] These words of Linton echo those of Lamennais:

> Violence is evil; and yet it is just to resist wrong even to the death.[2]
> I have seen millions of men, and many of them the wise and noble and intelligent bowing to the caprice of an ordinary child.[3]

Linton's use of the refrain 'Child of Mortality why mournest thou?' is in imitation of Lamennais's 'L'exilé partout est seul'.[4] Like Lamennais, he sees visions of the past, present, and future, and of man in chains rising to fight his oppressors in order to achieve the idyllic age of freedom, love, and leisure.[5] Examples could be multiplied, but these suffice to show that Lamennais's style had taken a hold upon Linton.

[1] *Revelations*, I, 11; *Paroles*, XIII, 9.
[2] *Revelations*, I, 16; *Paroles*, XIX, 11.
[3] *Revelations*, I, 4; *Paroles*, XIX, 4.
[4] *Revelations*, I, 17; *Paroles*, XLI.
[5] *Revelations*, II, 7; *Paroles*, XI, 34–38.

Full of enthusiasm for his hero, Linton determined to translate and publish his writings for the benefit of Englishmen of a like mind with himself. In the following year (1840) appeared *Modern Slavery*, a translation of *De l'esclavage moderne* (1839), with certain very moderate explanatory notes. Linton's only real addition to Lamennais's work was an appendix in which he said that although the day of liberty was in sight, there remained one glaring case of slavery to be dealt with, the slavery of women; the essential preliminary to their emancipation was that they should be taught to desire freedom. Linton must have felt strongly about this subject because he devoted a chapter of the *Revelations* to it.[1]

The publisher and the bookseller of *Modern Slavery* came from the same circle of Chartist agitation as Linton himself. James Watson, the publisher, who had his office at 15 City Road, Finsbury, and who, together with Hetherington, Cleave, and Heywood, was prominent in the fight for unstamped newspapers, had been a pious man, but later became a free-thinker and started to publish works which tended to undermine established religion. Among them were the works of Thomas Paine, Owen, Volney, and Godwin.[2] It was in this company that *Modern Slavery* appeared. Whether it achieved a large circulation we have no means of knowing, but apart from the allusions to it in Linton's own works, there is one comment on it which is of some importance. It is by G. Julian Harney in the *Democratic Review*[3] and is part of Harney's campaign to popularize the French reformers with English readers. It certainly does that in terms which are, according to Harring's categories, likely to appeal to Englishmen. Harney describes *Modern Slavery* as a much more successful attempt than the *Words* had been to paint a factual picture of the condition of the people. *Modern Slavery* was still being advertised for sale in 1855—'Price Four Pence. An excellent exposition of the present condition of the working classes'.[4] The bookseller, Henry Hetherington, who operated from 126 The Strand, had published a translation of *Le Livre du peuple* two years earlier and was later to become one of the leading Chartists.

[1] *Revelations*, I, 8.
[2] Linton, *James Watson*, &c., pp. 21 f.
[3] *Democratic Review*, January 1850, p. 314.
[4] *English Republic*, iv, 1855, opp. p. 108.

It was to Linton that Lamennais owed the publicizing of his later ideas in England. These appeared in several papers, all intended for the people. The *Red Republican*, edited by Harney, which drew much of its material from the Continent—Ledru Rollin and Mazzini were among its contributors—first published Linton's political manifesto.[1] This was quite simply 'Equality, Liberty and Humanity (or Fraternity)', in that order. Equality was to be obtained through universal suffrage. Liberty of all sorts was to be guaranteed by the equality already obtained. Humanity was the result of these two: it included collective progress, mutual support, and the steady advance from aspiration to acquirement, higher and ever higher. He explained that it was Lamennais who had taught him to put Equality before Liberty, since liberty to build is only a deception until the ground is cleared by equality. But it was from Mazzini that he had learnt to prefer Humanity to Fraternity. Linton had not swallowed Lamennais's ideas whole. He was still cautious of what he regarded as Lamennais's excessive dogmatism. He knew that for Lamennais Fraternity meant that all men were brothers under the Fatherhood of God, and although he acknowledged the importance of God, he was not willing to make his whole philosophy depend on it. He therefore put the emphasis on the effort and activity of man and relegated God to the background.

Of the many papers which Linton edited it was the *English Republic* which gave the fullest account of Lamennais's thought.[2] Apart from the space-filling quotations and the extracts from the *Paroles*,[3] there were two articles from the *Peuple constituant* which gave the essence of Lamennais's later views. 'Religion, Family, Property: Who are the Friends of Order?' expounded Lamennais's attitude to those three cardinal points which distinguished him in various ways from other socialists of the day.[4] The other essay was important as a résumé of his attitude to labour in relation to the ideas of other socialists and communists in this matter.[5]

When Lamennais died, Linton wrote an eloquent essay to commemorate him: 'The noblest Frenchman of them all—even

[1] *Red Republican*, Saturday 21 September 1850, p. 110.

[2] *English Republic*, 1851–5. The title-page always bore the motto, 'God and the People'.

[3] ibid., 1851, p. 264; 1852, pp. 29–32.

[4] ibid., 1852, pp. 5–8.

[5] ibid., pp. 285–90, a translation of *Question du travail* (from *Peuple constituant*, Paris, 1848).

if France was herself again, and all her nobles restored to her—the friend of Mazzini and "George Sand", the venerable Lamennais, is no more'.[1] The depth of Linton's fervour can be judged from these words: 'Never since the conversion of Saint Paul has the good cause won over a purer or more puissant soul; never has the people's right been upheld, or the world's duty inculcated, by an apostle more fervid, more unweariable, more sincere'.[2] The rest of the essay was in the same vein and testified not only to Linton's personal loss but also to his belief in the enduring value of Lamennais's teaching.

The *English Republic* did not have a great circulation and Linton had to discontinue it in 1855. It must, however, have made an impression in some circles, because, as we have already seen, it was cited over thirty years later as 'the once well-known Republican Tracts of W. J. Linton'.[3]

A friend of Linton's who moved in the same circles, shared many of the same friends, but had a much wider influence, was Giuseppe Mazzini. He too had been greatly impressed by the *Paroles*, not so much because that work had opened his eyes to something he had not seen before, but because it showed in a remarkable way how similar were his views and those of Lamennais. Already before the publication of the *Paroles*, Mazzini had looked to Lamennais to give a lead in imbuing Catholicism with democracy, in providing a strong combination of religion and the power of the people.[4] The *Paroles* showed him that his trust had not been misplaced; the two began to correspond;[5] they met more than once,[6] and thereafter Mazzini had a firm admiration for Lamennais and did all he could to show his real significance.

In 1837 Mazzini came to England and for several years lived by the little he could earn from his pen. His tendency to generalize, his religious fervour, and his preference for duties above rights, did not endear him to the mass of English radicals, but he acquired a small number of English friends, among whom were Linton, Holyoake, and the Carlyles, as well as many Italian ones.

[1] *English Republic*, iii, 1854, p. 148.
[2] ibid., p. 152. [3] Above, p. 161.
[4] Joseph Mazzini, *The Pope in the 19th Century*, London, 1851 (the article is quoted from *Italia del Popolo*, 1849, and was written in 1832).
[5] Bolton King, *Life of Mazzini*, London (Everyman), 1938, pp. 89 f.
[6] It was through Mazzini that Linton met Lamennais (Linton, *Memories*, London, 1895, p. 104).

Much of his literary work appeared in the *Monthly Chronicle*. This was a serious monthly started by Dr. Dionysius Lardner, a prolific writer of popular scientific works and handy manuals of instruction.[1] It was here that Mazzini published the first article in English which tried seriously to appraise Lamennais's contribution to thought, although it erred (as did everything that Mazzini wrote about Lamennais) on the side of adulation.[2] It contained several passages like the following:

M. Lamennais occupies a rank so elevated as a philosopher, as a writer, and in France, as a political power, his progress is so intimately allied to that of the age, that for those even who conceive nothing of the good there is in studying the spectacle of virtuous genius, it must be of considerable importance to know the proper estimate of a man who has such great, and who, one day or other, will have still greater influence on France and the rising generation of Europe.[3]

The purpose of the article was to set Lamennais in a more favourable light with Englishmen after the treatment he had hitherto received:

We have seen this man transformed by one of our reviews[4] into a creature of blood, into a preacher of anarchy. Moreover, each of his publications has been judged separately as a work of art or of politics; never, that we are aware of, has this vast and fertile intelligence been estimated as a whole.[5]

This was something new. Mazzini was right in claiming that so far Lamennais's works had been judged individually; it was almost inevitable that this should be so. Mazzini was the first person, in England at any rate, to assess Lamennais's character as a

[1] E. B. de Fonblanque, *Life and Labours of Albany Fonblanque*, London, 1874, p. 40.

[2] *Monthly Chronicle*, iii, 1839, pp. 317–28. This has been reprinted several times since: *Life and Writings of Joseph Mazzini*, vi, 1870, pp. 1–31; in the Camelot series, *Selected Essays*, ed. with an introduction by W. Clarke, 1887, pp. 59–82; and as a preface to the 1891 translation of the *Paroles* and *Du passé* by L. E. Martineau. One bookish weekly commented on Mazzini's words that 'something more than vague rhetoric is wanted to make the reader of today understand Lamennais and his position' (*Academy*, 3 October 1891, p. 280); it was used as the basis of Linton's chapter on Lamennais in his *European Republicans*, London, 1893, pp. 193–222.

[3] *Monthly Chronicle*, iii, 1839, p. 319.

[4] Probably the *Quarterly*.

[5] op. cit., p. 319.

whole. It was a very good attempt. He saw Lamennais as the exemplification of the double impulse of faith and conscience in humanity.[1] Roughly speaking, his early productions represented the working of faith and the later ones the working of conscience. Both were present all the time, and all the time he had but 'one sole and sacred thought'—'the welfare of the people by the means of belief'.[2] But in his first period faith had been paramount and had encouraged submission and humility, while in his second conscience rose up to assert the claims of justice and love.

Several other articles by Mazzini in the same journal ascribed to Lamennais the first place in the European literature of the day. In the 'Present State of French Literature'[3] he expressed the opinion that all that was being written in France was worthless rubbish, with the exception of the works of Lamennais and George Sand, on whom the whole of future literature would depend,[4] and when writing of George Sand he went even further and ranked Lamennais first among French writers.[5] In an article on the State and Prospects of Italy[6] he contrasted the attitude of the typical Italian priest to the misery around him with Lamennais's 'sacred indignation'. An article on Young Europe breathed his spirit and showed similar enthusiasm for Lamennais. He had spoken 'words of comfort to the world', with 'the vigour of new-born life'. He was the 'foreteller of joy whilst encompassed by sorrow'. Regeneration was written on his brow, and he was 'one of the beacons of the era'.[7]

In addition to these journalistic essays, Mazzini set out his ideas on religion and politics in two short treatises, *Faith and the Future* and *The Duties of Man*. The former was written in 1835 and fragments of it first appeared in English translation in Smith's *Shepherd*.[8] It is influenced by the thought of the *Paroles*, though

[1] op. cit., p. 321. Bolton King (op. cit., pp. 240–5) analyses Mazzini's concepts of tradition (which is similar to 'faith' in the sense in which he uses it in the articles on Lamennais) and conscience, as 'the two wings given to the human soul to reach to truth' (p. 240).

[2] *Monthly Chronicle*, iii, 1839, p. 328.

[3] ibid., p. 219.

[4] A typical phrase (among many) is: 'Lamennais, whose inspiration, deeply religious, popular and prophetic, unites in their highest strength the three most essential characteristics of true poetry' (ibid., p. 219).

[5] ibid., iv, 1839, p. 40. He had not changed his opinion when he wrote in the *People's Journal* eight years later (*People's Journal*, 1847, iii, p. 132).

[6] *Monthly Chronicle*, iii, 1839, p. 411; cf. *Tait's*, vii, June 1840, p. 389.

[7] *Monthly Chronicle*, vii, 1841, p. 469.

[8] On Smith see Appendix B, pp. 203 f.

not by its form, but made little impression in England.[1] *The Duties of Man* was written in 1843 and first published in England in Mazzini's paper for the Italian exiles, *L'Apostolato Popolare*, and thereafter several translations appeared.[2] This work also acknowledged Mazzini's debt to Lamennais[3] and resembled Lamennais's later writings more closely.

How wide was Mazzini's influence with the English is difficult to assess. *Faith and the Future* did not enjoy popularity in England but *The Duties of Man* has exercised a subtle influence on radical thought.[4] His article on Lamennais was well known. It did not, however, at all affect the inaccuracy of other writers in the *Monthly Chronicle* when they dealt with Lamennais. One said: 'The abolition of the institution of private property as the source of all selfishness, inequality, misery and crime, is at the bottom of all their [i.e. French socialist] systems, and openly avowed by Lammenais [*sic*] and other eloquent writers of the party'.[5] This misrepresentation of Lamennais's views on property was repeated in a later letter, in which it was said that Lamennais 'boldly preaches a crusade against property as the root of all evil, and links up his system of Catholicism with a scheme for the abolition of all outward distinctions, . . . unbounded toleration and unlimited liberty of thought'.[6] The writer made his comments seem even more curious by linking them with orthodox papal Catholicism. This extreme socialism, he said, was going too far for Rome's liking: 'nevertheless, the abbé goes on in spite of Papal prohibitions, making converts to the cause of Catholicism, and extending the boundaries of the church, while he defies its authority'.[7]

On the other hand, the same articles have an illuminating comparison between Lamennais and two English reformers,

[1] Harring maintained that after the failure of the *Paroles* in England, no publisher would undertake a translation of *Faith and the Future* (*Skizze aus London*, 1838, p. 81).

[2] Mazzini, *Life and Writings*, 1867, iv, pp. 204–378, translated by Mme Venturi and H. S. King, London, 1877; Everyman edition, London, 1907.

[3] e.g. *Life and Writings*, iv, p. 209 and p. 313.

[4] e.g. Gilbert Murray in a *Fragment of Autobiography* (*Sunday Times*, 31 January 1960) said that his wife was well versed in *The Duties of Man*.

[5] *Monthly Chronicle*, vi, 1840, p. 201.

[6] ibid., p. 416.

[7] ibid.

Richard Oastler[1] and Joseph Rayner Stephens.[2] In view of the *Monthly Chronicle*'s complete misunderstanding of Lamennais's teaching on property, it is doubtful if this comparison was as deliberate as it was apt. Mazzini probably succeeded in conveying a tolerably accurate picture of Lamennais to only a few interested Englishmen.

There is, however, a notable contrast with this in his effect on his compatriots in London. Through *L'Apostolato Popolare*[3]

[1] Oastler was a Tory, a supporter of the Established Church, and a greatly admired man. He himself was poor and devoted most of his life to a one-man campaign against the Poor Laws. In 1841 he was imprisoned for debt and spent his two years in the Fleet Gaol writing and publishing the *Fleet Papers* (being letters to Thomas Thornhill, Esq., from Fleet Prison, 1841–2), attacks upon the Poor Law. He had it in common with Lamennais that he upheld the rights of property.

[2] Stephens's resemblances to Lamennais were also noticed by G. J. Holyoake (*Life of Joseph Rayner Stephens, Preacher and Political Orator*, London and Edinburgh, 1881, pp. 40 f.). Stephens was a Methodist minister who had spent some time in Stockholm. Here in 1829 he had become friendly with Montalembert and may have had some influence upon him. The two were on terms of fairly close friendship, and a long letter written by Montalembert to Stephens is very revealing for the period of his life shortly before he became associated with Lamennais and the *Avenir*. It is full of self-pity, love-sickness, a deep desire for Stephens's friendship, and includes this passage: ' "Remember that I rely upon you"! Our union, our friendship, is a debt we owe to the noble cause of *faith*, religious, moral and political, which we have both embraced, which you proclaim from the altar of the Most High, and which I may perhaps also defend in my country's presence. Let there be between us a tie of sacred sympathy—a tie formed by faith in the same truths, and love for the same virtues—a tie which may yield us some comfort in this world, and not be quite useless to our fate in the next' (Holyoake, op. cit., p. 39). Back in England Stephens was forced to resign his position as a Methodist minister after being condemned for preaching the separation of Church and State. In December 1838 he was arrested for his vehement attacks on the Poor Law and his advocacy of the 'Ten Hours Bill', and was accused of using force to support his opinions. He conducted his own defence. In his speech he said that he had always opposed the opinions of Paine and Carlile. He rejected that liberalism which sought happiness for the greater number at the expense of the few. He concluded that the source of all power was not the people but God. He was sentenced to eighteen months' imprisonment. Stephens *did* have a great deal in common with Lamennais, not only in his life and teaching, where surprising similarities exist in spite of the difference of their religious backgrounds, but also in the fact that Montalembert was drawn to both of them within eighteen months. (Montalembert's first visit to Lamennais was on 5 November 1830.)

[3] For some of the time this was published by Cleave of Shoe Lane, Fleet Street, who was allied with Cousins and Hetherington in the Chartist cause.

they watched Lamennais's career with such interest that when he was imprisoned in 1840 they sent him a seal as a symbol of their firm adhesion to the principles for which he endured persecution. Lamennais's reply is already familiar,[1] but Mazzini's letter is not and shows not only the warmth of his personal affection but also the extent to which the exiled Italians identified themselves with Lamennais.[2]

Another of these indefatigable journalists, who was greatly influenced by the *Paroles* and did his best to make it better known in England, was George Julian Harney, one of the most cosmopolitan of the Chartist leaders.[3] In an article that he wrote in later life[4] he said he treasured a neatly bound, thin octavo volume, the pages showing abundance of margin and blank space between the chapters, an early edition of the *Paroles*,[5] and certainly its influence can be clearly seen in the pages of the papers with which he was associated, the *Red Republican*, the *Vanguard*, the *London Democrat*, *The Friend of the People*, and the *Democratic Review*.[6] It would, however, not be right to lay too much stress upon this fact, because most of the contributions to Harney's journals were from foreign correspondents. He felt strongly about the insularity of British socialists and did his best to correct it:

Whatever the cause, and no matter who is to blame, the fact that the writings of such men as Louis Blanc, Proudhon, Considérant, Lamennais, etc. are almost, or entirely unknown in England, is a fact to be regretted. Sound knowledge will make but slow progress in this country as long as the writings of the Continental Social Reformers are untranslated, and, consequently, unknown to the British masses.[7]

Six months later it seems that he felt he had had some success, for in an account of the later works of Lamennais he called him 'the well-known and much-admired Abbé de Lamennais' and 'the most truly noble of living men'.[8] Harney's veneration for

[1] *O.P.* ii, p. 473.
[2] *L'Apostolato Popolare*, 25 July 1841, pp. 12 f. (letter dated 22 November 1840).
[3] G. D. H. Cole, *Chartist Portraits*, London, 1941, p. 268.
[4] *Open Court*, Chicago, 24 September 1891, p. 2959.
[5] He claimed that it was dated 1833 and did not bear the name of the author (ibid.).
[6] *The Friend of the People* printed translations of chs. 5, most of 6, 7, 20, 21 and most of 22 (1851, pp. 177, 196, 199, 271 f.).
[7] *Democratic Review*, No. 1, June 1849, pp. 33 f.
[8] ibid., January 1850, p. 313.

Lamennais grew with time, and by 1891 he could call him 'The Christian Saint in our Republican Calendar'.[1]

The friends of Linton and Mazzini, the agitators and political radicals of the 1830's and 1840's who constituted the small circle of people who read and were influenced by the *Paroles* when it appeared, were also those at whom the next translation, that of *Le Livre du peuple*, was aimed.

Le Livre du peuple appeared in France in 1837, and was first translated into English by J. H. Lorymer in 1838. It was sold at a shilling, or for those who could not afford that at once, in four parts at 3*d*. each.[2] It was published by Hetherington and Lorymer jointly.[3]

Lamennais had been much better served by the translator of the *Paroles* than he was by Lorymer. Lorymer seems to have been the extreme and destructive type of reformer. The *Republican*, which he controlled, was loud in its demand for radical reform. Banner headlines and very large print, unusual for those times, played their part in the campaign. The *London Democrat* of 1839, in which he was associated with G. J. Harney, was one of the most inflammatory of the radical papers.[4] 'THE REVENGE—the too long withheld revenge—of the people will soon be accomplished'—sentiments of this sort, rare in the press of the time, underline the destructive nature of his thought.[5]

The notes that Lorymer scattered through his translation show that he had a petty and ill-stocked mind. For example, Lamennais asserts that only good comes from God. Lorymer replies that, God being the creator of all, both good and evil must come from him.[6] This superficial way of dealing with the oldest of theological problems continues throughout the book, until it is difficult to see why Lorymer thought it worth his while to translate it at all. The gulf which existed between his way of thinking and Lamennais's is clearly seen in his comments on chapters XI

[1] *Open Court*, 1891, p. 2959.

[2] *Cleave's Penny Gazette of Variety*, i, No. 24, Saturday 24 March 1838.

[3] *Book of the People* by F. Lamennais (Author of 'Les Paroles d'un Croyant' &c.) translated with notes by J. H. Lorymer, London, H. Hetherington, 126 Strand, and J. H. Lorymer, 188 Strand, 1838.

[4] *London Democrat*, Letters addressed to the people by G. J. Harney and J. H. Lorymer, 13 April—8 June 1839.

[5] ibid., p. 66.

[6] *Book of the People*, ch. i, p. 1.

and XII, which he thinks are superfluous. Chapter XI deals with brotherly love, forgiveness (which Lorymer thinks is silly because it only provides encouragement to further commission of wrong),[1] and the striving within man to make the angel in him predominate over the animal. Chapter XII deals with family duties. Lorymer found these either unnecessary or incomprehensible, although in fact they are the core of Lamennais's teaching. Linton was quick to defend Lamennais and complained of Lorymer's very sectarian notes.[2] They were also disapproved of by another reviewer, in *Cleave's Penny Gazette of Variety*. He said that Lamennais was a writer of great acuteness and benevolence, but that the notes of the translator added nothing to the value of the work. 'They are flippant in style, superficial in reasoning, and in many cases betray an extraordinary lack of information on the subjects to which they relate'.[3] It would not be too harsh to say that Lorymer was the least pleasant and least fair of the radicals. His unpleasantness may have been one of the reasons for the failure of *Le Livre du peuple* to share the success of the *Paroles*. Whatever the reason, it remained a relatively unknown work among those for whom it was intended.[4]

Hitherto it has been supposed[5] that Lorymer's translation was the only one into English in this country. There was, however, at least[6] one other. It appeared the year after Lorymer's from Hedderwick's in Glasgow and Simpkin and Co. in London.[7] A notice of it appeared in the *Christian Reformer*, a unitarian review published by J. Hedderwick, a prominent unitarian who had achieved great success as a printer. He was appointed Queen's

[1] *Book of the People*, ch. xi, p. 49.

[2] *National*, 1839, p. 367.

[3] *Cleave's*, &c., i, No. 25, Saturday 31 March 1838.

[4] Many who had been acquainted with Lamennais's ideas in earlier times still watched his work. *Le Livre du peuple* (though probably not its translation) did not escape them (*Church of England Quarterly Review*, xxii, 1847, pp. 483 f.).

[5] F. Duine, *Essai de bibliographie de La Mennais*, and H. Talvart and J. Place, *Bibliographie des auteurs modernes de langue française*, &c., xi, *ad loc.* mention only Lorymer. The British Museum, Bodleian, and Cambridge University libraries have no record of any other translation.

[6] There may have been a third. The *English Catalogue*, records one published by William S. Orr and Co., 147 The Strand, 1839, 1*s.* 4*d.*—24 mo., of which there is no trace elsewhere.

[7] F. De Lamennais. *The Book of the People*. Translated from the French. Pocket Edition, pp. 87, Glasgow and London, 1839.

Printer for Glasgow in 1839, and printed chiefly religious books and periodicals.[1] Of Lamennais he said:

The ex-Abbé Lamennais, who once preached a crusade against liberalism and for the restoration of the papal dominion, is now the champion of democracy and of the religion of equality and philanthropy. His writings are said to produce a great effect in France. They consist of lofty declamation, oracular philosophic dicta, familiar imagery, appeals to the bitter experience of the masses, and millenial anticipations,—the whole tinged with the mysticism which has so great a charm for a class of modern readers.[2]

There followed a quotation of five lines in support of the abolition of capital punishment. Two years later, in the same magazine, an article on capital punishment quoted *Le Livre du peuple* once more in the same sense.[3] Agitation for this cause was much more an expression of radical views than it is today. Several years later still a letter to the same paper drew the attention of unitarians to Lamennais's translation of the Gospels and claimed to prove with a series of very obscure quotations that the views expressed in the notes to this translation presupposed unitarian sentiments.[4]

In view of the fact that the great unitarian Charles Beard wrote at some length about Lamennais,[5] it is possible that during his lifetime unitarians tried to obtain what support they could from his teaching. They were a more considerable body of religious opinion than they are now and played their own part in the politics of Dissent, which was closely associated with radicalism. Apart from these interesting hints, however, there is not much to suggest that Lamennais was any great help to them. Certainly the emphasis on trinitarianism in his later theology was far from their theological outlook, even if their political conclusions were similar.

These attempts to extract a practical programme from Lamennais's later works were, for the most part, ineffective. The need

[1] *Christian Pioneer*, November 1844, pp. 531 f.
[2] *Christian Reformer*, vi, 1839, p. 780.
[3] ibid., viii, 1841, p. 701.
[4] ibid., ii (N.S.), 1846, pp. 237 f. Letter dated London, 17 February 1846, and signed 'R.H.'.
[5] *Theological Review*, July 1873, pp. 339–64, and January 1874, pp. 70–98, 'A Group of French Friends'; see also 'Eugénie de Guérin', 1866, iii, pp. 501–26. The rest of the review associated Lamennais with other theological movements: e.g., Liberal Catholicism (iii, 1866, p. 455); Old Catholics (ix, 1872, p. 69); Vatican decrees (xii, 1875, p. 276).

which, before Kingsley, was felt by radicals and Chartists, and which Lamennais fulfilled, was not for a political policy but for its religious setting. It was this about Lamennais's work which affected Mazzini and his sympathizers, and which even touched the secularist Holyoake.

In its mildest form this attitude was passed on to the people through the family magazine of the day. The outstanding examples of this type were *Howitt's Journal of Literature and Popular Progress* and the *People's Journal.* These were not particularly meant to keep the people up to date with contemporary events, but rather to entertain and to make them aware of their potential power. It was in 1847 that the first picture of Lamennais appeared in the English press,[1] a large engraving in which H. Harrison portrayed him wearing an unpriestly redingote with a waistcoat and scarf.[2] This accompanied an article about him by Dr. Samuel Smiles, the famous author of many popular biographies, and the exponent of the 'self-help' philosophy. The keynote of the article, as indeed of the magazine, was progress. Lamennais was placed in the highest rank of the men of progress. He had worked for the elevation and emancipation of the universal people. He had fought for love, liberty, peace, and brotherhood. He was read everywhere in Europe, by rich and poor alike. He was a fit subject for superlatives: 'In Félicité Lamennais we find one of the most earnest of living men in the cause of human progress, one of the most courageous thinkers and writers, and one of the least selfish and most self-denying spirits of the age'.[3] Dr. Smiles, who had no great liking for the French people generally, did not spare himself in his praise of this Frenchman, and this article must have done much to clothe the skeletons of Lamennais's translated works with some biographical flesh. This is even more true of an article in the *People's Journal* by one Lacigogne,[4] which was less concerned with his ideas and ideals than with his surroundings, his street and his room. It described an intimate conversation with Lamennais, especially on subjects which could be expected to appeal to the average reader: the evils resulting from the lack of

[1] A crude engraving had accompanied Mazzini's article on Lamennais in *L'Apostolato Popolare*, 25 July 1841, p. 12.

[2] *Howitt's Journal*, ii, No. 28, 10 July 1847, p. 17.

[3] ibid., pp. 21 f.

[4] *People's Journal*, iv, pp. 205–9.

family life and the need for freedom. It established Lamennais as a celebrated sage favourable to the people's cause.

Outside this small circle of popular radicals and their sympathizers, Lamennais was little known. None of the poets or men of letters who claimed radical views took any notice of him, with the exception of Leigh Hunt,[1] who read him because he, Robert Owen, Parker, Foxton, and [probably Francis] Newman were 'brave and good hearts, and self-sacrificing consciences prepared to carry it [Christianity] as high as it can go, and thinking no earthly consideration paramount to the attainment of its heavenly ends . . .'.[2] and, later, John Payne, who shared Lamennais's outlook in many respects, although he was more interested in him from the literary than from the political or religious point of view.[3]

Later translations took Lamennais well outside revolutionary circles. The *Paroles* was translated several times[4]: in 1845 by the Reverend Edward Smith Pryce, a disestablishmentarian on the Church's left wing but scarcely qualified as an agitator[5]; in 1848 by an anonymous translator who, although he wished to take advantage of the 1848 revolutions, gently dissociated himself from the opinions of 'one of the greatest agitators of the epoch'[6]; and in 1891 by L. E. Martineau, who trusted that 'so splendid an example of undaunted faith and perseverance [would] be a help and encouragement to many an earnest though stumbling wayfarer along the road of progress'.[7] Martineau wrote on behalf of the Fabian Society.[8] It was perhaps fitting that Lamennais, who

[1] The *Avenir* had appreciated Hunt's (and Carlyle's) importance as early as 1830 (*Avenir*, 24 November 1830; *A.A.* i, p. 305).

[2] *The Autobiography of Leigh Hunt*, London, 1860, p. 436.

[3] J. Payne, *Songs of Life and Death*, London, 1872, pp. 120–33, 199–211; E. Starkie, *From Gautier to Eliot*, pp. 36 f.

[4] This takes no account of the translation by the Irish patriot, Garrad Dierlagh: *Words of a Believer*, translated by the author of *Erin's Island*, Paris (Belin), 1834.

[5] *Words of a Believer*, London, 1845. In the preface Pryce said that it contained 'many truths of great importance to man's social and religious well-being . . . presented in a form both powerful and attractive'.

[6] Translation of a preface by Loménie (F. Duine, *Essai de bibliographie de Félicité Robert de la Mennais*, 1923, p. 94) to the *Words of a Believer*—by the Abbé F. de Lamennais, Member of the National Assembly, London, 1848.

[7] Translator's preface to *Words of a Believer and the Past and Future of the People*, by F. Lamennais. Translated by L. E. Martineau. With a Memoir of Lamennais [by Mazzini], London, 1891.

[8] *Queen's Quarterly*, Kingston, U.S.A., xxvi, 1919, p. 444.

had been invoked to substantiate the claims of many types of agitators, should end the century by being used by those who worked for the gradual but relentless progress of society.[1]

It remains to consider what part, if any, Lamennais played in the development of communism in England.

The history of communism in England before Marx is very obscure and needs a careful study of its own. Some may find it difficult to distinguish between the more extreme utterances of what we have called the 'agitators' and communists proper, but nevertheless the distinction must be made. The agitators were not organized, neither did they subscribe to any one theory of society. They were concerned only with improving and if necessary changing the existing situation, and with awakening the people to a sense of their potentiality.

Communists, on the other hand, were organized according to a set political theory. Utopian communism was best represented in England by Robert Owen, but the failure of his experiments led to other attempts to promote a communistic way of life.

There were several of these, but before the advent of Marx the best known and the most widely recognized were those which had their origin on the Continent. One such was the *Bund der Gerechten*, which had been founded in Paris in 1836 by several hundred seceders from another secret society, the *Bund der Geächteten*.[2] Both of these societies were greatly influenced by the *Paroles*[3] and are even said to have adopted the *Paroles* for a short time as the basis of their plan of action.[4] Wilhelm Weitling, who after the *Paroles* became a firm disciple of Lamennais and who was to be one of the leaders of this type of communism for the next few years, joined the *Bund der Gerechten* in 1837.[5] In February 1840, a branch of the *Bund* was formed in London under the guise of the *London German Workers' Union*.[6] This branch eventually became the centre of the *Bund*'s activities when the Paris branch was closed down because of rioting.

[1] J. Poisson, *Le Romantisme social de Lamennais, essai sur la métaphysique des deux sociétés, 1833-1854*, Paris, 1932, pp. 23–29.

[2] See C. F. Wittke, *The Utopian Communist, a biography of Wilhelm Weitling*, Baton Rouge, Louisiana, 1950. [3] ibid., p. 20.

[4] *Science and Society*, xii, 1948, 'Marx and the Utopian Wilhelm Weitling' by Hans Mühlestein, pp. 115 f.

[5] Wittke, op. cit., p. 20.

[6] B. Nicolaievsky and Otto Maenchen-Helfen, *Karl Marx, Man and Fighter*, London, 1936, p. 109.

It would be reasonable to suppose that this London branch continued the policy of its parent in Paris, and that it paid high regard to Lamennais and the spirit of his later writing, but this appears not to have been the case, at least to start with. It very soon came under the control of Karl Schapper, the leader of the German members of the *Bund*, who was more interested in economic communism of the Marxist sort than in the vague utopian ideals of Weitling and Lamennais.

Schapper, however, did not have things all his own way. The leading journalist of the movement was Goodwyn Barmby. He edited the communist weekly *New Moral World*, the *Promethean or Communitarian Apostle*, and the *London Communist Chronicle*, which, although beyond advertising the English translations of the *Paroles* they did little openly to further Lamennais's ideas,[1] were yet conducted with the vagueness and rhetorical generalization which characterized the *Livre du peuple*. The *Promethean*, for example, abounded in theorizings of this sort: 'Nature is combined in complete unity, and so should society be. Love, the one in all, should rule the world'.[2] Barmby tried to do what Lamennais did, but with less precision: to weave humanitarian ideals into the pattern of Christian doctrine while denying the dogmatic assumptions from which the ideals themselves sprang.[3] Needless to say, Barmby was a supporter of Weitling and gave him an enthusiastic welcome when he came to England in the summer of 1844. He compared the impact of Weitling's *Evangelium* (which had appeared in 1843, owed a lot to Lamennais, but was repudiated by him)[4] to the impact of the *Paroles*.[5]

The nature of the conflict among communists in England had already been made apparent by Friedrich Engels, who was writing at that time for the *New Moral World*. He saw that what was usually called communism meant different things in different countries. Thus for the English it was something practical, for the French something political, and for the Germans something philosophical. But he saw a further difference in that the communism of devout England was mainly atheistic and the communism of infidel France mainly Christian. He therefore undertook to

[1] *Promethean*, i, 1842, Nos. 2 and 3, pp. 40 and 56.

[2] ibid., i, No. 1, p. 2.

[3] He refers to Christ as the half man, half God, Joshua ben Joseph (ibid., p. 3).

[4] Wittke, op. cit., p. 77.

[5] Th. Frost, *Forty Years' Recollections*, London, 1880, p. 60.

describe the communists of the Continent,[1] among whom he included Lamennais,[2] with a view to setting them in their proper context. Although he did not actually say so, it is clear that he was disturbed that the Christian motives of some of the Continental revolutionaries had been distorted and misused, largely through the ignorance of Englishmen, and allowed to degenerate into sentimentality, which held back real economic progress.

In spite of this warning, Weitling was warmly greeted when he arrived in London. G. J. Holyoake said: 'Not only will the interchange of valuable ideas, hitherto finding no vent, necessarily work important changes, but the refined ardour of our German friend will infuse a spirit of poetry over the hitherto dull and tame character of English Communism'.[3] Holyoake was one of those who welcomed the influence of ideas expressed in the manner of Lamennais.[4]

There is, however, no evidence that Weitling ever gained the ascendancy over the communists in London.[5] In spite of the considerable body of support which he seems to have had before his arrival, he was constantly defeated on issues which affected the leadership by the more practical Schapper.

The views of Weitling and of his disciple Kriege were effectively killed by the Brussels conference of 11th May 1846. The pretext for this meeting was the continued publication in the U.S.A. by Kriege of a communistic journal, the *Volkstribun*. The *Volkstribun* was an embarrassment to serious-minded communists because it refused, as it seemed to its opponents, to face facts, but concentrated on vague philosophizing. All those present at the meeting,[6] with the exception of Weitling, agreed that the *Volkstribun* was not really communistic at all, that its childish pomposity was

[1] *New Moral World*, v, 3rd series, 4 November 1843, No. 19, pp. 145 f., 'The Progress of Social Reform on the Continent', reprinted in *Marx-Engels Gesamtausgabe*, Abt. I, Bd. ii, pp. 435–42. I have been unable to see the original, as this number is missing from the files in the principal libraries. A facsimile is printed in the *Marx-Engels Gesamtausgabe*.

[2] *Marx-Engels Gesamtausgabe*, I, ii, p. 442.

[3] *The Movement*, ed. G. J. Holyoake assisted by M. Q. Ryall, 1843-5, p. 367.

[4] His journal, *The Reasoner*, printed a glowing tribute to Lamennais when he died (Sunday 12 March 1854, p. 182).

[5] Wittke, op. cit., pp. 101 f.

[6] For the full texts and details of the participants, see *Marx-Engels Gesamtausgabe*, I, vi, pp. 3–21.

compromising and that its 'enthusiasm' was demoralizing. A letter was sent to Kriege explaining these resolutions in greater detail. Among the explanations are two of especial interest. The letter accuses Kriege of defending people like Lamennais and Börne against others like Proudhon and Cabet:

Dass die deutschen Kommunisten eben so weit über Börne hinaus sind, wie die französischen über Lamennais, hätte Kriege schon in Deutschland, Brüssel und London lernen können.[1]

The final blow was even more forthright:

Wenn Kriege nichts Besseres vorzubringen weiss, als diese erbärmlich stilisierten Sentimentalitäten, so täte er allerdings klüger, seinen 'Vater Lamennais' in jeder Nummer des Volkstribunen aber- und abermals zu übersetzen.[2]

These explicit condemnations show that the name of Lamennais was still prominent among certain communists, on the Continent,[3] in England, and in the U.S.A., but that for orthodox communists it was anathema from that time onwards. Certainly British communists, who were more concerned with facts than with theories or even ideals, paid no further attention to him. Even if they, following the example of the Chartist Harney, had done so, they would have deferred to his reputation but differed from his ideas. Lamennais, at least at the time of the *Livre du peuple*, saw in primitive Christianity the ideal form of communism; on the other hand, the communists who praised him believed first in communism and supported their belief by appealing to Christianity.[4]

[1] *Marx-Engels Gesamtausgabe*, I, vi, p. 10.

[2] ibid., p. 19.

[3] Marx had wanted Lamennais to edit the Paris edition of a bilingual review, *Annales franco-allemandes*. In refusing, Lamennais had concealed his socialism in what was for Marx's emissary, Ruge, a metaphysical haze (A. Ruge, *Zwei Jahre in Paris*, Leipzig, 1846, i, pp. 146–51).

[4] A. Cornu, *Karl Marx et Friedrich Engels*, Paris, 1958, ii, pp. 148 f.

VII

LAMENNAIS IN THE TWENTIETH CENTURY

'It would be difficult', wrote W. E. H. Lecky, 'to find in all literature more fiery, more eloquent and more uncompromising denunciations of the existing fabric of society than are contained in the later writings of Lamennais'.[1] Because the fabric of society which Lamennais denounced has largely crumbled, he has in many ways been vindicated as a true prophet[2]; and because his revolutionary ideas were rooted in his religious beliefs, interest in them has remained, despite the changed circumstances.[3] Above all, his striking personality has continued in this country to invite closer attention to his teaching.

As far as Continental politics are concerned, the line of development between Lamennais and modern Christian democracy has been drawn and commented upon.[4] The programme of the *Avenir*, worked out as it was within the context of the revolutionary Europe of 1830, has much in common with the programme of those Christians whose concern for the social order springs from their belief. In England, however, things have developed differently. No political party is more noticeably representative of Christian beliefs about the social order than any other, and it is certainly doubtful whether Lamennais can, for example, meaningfully be called 'a distant forerunner of the British Labour Party'.[5]

[1] W. E. H. Lecky, *Democracy and Liberty*, ii, London, 1896, pp. 221 f.

[2] Two American authors have taken this view and claimed to see in Lamennais's teaching warnings about the future of democratic society: R. Roberts, 'A neglected Apostle of Liberty' in *The Nation*, New York, 1918, 14 February, p. 180, and 28 February, p. 233; and W. G. Jordan, 'A Modern Prophet—Lamennais' in the *Queen's Quarterly*, Kingston, U.S.A., xxvi, April-June 1919, pp. 432–47.

[3] e.g. Tom Bryan, *Visions of the People, Taken from Lamennais' 'Words of a Believer'*, London, 1914.

[4] Michael P. Fogarty, *Christian Democracy in Western Europe, 1820–1953*, London, 1957, pp. 155 f.; R. Havard de la Montagne, *Histoire de la démocratie chrétienne de Lamennais à Georges Bidault*, Paris, 1948.

[5] Philip Spencer, 'Prophet without dishonour' in *The Listener*, 25 March 1954, p. 537.

In France Louis de Villefosse has derided those who have treated Lamennais as the precursor of Bidault and Adenauer.[1] He has preferred to regard him less as a reformer than as a revolutionary, the first Christian revolutionary.[2] This view was also taken in England by G. D. H. Cole. He wrote enthusiastically of Lamennais's role in preparing for the socialist revolution.[3] He placed less emphasis upon Lamennais's foreshadowing of modern Trade Unionism and co-operation (in which Lamennais was by no means alone) than upon the revolutionary nature of his teaching. In this way he diminished the difference between Lamennais and Marx. 'Lamennais', he claimed, 'influenced Marx a good deal more than Marx himself realised'.[4] For him, 'one of the greatest documents in the history of the idea of the class struggle'[5] was Lamennais's 'striking essay',[6] *De l'esclavage moderne*, the language of which he likened to that of the *Communist Manifesto*. Several years earlier Harold Laski had made a similar comparison when he called the *Paroles* 'a lyrical version of the *Communist Manifesto*'.[7] Cole, on the other hand, did not see the *Paroles* in this light. For him it was a human work, 'throbbing with pity for the sufferings of the poor and with anger against the evil-doing of the powerful, and fervently calling upon the workers to join forces in order to throw off the yoke of the servitude that bears them down and denies to them the elemental rights of men'.[8]

Cole was careful not to attribute to Lamennais a later social theory which he did not hold.[9] His importance as a forerunner of socialism lay principally in his passionate interest in the welfare of the people, allied as this was with his religious belief. 'His thought was, from first to last, profoundly religious: he could not understand any morality that was not rooted in faith in God'.[10] This is true as far as it goes, but it does not go far enough in considering what Lamennais meant when he talked in the later part of his life of 'faith' and 'God'.

[1] L. de Villefosse, 'Lamennais dans son époque et dans la nôtre' in *Europe*, February-March 1954, p. 18.

[2] ibid., p. 24.

[3] G. D. H. Cole, *Socialist Thought, the Forerunners 1789–1850*, London, 1953, pp. 189–200.

[4] ibid., p. 199.

[5] ibid.

[6] ibid., p. 193.

[7] H. J. Laski, *Authority in the Modern State* (1919), New Haven, 1927, p. 255.

[8] Cole, op. cit., p. 192.

[9] ibid., p. 189.

[10] ibid., p. 198.

There is a similar ambiguity about Cole's reference to Lamennais as the direct progenitor of much Christian Socialist doctrine.[1] Interested though some Christian Socialists were in his socialism, Lamennais came to it at a stage in his life when his theology had ceased to hold much interest for later generations of Christians. Miss Ruth Kenyon, one of the editors of *Christendom, a Journal of Christian Sociology*, claimed that the real point of contact between Lamennais and the socialist strain in the Anglo-Catholic movement was not his political beliefs but his theology of the 1830 period. The balance of the transcendental and the immanental, the awareness that the divine society had a mission within the world, was, she believed, the message of the *Avenir* and Hurrell Froude, of Stewart Headlam and the *Lux Mundi* group of liberal Anglican Catholics, and later of Canon P. E. T. Widdrington and the Church Socialist League.[2] Canon Widdrington himself showed the historical differences between the situation on the Continent and the situation in England at the beginning of the Oxford movement. He even set it on record that in matters of politics he believed Lamennais to be wrong: 'History will probably confirm Pius IX's opinion of Liberalism rather than that of Lamennais'.[3] But he acknowledged that the questions which the Christian sociologist must continually ask, 'What is the Church and what ought to be the relation of the Church to society?' were first posed on the Continent.[4] For that reason Christian Socialists should find Lamennais's life instructive still.

This tension between the transcendental and the immanental was seen rather differently by Harold Laski. In one of the best treatments of Lamennais in England, *Authority in the Modern State*, he used Lamennais to describe the dilemma of the nineteenth century. 'He remains as the champion of two mighty causes which still battle for the empire of the mind'.[5] These two were order and liberty. Laski saw Lamennais as a valuable example of one who perceived clearly and rejected the errors of the French Revolution, who strained every nerve to re-establish in French

[1] Cole, op. cit., p. 199, above, p. 152.

[2] Ruth Kenyon, 'The Social Aspect of the Catholic Revival' in *Northern Catholicism*, ed. N. P. Williams, London, 1933, pp. 367–400.

[3] P. E. T. Widdrington, 'The Social Mission of the Catholic Revival, I—Our Inheritance' in *Christendom*, June 1932, ii, No. 6, p. 98, note 6.

[4] ibid., pp. 95 f. See also W. G. Peck, *The Social Implications of the Oxford Movement*, New York, 1933.

[5] Laski, op. cit., p. 190.

life the sense of order which the Revolution had destroyed, but who at the same time recognized that it contained political truths fundamental to a creative understanding of modern life. 'There is a sense indeed in which his career is little less than the mirror of his age'.[1]

Perhaps it was *this* tension which evoked a response in Anglican theology. The religion and theology of the Church of England during this century have been moulded by the thought of the Oxford movement—not by the Anglican papalists, who sought to restore order to the Church at the expense of liberty, but by the liberal Catholics, who wanted to strengthen teaching about the Church and the sacraments, while at the same time encouraging scientific study of the Bible and the Fathers. A combination of sound scholarship and Catholic outlook has been characteristic of many of the best Anglican scholars of this century.

The shape of Anglican theology in these years has been largely influenced by the work of Bishop Gore. We may agree with Dr. Carpenter when he says, 'Whatever place future historians assign Charles Gore, it must be acknowledged that he was virtually without parallel as a theological force in his own time and that his method and approach to theology continue to exercise a not inconsiderable influence in Anglican thought'.[2] The method referred to is one unfettered by any imposed pattern of thought, but controlled by Scripture and the tradition of the Church. Gore was impatient of any doctrinal rigidity which tried to assert that one pattern of truth had to be accepted or rejected as it stood. For him it was more important that a truth should be understood than that it was expressed in traditional language.

At first sight it might seem that Lamennais is anything but liberal in this sense of the word, and that Gore's high view of reason contrasts strongly with Lamennais's disdain of it. And yet on this vital point it is remarkable how closely Gore's thought coincides with that of the author of the *Essai sur l'indifférence*. Gore's idea of development is not greatly different from that which appears in the *Essai* and which is developed in the *Avenir*. According to Gore, it is the function of the Church 'to enter boldly into the thought and imagination and science of its time, adopting,

[1] Laski, op. cit., p. 189.

[2] James Carpenter, *Gore: a Study in Liberal Catholic Thought*, London, 1960, p. 10.

appropriating or rejecting, and so fashioning its theology, which will be in a measure different for every epoch and for every century'.[1]

This similarity is probably not accidental. As early as 1895 Gore was conducting a correspondence with Wilfrid Ward about Lamennais and Newman's idea of development.[2] Regrettably all trace of this correspondence is now lost, except for one letter which summarizes his view of development with admirable clarity: 'I see two processes. (1) A dogmatic development always tending to increased definition and therefore limitation. (2) A continual checking of this process by historical criticism and Biblical counterpoise'.[3] If this correspondence had survived we should have been able to judge how far Lamennais's mode of thought appealed to Gore. Gore had been a founder-member of the C.S.U., whose publication, *The Economic Review*, had shown respect for Lamennais's social teaching,[4] and as late as 1923 Gore recorded in his diary that he had read *Paroles d'un croyant*.[5]

The affinities between the two men were great: both were prophets, both were accused of unorthodoxy, both were deeply concerned with social problems, and both were convinced of the mission of the Church to society. There was some truth in Hensley Henson's remark, made apropos of Gore's contribution to *Lux Mundi*, that 'he would play in the Church of England a part similar to that which, earlier in the century, Lamennais had played *mutatis mutandis* in the Church of France'.[6] In these circumstances it is not surprising that when C. S. Phillips's book *The Church in France 1789–1848* appeared in 1929, one of its reviewers opined that 'most readers will probably prefer the chapters dealing with Lamennais',[7] 'by far the most celebrated of the prophets of the Counter-Revolution—the brilliant, wayward, unhappy genius . . . that "pilgrim of eternity" who sought

[1] Gore, 'Dogma in the Early Church' in *History in Dogma and Thought*, ed. W. R. Matthews, p. 74, cited Carpenter, op. cit., p. 130.

[2] G. L. Prestige, *Life of Charles Gore*, London, 1935, p. 173.

[3] Letter dated 22 November (1895?) in the possession of Mrs. Sheed, Messrs. Sheed and Ward, London.

[4] See above, p. 158.

[5] Prestige, *Life of Charles Gore*, p. 470.

[6] H. Henson, *Retrospect of an Unimportant Life*, i, London, 1942, p. 155.

[7] Canon H. Maynard Smith, *Church Quarterly Review*, April 1930, p. 172.

truth at the bottom of every well in turn, yet seemed doomed never to find it'.[1]

In recent years an interesting attitude to the general lines of Lamennais's thought has been adopted by the Church of Rome. Although respectful tribute has been paid to the *Essai sur l'indifférence*[2] (and indeed there is less reason now than in 1870 to see its teaching as dangerous) it has had little influence upon Catholic apologetic in recent times. Similarly, in social questions, Roman Catholicism in this country has been little affected by Continental Christian democracy.[3] But in the matter of relations between Church and State and in the wider question of religious liberty, the temper of Lamennais's mind has been matched in modern times.

Both Gregory XVI[4] and Pius IX[5] condemned the teaching of the *Avenir* and many of the implications of its teaching on these questions. In recent years, however, both Lamennais's ideal of an autonomous Church within a secular State and his complementary view of religious liberty have gained such widespread acceptance that they have been given conciliar authority. For long it has been held that religious toleration and the total separation of Church and State, as practised in the U.S.A., are allowable as long as they produce healthy results,[6] but recently a more positive approach has been discernible. Father John Courtney Murray, S.J., an authority on relations between Church and State, has argued that the sort of state envisaged by the constitution of the U.S.A. is that which is most likely to offer 'to the Church as the Christian people a means, through its free political institutions, of achieving harmony between law and social organization and the demands of their Christian conscience'.[7] Father Murray makes

[1] C. S. Phillips, *The Church in France 1789–1848*, London, 1929, p. 216.

[2] H. G. Schenk, 'Lamennais 1782–1854' in *The Month*, January 1954, p. 157.

[3] H. Somerville, *Studies in the Catholic Social Movement*, London, 1933, does not mention Lamennais at all.

[4] *Mirari vos*, 15 August 1832, H. Denzinger, *Enchiridion Symbolorum*, Freiburg, 1937, paras. 1614–16.

[5] *Syllabus errorum*, 8 December 1864, Denzinger, op. cit., paras. 1715–18 and 1755.

[6] E. E. Y. Hales, *The Catholic Church in the Modern World*, New York, 1960, pp. 94 f.; J. Lecler, S.J., *The Two Sovereignties*, London, 1952, pp. 174 f. (translated from *L'Église et la souveraineté de l'État*, Paris, 1946).

[7] Vidler, pp. 273 f., who quotes from *Thought: Fordham University Quarterly*, xxvi, No. 102 (1951), p. 447. See also J. C. Murray, *We Hold These Truths*, London, 1960.

this claim, which amounts to a plea for the separation of Church and State according to the American pattern, not as a rebel aligning himself with Lamennais against the nineteenth-century popes, but as one who believes that the Church's condemnation of the teaching of the *Avenir* was based upon acquaintance with the absolutist States of the Continent.[1] Father Murray's preference for a free Church in a free State is more closely akin to that of Lamennais and Montalembert than to that of Cavour. He is still not without opposition.[2] Yet, the fact that he was invited to the second session of the Vatican Council and that he was largely responsible for drafting the decree on religious liberty leaves no room for doubt that Pius IX's bald condemnation of the proposition 'ecclesia a statu statusque ab Ecclesia seiungendus est'[3] was not the last word on the subject.

It would be unwise to attribute this development in the outlook of the Roman Catholic Church (and it is a development no longer confined to the U.S.A.) principally or even partly to Lamennais; but it is a further indication that, although most of his writings have now been overtaken by events, many of the problems with which he wrestled still remain to be solved.

Dr. Vidler concluded his *Prophecy and Papacy* with a reflection on the perennial tension in history between the priest and the prophet.[4] This tension is particularly relevant to the early years of Lamennais's life, which Vidler was studying, and is illustrated by Lamennais's relation to the growth of English Roman Catholicism between Emancipation and the first Vatican Council. During that time the ferment in all forms of thought was so great that, in order to preserve her stability, the Church had to lay unusual emphasis upon her priestly function and upon the virtue of obedience. On one level, Lamennais was a victim of this struggle.

Another nineteenth-century tension, which appears more clearly in the way his views were received in England, is the tension between scepticism and faith. A reviewer of Sir Harold

[1] See his articles in *Theological Studies*, xiv, 1953, 'Leo XIII on Church and State', pp. 1–30; 'Leo XIII: Separation of Church and State', pp. 145–214; 'Leo XIII: Two Concepts of Government', pp. 551–67.

[2] See Vidler, p. 274; M. Novak, *The Open Church*, London, 1964, pp. 257 f.; X. Rynne, *The Second Session*, London, 1964, p. 192.

[3] Denzinger, *Enchiridion Symbolorum*, para. 1755, p. 488.

[4] Vidler, pp. 275–84.

Nicolson's *Sainte-Beuve* complained that the problem of the 'Unwilling Sceptic' had been inadequately dealt with and that too little had been said about Lamennais.[1] This is the thread which runs through all Lamennais's works, for they derive their consistency from their author's overwhelming desire to bring about the regeneration of society, and from his persistence in expressing himself in religous terms. But the religion had to change in order to fit the facts of society.

This obsession with the welfare of man at the expense of a direct and simple faith in Christian truth was the spectre haunting every type of religious movement in the nineteenth century. It was the 'ill flavour' which Newman noticed about Lamennais's teaching.[2] It was the 'literature of desperation' which Carlyle deplored.[3] It was the 'unhealthy eloquence' condemned by Acton.[4] All those who read Lamennais were aware, consciously or unconsciously, that the lucid expositions and trenchant commentaries on the age were not all that they appeared to be: they were a cover for very disturbing doubts. This did not affect the validity of the policies and even of the doctrines which Lamennais advocated, but it did leave his readers with a sense of apprehension. Outward forms were being retained but their religious content was being gradually changed.

This tension between faith and scepticism was what troubled the Tractarians about him and what made those of them who were sympathetic to him as a person return time and time again to the 'tragedy' of his life.[5] It was not simply a personal tragedy. It summed up what they could dimly foresee as a danger to faith in the future. The same was even more true of the English liberal Catholics, who were very uneasy about Lamennais's middle 'liberal' period and yet deplored his early ultramontanism.

[1] *The Listener*, June 1957, p. 967.
[2] Above, p. 109.
[3] Above, p. 41.
[4] Above, p. 135.
[5] In 1860, when Dr. Rowland Williams was being assailed on all sides for his essay on Biblical Criticism in *Essays and Reviews*, he turned to Lamennais: 'Read a little of *Paroles d'un Croyant* by Lamennais. The book is a remarkable one for a Romish priest to have got to, but quite one-sided and inconsiderate in its declamation against wealth and government.' But the main part is still to come: he uses Lamennais as the source of a meditation on whether it is better to resign a sacred function when one finds one's self out of sympathy with the Church or to adhere inconsistently (*Life and Letters of Rowland Williams*, 2 vols., London, 1874, ii, p. 13).

The tension in their sphere of activity was not between faith and scepticism (as it was, however, for liberal *Protestants*) but between faith and science. They were certain that ultimately these two could be reconciled. They were only anxious to avoid any action by either side which would make that outcome impossible. Lamennais was a threat to reconciliation, because he introduced doubt by undermining first science and then faith. It was this double action which Acton was regretting when he referred to the 'subtle influence of the theories of Lamennais',[1] and which eventually made Lamennais so congenial to the modernists. For it was in modernism that outward forms and personal piety were combined with scepticism in matters of belief. This was no mere insincerity. It was an attempt to express in terms of contemporary thought the view that Christianity was standing at a cross-roads.

The only realm in which this tension was not strongly felt was among socialists, and it was as a man of the Left that Lamennais was most superficially portrayed in England. Engels grasped and condemned (and, on his own premisses, rightly condemned) the contradiction in Lamennais's social theories,[2] which were more personal to Lamennais himself than his truly religious beliefs. Mazzini alone was more perceptive than the other popular reformers. He saw the tension and described it as the 'double impulse' of faith and conscience.[3] The fact that at the century's end interest in Lamennais was not diminishing may be interpreted in a number of ways. It may be interpreted as an academic examination of the past; or as an attempt to justify certain lines of belief or action already taken by reference to past disputes; or simply as interest in a person who was more than usually involved in the century's movements of thought. These explanations are justified by some of the facts. But behind them all is the awareness, at least as far as England was concerned, that Lamennais in some way epitomized the century; that in his life was the century's struggle between scepticism and faith, and that that struggle would not be concluded merely by the complete victory of one side or the other. In the last century this tension was still felt to be revolutionary. Now it has sunk deep into common belief and is accepted by many Christians as part of the nature of religion itself.

[1] Above, p. 135. [2] Above, p. 184.
[3] Above, p. 173.

Laski summed up the impression that Lamennais's life had made, at least in England, in these words:

> It is the dramatic quality of his challenge to those whom he had so splendidly led which gives him in the nineteenth century a place at once exceptional and important. He dare not be forgotten so long as men are willing to examine the principles upon which their life is founded. For few have faced so courageously the difficulties of existence. None has suffered more nobly in the effort to confound them.[1]

[1] H. J. Laski, *Authority in the Modern State*, p. 190.

APPENDIX A

Unpublished letter from Lamennais to MacCarthy among the Houghton MSS, at Trinity College, Cambridge

La Chenaie, le 9 decbre, 1832

Vous savez d'avance, mon cher enfant, combien votre lettre du 15 novembre m'a fait de plaisir sous plusieurs rapports. D'un autre côté elle m'afflige, et bien vivement, pour ce que vous me dites de vos chagrins personnels. Je prie Dieu du fond de mon ame [*sic*] qu'il les adoucisse, ou, si ce n'est pas sa sainte volonté, qu'il vous accorde la grâce nécessaire, pour qu'ils déviennent [*sic*] par la patience, la résignation, l'amour avec lesquels vous les supporterez, cette Croix Salutaire que doivent porter, à la suite de Jésus-Christ, tous ses vrais disciples. La souffrance est plus que jamais leur état en ce monde. Ce temps est pour eux en réalité le temps de la Passion.[1] Voyez ce qui se passe, et dites-moi si rien jamais ressembla plus aux derniers jours de la synagogue, et si le Christ moqué des uns, trahi des autres, persécuté par tous, ne monte pas, sous nos yeux, une séconde [*sic*] fois sur le Calvaire? Aussi la race humaine éprouve-t-elle en soi quelque chose d'extraordinaire. On dirait que la vie lui échappe avec la vérité. Il y a dans le fond des cœurs comme une angoisse inexprimable, et de temps en temps il en sort des cris qui font frissonner. Cela se voit mieux encore ici que là où vous êtes. Les uns, sentant que tout s'ébranle, se cramponnent dans les ténèbres au monde matériel; les autres gravissent sur les montagnes pour découvrir dans le ciel désert les premiers rayons d'un nouveau soleil. Il y a des pleurs, des rires effrayants, des gémissements sourds et concentrés, des prières, des blasphèmes, des silences qui glacent l'ame [*sic*], et puis tout d'un coup une grande voix, une voix universelle: *Ut quid derelequisti me!*[2] N'en doutons pas cette

[1] cf. a letter to the Comtesse de Senfft, 15 March 1833: 'L'humanité est partout dans un état extraordinaire d'angoisse. Pour moi, je regarde le temps où nous sommes comme les heures de sa passion: entrez dans les détails et vous verrez si quelque chose y manque. Le genre humain est sur la croix et j'en conclus que le salut est proche' (cited Le Hir, *Paroles d'un croyant*, Paris, 1949, pp. 58 f.).

[2] In a letter to Milnes, 26 January 1833, MacCarthy cites this passage: 'What do you think about this? For my part I am afraid to think about anything.' The reference is to Matt. xxvii. 46 and Mark xv. 34.

époque étonnante et sinistre marquera dans le cours des âges un moment solennel. Est-ce le travail de l'enfantement? Est-ce l'agonie de la fin? Dieu le sait. Il me semble, pour moi, que le genre humain n'a pas, à beaucoup près, accompli encore ses destinées terrestres, qu'il doit, avant de mourir, révenir [*sic*] pour Jésus-Christ à l'unité de son origine, et que dès lors, la révolution qui s'opère sous nos regards, n'est que le commencement d'un nouveau cycle, d'une nouvelle période de son existence. Quels changements amènera-t-elle dans ce qui est, dans ce qui a été? Il est difficile, impossible de le dire. Seulement, on est chaque jour forcément conduit à penser qu'ils seront plus vastes, plus profonds qu'on ne l'imaginoit la veille. De là cette anxiété dont je parlois tout-à-l'heure et qui augmente sans cesse. Ce n'est pas telle idée, telle opinion plus ou moins répandue qui me frappe, mais l'ébranlement universel de toutes les opinions et de toutes les idées, une certaine impuissance de s'attacher à rien, de se reposer en rien de connu. Les hommes étouffent dans le vieux monde qu'ont habité leurs pères. Ce n'est pas raisonnement, calcul, volonté délibérée, mais le résultat d'une cause sécrète [*sic*], cachée dans les entrailles de l'humanité, de je ne sais quoi d'instinctif, d'organique si on peut le dire. Or, voyant cela, il est entièrement hors de mon pouvoir de m'intéresser beaucoup desormais [*sic*] à tout ce qui regarde l'affaire qui m'avoit conduit à Rome. Il s'agit aujourd'hui de bien autre chose, et quoique nous ne devions pas, dans l'ordre de la Providence, négliger rien de ce qui, de près ou de loin, peut ressembler à un devoir, néanmoins les questions sur lesquelles on me chicane, sont enveloppées dans tout autres questions et paroissent si petites dans celles-ci, qu'il n'y a pas lieu de s'en occuper avec la suite et l'activité qu'on mettroit à une chose d'importance. Le mouvement de la société, qui devient plus rapide d'heure en heure, les laissera bientôt en arrière. Toutefois, je le regrète [*sic*], il nous reste toujours néanmoins une sorte de devoir personnel à remplir, et pour faire jusqu'au bout ce que Dieu semblera demander de nous à cet egard, il nous sera fort utile, mon cher enfant, que vous veuilliez bien continuer de m'avertir de ce qui se passe à Rome, des démarches de nos adversaires, des jugements qu'on en porte, et des dispositions particulières du Pape. Peut-être lui adresserons-nous un travail sur la censure épiscopale, avec un autre mémoire sur un point de doctrine, au sujet duquel il seroit, à mon avis, très-important que les catholiques sussent exactement à quoi s'en tenir. Mais je n'ai encore aucun parti décidément pris sur tout cela. Ecrivez-moi le plus souvent et le plus longuement que vous le pourrez. Vos lettres me consolent; elles font que nous sommes moins séparés. Notre petite colonie de la Chenaie s'est augmentée de deux personnes, et j'en attends encore deux autres. Que deviendra ce frêle et imperceptible germe? Ce que Dieu voudra: nous n'en savons que cela, et cela doit nous suffire. Ménagez votre santé; chauffez-vous, quoiqu'en disent les romains, qui croient faire merveille de boire par tous les pores la moiteur glacée de leur humide hiver. Ici, point de gelée jusqu'à présent, mais une température fort douce. Ce seroit presque le printemps, si l'air étoit plus sec. Il y a bien de l'affinité entre la grande et la petite Bretagne, et je le sais surtout à la tendresse que m'inspire mon cher enfant.

[The letter is unsigned.]

Three words on the outside are difficult to decipher:

Al ? ? ? C. Maccarthy,
al Collegio degli Inglesi,
Roma.

APPENDIX B

The First English Translation of the Paroles

The *Paroles* was published on 30th April 1834.[1] On 8th June Lamennais wrote to Montalembert saying that two translations of the book, one Italian and one English, had already been made.[2] As far as the English one was concerned, it seems that Lamennais's information was inaccurate. In a letter of 21st June MacCarthy wrote to Lamennais:

J'ai fait dernièrement la connaissance d'un savant anglais, le docteur Foster [*sic*], homme très remarquable sous tous les rapports. Il s'est fait catholique il y a quelques ans, et s'est beaucoup occupé de vos ouvrages, qu'il a répandus entre ses amis et ses connaissances, surtout à Cambridge. Il a même publié, je crois, une démonstration de votre doctrine sur le fondement de la certitude, avec des illustrations fort curieuses. Il est astronome de profession, et l'ami intime de Herschel.[3]

MacCarthy went on to call him 'l'Anglais le plus avancé que j'aie rencontré jusqu'ici dans les matières philosophiques'.[4] He reminded Lamennais that Forster had sent him from Brussels a large parcel of books which had never been acknowledged.[5] He concluded: 'Il a maintenant le projet de traduire le livre que vous venez de publier, et de le répandre en Angleterre'.[6] After having received this letter Lamennais wrote, on 9th July: 'Une dame anglaise et un savant très distingué nommé Forster, ami d'Herschell, ont dû aussi ou doivent le traduire en anglais'.[7]

Lamennais therefore mentions two translators: Dr. Forster, about whom he had heard from MacCarthy, and 'une dame anglaise'. We do not know from whom he heard about the latter. To these two we may add the Reverend J. E. Smith, who was mentioned by G. J. Harney as the probable translator.[8]

[1] See the reference in Vidler, p. 244.

[2] *L. à M.*, p. 281 (8 June 1834) and p. 289 (25 June 1834). On 15 June he wrote to L. de Potter that translations of the *Paroles* into English, Italian, Swedish, Dutch, and Polish had already been announced (*Revue de France*, v, 1935, p. 634).

[3] *Portefeuille*, pp. 152 f.

[4] ibid., p. 153.

[5] Lamennais said that he had not received this, nor had he had any letter from the doctor (*Revue bleue*, ix, January-June 1898, p. 492, letter to d'Alzon, 22 July 1834).

[6] *Portefeuille*, p. 153.

[7] *L. à M.*, p. 299.

[8] *Open Court*, 1891, p. 2960.

Dr. Forster

Thomas Ignatius Maria Forster, M.D., was born in 1789 and died in 1860.[1] Between 1820 and 1824 he was preparing the *Perennial Calendar*, a collection of miscellaneous information about flowers, physical oddities, feasts, and saints, published under each day of the year. His studies in connection with this work converted him to Roman Catholicism. From 1833 onwards he spent most of his time at Bruges. He published several curious works, including *Recueil de ma vie, mes ouvrages et mes pensées* (Frankfurt, 1835; 3rd edition, Brussels, 1837), the autobiographical part of which contains no reference to Lamennais, although there is this passage about him under the heading 'Méditation philosophique':

Ce savant homme M. l'abbé de La Mennais me semble être tombé dans une grande erreur quand il propose à l'individu de faire fonder toute croyance individuelle sur la tradition générale: il est vrai qu'en examinant la vérité de certaines propositions, en particulier, nous devons nous appuyer sur l'opinion publique. Il est vrai aussi que la croyance en Dieu et bien d'autres vérités nous sont enseignées par la tradition. Mais si nous poussons notre sophisme encore un peu plus loin, il est facile de voir l'imperfection de cette épreuve. Car avant de se fier au témoignage, il faut s'assurer de l'existence des témoins!

Pour vous faire voir, lecteur philosophique, l'absurdité ou au moins la faillibilité de cet argument, il faut vous entretenir des songes . . . Celle-ci est la plus horrible forme du scepticisme à laquelle notre raison orgueilleuse peut nous conduire.[2]

The only quotations are from works written by Lamennais while he was still comparatively orthodox.[3]

Forster's rigid ultramontanism, which remained after 1834 as before, suggests that he was not a probable person to have undertaken to translate the *Paroles*. Since there is no evidence, and, indeed, in view of the above passage, it is extremely unlikely that MacCarthy's information about Forster's interest in Lamennais is accurate, and since in other respects MacCarthy's information is far from reliable, we can conclude that MacCarthy was wrong in believing that Dr. Forster was the translator.

[1] Biographical details from *D.N.B.*, *ad loc.*

[2] *Recueil*, &c., Brussels, 1837, pp. 44 f.

[3] Forster, *Epistolarium or Fasciculi of Curious Letters*, &c., Bruges, 1845, pp. 32 and 92.

'Une dame anglaise'

On 26th July an announcement appeared in the *Crisis* (The National Co-operative Trades' Union Gazette) of the forthcoming publication of the *Words of a Believer*, 'translated into English by a Lady'. It assured the public that the abbé had formerly been the right-hand man of His Holiness. The work was 'calculated to give satisfaction to all parties' because it taught 'the doctrines of a new and more equable [*sic*] state of society'. Nevertheless it abode 'by the original and fundamental principles and precepts of the Christian religion'.[1]

As far as we know, there has been no speculation among scholars about the identity of this lady, because until recently there have been no clues. But in the unpublished Memoirs of Gertrude Tennant there is a passage which reveals that when only fifteen years old she determined to translate the *Paroles* in order to ensure that her name was ever associated with Lamennais. Born on 9th November 1819, married in 1847 to Charles Tennant, M.P. for St. Albans, and dying in 1918, she was the daughter of Admiral Collier, who, as a Captain, lived in France to escape his creditors.[2] This is the account of her introduction to Lamennais's work:

Among my pleasant recollections were the occasional visits of an old French lady. She came curtseying in, with a large flat green band-box under her shawl. In it was carefully packed odd ends of ancient black and white lace, all for sale. She was poor, very old-fashioned and provincial-looking, but quite a gentlewoman. Her name was Robert. Madame Robert we found was a near relative of Lamennais.

Her visits delighted me. I always got a chair, untied her band-box, admired her lace—and she called me a charmante fillette for my trouble. Her little bills were made out in a exquisite Italian handwriting. My mother desired me to try and write like that. Madame Robert said, 'You must not copy my handwriting but dear Féli's'. She brought me a letter of dear Féli—who was no less than l'abbé Lamennais. He was christened Félicité.

We were very ignorant of Lamennais's fame, for my parents lived in an English world, but Madame Robert interested me in him. She told

[1] *Crisis*, 26 July 1834, p. 128, and thereafter weekly until 16 August, the day of publication.

[2] *French Studies*, viii, No. 2, April 1954, p. 98, 'New Light on Flaubert's Youth' by the late Philip Spencer, to whom I am indebted for drawing my attention to the information about Gertrude Tennant.

me how learned, how poor, how lonely, how desolate he was, how great his bodily and mental suffering were—and so I thought I would befriend him and patronize him, and asked Madame Robert if she would bring him. She laughed and said, 'My child, he is the most remarkable man in France. Do you think he would go about with an old woman like me?—though he is my near relation!' And this increased my desire to know Lamennais. I knew my father and mother would think a poor old French abbé not worth their notice, so that I grew tall and straight, held my head up and looked distingué. I was left very much to my own devices—'wholesome neglect' was the order of the day. But I was determined to get acquainted with Lamennais and read his books. I deposited my solitary 5 franc piece at a little circulating library—and paid 2 sous a volume—for Lamennais's Indifférence en matière de religion, of which I did not follow intelligently one sentence. But a tiny volume fell into my hands entitled Paroles d'un Croyant, but which was much read—was understood and misunderstood by many thinking men in those days. I thought it superhumanly divine and was too ignorant and childish to detect the false wisdom of that little volume some went so far as to call a 'sacred poem'. I determined to translate it. The sentences were short, and the sentiments and language highflown! One evening, quite carried away by my enthusiasm, I startled my parents by reading aloud unasked and mal à propos portions of Chapter beginning [*sic*]

My father looked up, listened to a few sentences, and said 'It is damn French revolutionary nonsense'. My mother, with cold contempt on her beautiful face, said in a chilling voice, 'You had better mend your stockings'. I shuffled away my papers, determined in my own mind to know l'abbé Lamennais and show him my translation. He would admire it and would appreciate me and my name would be associated for ever with his etc. etc. etc. And so I set to work to gain my object.[1]

Here the text ends. From this note in a commonplace book we know that she did eventually meet him:

Lamennais I saw at Mme. Robert's a very poor woman some relative of his I fancy. She begged my mother to buy a Black Lace Veil from her—I have it now—at her little lodging I saw Lamennais a little shabby meagre chetif [*sic*] man—an immense head & forehead & eyes like flame. dressed like a [*sic*] old coat—blue stockings, hob-nailed shoes.[2]

[1] From the unpublished memoirs of Gertrude Tennant, pp. 163–5 (*c.* 1880?).

[2] Gertrude Tennant, MS. commonplace book (*Almanack* for 1847).

Whether she finished the translation, and, if so, whether it was the one which Cousins published, we do not know. Two considerations make it improbable. The first is that Cousins announced in July that a translation was being prepared by a Lady. This means that in the course of, at the most, two and a half months, Gertrude Collier, who was only 14½ at the time, had conceived the idea of translating the *Paroles* and had had her proposal accepted by a publisher in England. There is no mention of this in the (admittedly unfinished) memoirs. The second is that Gertrude, the daughter of an impoverished but genteel family, was scarcely likely at her age to have the means of communicating with one of the best-known free-thinking publishers in London.

The Reverend J. E. Smith

Smith (1801–57) was popularly known as 'Shepherd Smith' on account of his magazine, *The Shepherd*. His churchmanship was indefinite but with a distinct bias towards the institutional and Catholic rather than the reforming and Protestant. He was unattached to any Christian body.[1]

A glance at *The Shepherd* confirms the suggestion that Smith was just the sort of man to translate the *Paroles*. His contribution to the prevailing atmosphere of doubt and revolt was a grandiose form of pantheism. He used such scientific information as he could muster to prove the unity of nature and therefore the immanence of God. He constantly treated religion as a social principle with the result that he believed that it reached the peak of its achievement with the perfection of society.[2] This view of the nature of religion led to millenarianism.[3] *The Shepherd* preached the need for authority. This authority was to be found in the spirit of society.[4] The idea of the perfectibility of man and of religion as simply a social principle led irresistibly to the conclusion: 'man is naturally disposed to virtue; society is artificially adapted for vice'.[5] Christ was not to be sought within

[1] G. C. Binyon, *The Christian Socialist Movement in England*, London, 1931, p. 43.

[2] e.g. *The Shepherd*, 19 August 1837, p. 61: 'It is only as a social principle that we advocate the cause of religion'.

[3] ibid., 26 August, p. 65.

[4] ibid., 16 September, p. 89.

[5] ibid., 18 November, p. 168.

one's self but within others. The recognition of Christ in others is 'the mutual feeling that binds society together and makes *all*'.[1] Smith summed all this up in a grand cosmology based on the dualism, space and time, good and evil, revelation and science, man and woman, the organic and inorganic elements in science, religion and politics.[2]

All this is remarkably similar to the later Lamennais, for whom also religion was a social principle, whose beliefs always led him to millenarianism, who preached the authority of the people, who believed in the perfectibility of man, who saw the unifying elements in society as religious ones (although he tended to identify them with the Spirit rather than with Christ), and who finally set down his beliefs in the form of a cosmological scheme, not dualistic but trinitarian.

That Smith knew about Lamennais there can be no doubt. In 1837 there appeared in *The Shepherd* extensive quotations from a translation of Harring's *Worte eines Menschen*, which was 'dedicated to the reader of La Menais' [*sic*] Words of a Believer' and was in crude imitation of his style.[3]

It is therefore quite possible that Smith, with his interest in all that was heterodox and vague in religion,[4] would have been attracted by the *Paroles* sufficiently to want to translate it. If he had done so there is nothing more natural than to suppose that B. D. Cousins would have published it, since he also published *The Shepherd*.

From the three candidates, therefore, we can exclude Dr. Forster. It is impossible to decide between the remaining two. Lamennais heard at an early date that a lady was translating his work. The advance notices of the translation made definite reference to a lady. We know that Gertrude Collier undertook a translation of the *Paroles*. But there are several good reasons for supposing that the 'lady' and Gertrude Collier may not have been the same person. On the other hand, there is no evidence, apart from Harney's statement (which must bear some weight, since Harney was in a good position to judge of these matters) that

[1] *The Shepherd*, 13 January 1838, p. 226.

[2] ibid., pp. 298–302.

[3] ibid., 1 January 1837, pp. 3 f.; see above, p. 165.

[4] Harring believed that the reason for *The Shepherd*'s ceasing publication was that it adhered too closely to the spirit of Mazzini's *Faith and the Future* (and therefore of the *Paroles*) (*Skizze aus London*, p. 81).

Smith was the translator. Indeed, the publisher's announcement (which may, however, have been motivated by other subtle considerations) counts against him. But on grounds of probability Smith wins, unless there was another lady translator whose name has not come to light.

BIBLIOGRAPHY

The fullest bibliographies of Lamennais and of literature about him are: F. Duine, *Essai de bibliographie de Félicité Robert de la Mennais*, 1923, and H. Talvart and J. Place, *Bibliographie des auteurs modernes de langue française*, xi, Paris, 1952, pp. 167–229.

A. ARCHIVES AND UNPUBLISHED DOCUMENTS

(1) British Museum: Subscription list in favour of eight Spanish officers, 1849;
letters from J. B. Robertson, A.-F. Rio, and Montalembert to W. E. Gladstone.

(2) Cambridge University Library: Acton papers: Lamennais file, (Add. 4970) and 'Dottrine dell' Abbe La-Mennais' by Paulo Polidori (Add. 4890(B), fos. 603–33).

(3) The Oratory, Birmingham: Letters, R. Simpson—J. H. Newman, Newman—Simpson, 11–14 April 1859.

(4) Public Record Office: Foreign Office Records (France), 1815, and Despatches of British Ambassadors in Paris (F.O. 27); Despatches from Rome (F.O. 43).

(5) Sheed and Ward Ltd.: Papers of Wilfrid Ward.

(6) In the possession of Mr. A. Coombe Tennant: Fragment of an unpublished memoir, and extract from MS. commonplace book, by Gertrude Tennant.

(7) Trinity College Library, Cambridge: Houghton MSS.

(8) Ushaw College, Durham: Cardinal Wiseman's letter to the Canons of the Cathedral Chapter of Westminster, privately printed, London, 1858.

(9) The Venerable English College, Rome: Letters from the Rev. H. C. Logan and Bishop Baines to Wiseman about MacCarthy, November, 1834.

(10) Westminster Diocesan Archives: Correspondence of Dr. Gradwell—Dr. Poynter; miscellaneous letters to Cardinal Wiseman.

B. LAMENNAIS

(1) *Works*

Œuvres complètes, 12 vols., Paris, 1836–7 (*O.C.*).

Essai sur l'indifférence en matière de religion (1817–23), Paris, 1819–23 (*Essai*).

L'Imitation de Jésus Christ, traduction nouvelle, &c. (1824), Tours, 1873.

Le Mémorial catholique, 1824.

Essai d'un système de philosophie catholique (*c.* 1830), ed. Y. Le Hir, Rennes, 1954.

Les Paroles d'un croyant (1834), ed. Y. Le Hir, Paris, 1949.

Paroles d'un croyant (1834), *Le Livre du peuple* (1837), *Une Voix de prison* (1843), *Du passé et de l'avenir du peuple* (1841), *De l'esclavage moderne* (1840), and *Mélanges*, in one volume, Paris (Garnier), n.d.

La Liberté trahie (*Du procès d'avril et de la république, 1834*), Paris, 1946.

Affaires de Rome, Paris, 1836–7.

Politique à l'usage du peuple, 2 vols., Paris, 1839.

Le Pays et le gouvernement, Paris, 1840.

Une Voix de prison (1843), ed. Y. Le Hir, Paris, 1954.

Discussions critiques et pensées diverses sur la religion et la philosophie, Paris, 1841.

Esquisse d'une philosophie, 4 vols., Paris, 1840–6.

De l'art et du beau (1841), Paris (Garnier), 1909.

Fragment inédit de l'Esquisse d'une philosophie (published by C. Maréchal in *Revue de métaphysique et de morale*, vi, 1898, pp. 704–25; vii, 1899, pp. 39–67).

Amschaspands et Darvands (1843), Paris, 1845.

Les Évangiles, traduction et commentaire (1846), ed. P. Harispe, Paris, 1928.

De la société première et de ses lois, ou De la religion, Paris, 1848.

Le Peuple constituant, 28 February–11 July 1848.

La Divine Comédie de Dante Alighieri (*Œuvres posthumes*, ed. E. D. Forgues), 3 vols., Paris, 1856.

(2) *Correspondence*

Annales de Bretagne, xxviii, 1912–13, pp. 178–202, inédites, published by F. Duine.

Blaize, A. (ed.), *Œuvres inédites de F. Lamennais*, 2 vols., Paris, 1866 (*O.I.*).

Le Contemporain, 3e série, xxiii, 1882, pp. 769–804, to a noblewoman.

Courcy, H. de (ed.), *Lettres inédites de J.-M. et F. de la Mennais adressées à Mgr. Bruté*, Nantes, 1862 (*L. à Bruté*).

Études, cxxii, January-March 1910, pp. 602–18; cxxiii, April-June 1910, pp. 239–54, to Ventura.

Forgues, E. (ed.), *Lettres inédites de Lamennais à Montalembert*, Paris, 1898 (*L. à M.*).

Correspondance inédite entre Lamennais et le Baron de Vitrolles, 1819–53, Paris, 1886.

Forgues, E. D., *Lamennais: Correspondance* (*Œuvres posthumes*), 2 vols., Paris, 1859 (*O.P.*).

Haussonville, Comte d', *Le Prêtre et l'ami, Lettres inédites de Lamennais à la Baronne Cottu 1818–54*, Paris, 1910 (*Cottu*).

Nouvelle Revue, xix, December 1882, pp. 715–52; xx, January 1883, pp. 53–90 and 335–58, to M. de Vitrolles.

Nouvelle Revue rétrospective, July-December 1903, pp. 73-96, 309–12.

Revue bleue, ix, 1898, pp. 450–5 and 489–92, to Emmanuel d'Alzon; xi, 1909, pp. 321–5 and 353–8, to various correspondents (including Eckstein).

Revue de France, v, September-October 1935, pp. 625–49, to Louis de Potter.

Revue de la littérature comparée, xiii, 1933, pp. 513–16, to the Spanish translator of the *Paroles d'un croyant.*

Revue de Paris, 12e année, iii, 1905, pp. 225–43 and 515–36, to Mme Yemeniz; 16e année, ii, 1909, pp. 321–48, to Mme Clément.

Revue des deux mondes, xxix, October 1905, pp. 765–99; xxx, November 1905, pp. 168–206, to M. Vuarin; li, June 1909, pp. 559–600, to Mme Cottu; xviii, November 1923, pp. 162–200 and 395–429.

Revue des questions historiques, cxxii, 1935, pp. 56–72 and 255–75, Letters (1819–25).

Revue d'histoire littéraire de la France, vi, 1899, pp. 271-276, to Baron de Ste.-Croix; xii, 1905, pp. 293-335, to Mme Clément.

Revue du monde catholique, cxxvi, 1895, pp. 953–87; cxxvii, pp. 37–49, 225–46 and 406–25; cxxviii, pp. 31–47 and 207–31, to Benoît d'Azy; cxlvii, 1901, pp. 5–15, 222–9 and 345–52, to M. Querret.

La Revue hebdomadaire, iv, April 1909, pp. 281–94, to Baron Cottu; x, October 1909, pp. 5–41, to Mme Ligeret de Chazey.

Roussel, A., *Lamennais d'après des documents inédits*, 2 vols., Rennes, 1893.

Studi Francesi, September-December 1957, 3, pp. 422–9, to von Haller.

Villerabel, A. du B. de la, *Confidences de La Mennais. Lettres inédites de 1821 à 1848*, Nantes-Paris, 1886.

Zeitschrift für französische Sprache und Literatur, xxix², 1905, pp. 86–89, to Alexis Gérard.

(3) *English Translations*

The Words of a Believer: and having thus spoken, &c, *translated from the French of l'Abbé de la Mennais*, London, B. D. Cousins, 18 Duke Street, Lincoln's Inn Fields, 1834.

The Words of a Believer, translated by the author of 'Erin's Island (Garrad Dierlagh), Paris, A. Belin, 1834.

The Book of the People by F. Lamennais, translated with Notes by J. H. Lorymer, London, Hetherington and Lorymer, 1838.

The Book of the People by F. De Lamennais. Translated from the French. Pocket edition, pp. 87, Glasgow and London, 1839 (reviewed in the *Christian Reformer*, vi, 1839, p. 780, but otherwise untraceable).

Modern Slavery, by the Abbé de Lamennais, London, J. Watson, 15 City Road, Finsbury, 1840 (notes signed 'W.J.L.', i.e. W. J. Linton).

The Words of a Believer, translated by Edward Smith Pryce, A. B., London, Aylott and Jones, 1845.

The Words of a Believer, by Abbé F. de Lamennais, Member of the National Assembly, London, H. G. Clarke and Co., 1848.

Words of a Believer and The Past and Future of the People by F. Lamennais. Translated by L. E. Martineau with a Memoir of Lamennais [by Mazzini], London, Chapman and Hall Ltd., 1891.

Essay on Indifference in Matters of Religion, by the Abbé F. de Lamennais, translated by Lord Stanley of Alderley, London, John Macqueen, 1895.

Words of a Believer, by Félicité de Lamennais, translated with an introduction by William G. Hutchison, London, S. C. Brown, Langham and Co. Ltd., 1905.

Visions of the People, Taken from Lamennais' 'Words of a Believer', introduced by Tom Bryan, London, 1914.

The People's Prophecy, by F. de Lamennais, translated by Cuthbert Reavely, London, Andrew Dakers Ltd., 1943 (*Paroles* and *Une Voix de prison*).

C. OTHER SOURCES

(1) *Periodicals and Newspapers*

(The dates after each title are intended only as a guide to stability and period of publication. The principal references to Lamennais are given in detail in the text.)

The Academy, 1869–1922.

L'Apostolato Popolare, 1840–43.

Athenaeum, 1828–1921.

Atlantic Monthly, 1857–

Autographic Mirror, 1864–6.

Bell's New Weekly Messenger, 1832–55.

Blackwood's Edinburgh Magazine, 1817–

British and Foreign Review, 1835–44.

British Critic, 1827–43, then the *English Review*, 1844–53.

British Magazine, 1832–49.
British Quarterly Review, 1845–86.
Brownson's Quarterly Review, 1844–64, 1872–5.
Catholic Gentleman's Magazine, 1818.
Catholic Miscellany and Monthly Repository of Information, 1822–30.
Catholic Spectator and Selector, or Catholicon, 3rd series, 1823–6.
Catholic Standard, 1849–55.
Century Illustrated Monthly Magazine (New York), 1881–1925.
Christian Examiner and Church of Ireland Magazine, 1825–69.
Christian Guardian and Church of England Magazine, 1802–52.
Christian Observer, 1802–77.
Christian Reformer (Unitarian), 1815–63.
Christian Remembrancer, 1819–68.
The Christian Socialist, 1850–51.
Christian Socialist: a Journal for Thoughtful Men, 1883–91.
Christian Times, 1848–58.
The Chronicle, 1867–8.
Church of England Quarterly Review, 1837–58.
Church Reformer, 1882–95.
Church Times, 1863–
Cleave's Penny Gazette of Variety, 1837–44.
Contemporary Review, 1866–
Cornhill Magazine, 1860–
The Crisis, 1832–4.
The Critic, London Literary Journal, 1843–63.
Democratic Review of British and Foreign Politics, History and Literature, 1849–50.
Dolman's Magazine, 1845–9.
Dublin Review, 1836– (now *Wiseman Review*).
The Ecclesiastic, 1846–7, then *The (Theologian and) Ecclesiastic*, 1847–50, then *The Ecclesiastic and Theologian*, 1850–62, then *The Ecclesiastic*, 1863–8.
Eclectic Review, 1805–68.
Economic Review, 1891–1914.
Edinburgh Review, 1802–1929.
English Churchman, 1843–
English Republic, 1851–5.
English Review, see *British Critic*.
The Examiner, 1808–81.
Foreign Quarterly Review, 1827–46.
Foreign Review and Continental Miscellany, 1828–30.
Fortnightly Review, 1865–1954.
Fraser's Magazine for Town and Country, 1830–82.

The Friend of the People, 1850–1.
Gentleman's Magazine, 1731–1907.
The Globe, 1803–1921.
Good Words, 1860–1906.
The Guardian, 1846–1951.
Herald of Peace, 1819–
Home and Foreign Review, 1862–4.
Howitt's Journal of Literature and Popular Progress, 1847–8.
The Labourer, 1847–8.
The Leader, 1850–60.
The Lion, 1828–9.
The Literary Churchman, 1855–92.
Literary Gazette and Journal of Belles Lettres, 1817–62.
London Democrat, 1839.
London Quarterly Review, 1853–
London Review, 1835–6.
The Modern Churchman, 1911–
The Month, 1864–
Monthly Chronicle, 1838–41.
Monthly Magazine, 1796–1843.
Monthly Repository, 1806–38.
Monthly Review, 1749–1844.
Morning Herald, 1780–1869.
Morning Post, 1772–1937.
The Movement, 1843–5.
The Nation (New York), 1865–
The National. A Library for the People, 1839.
National Review, 1883–1960.
New Monthly Magazine, 1814–84.
New Moral World and Official Gazette of the National Association of Industry, Humanity and Knowledge, 1834–45.
New Quarterly Review, 1852–62.
Nineteenth Century, 1877–1950.
North American Review (Boston, U.S.A.), 1815–1940.
North British Review, 1844–71.
Notes and Queries, 1849–
Open Court (Chicago), 1887–
Orthodox Journal, 1813–30.
Oxford and Cambridge Review, 1845–7.
The Patriot, 1832–66.
The People's Journal, 1846–9, later *The People's and Howitt's Journal*, 1849–51.
Politics for the People, 1848.

Poor Man's Guardian, 1831–5.
Promethean or Communitarian Apostle, 1842.
Prospective Review, 1845–55.
Putnam's Monthly Magazine (New York), 1853–70.
Quarterly Review, 1809–
Queen's Quarterly (Kingston, U.S.A.), 1893–
The Rambler, 1848–62, then *Home and Foreign Review*, 1862–4.
The Reasoner, 1846–72.
The Red Republican, 1850.
The Republican, 1831–2.
Saturday Review, 1855–1938.
The Shepherd, 1834–8.
The Spectator, 1828–
The Sun, 1792–1876.
The Tablet, 1840–
Tait's Edinburgh Magazine, 1832–61.
The Theologian, 1845–7, then *The* (*Theologian and*) *Ecclesiastic*, see *Ecclesiastic*.
Theological Review, 1864–79.
The Times, 1785–
Toynbee Journal and Students' Union Chronicle, 1885–6.
The Truth Seeker, 1846–50.
The Truthteller, 1825–9.
The Vanguard, 1853.
Voice of the People, 1848.
The Weekly Register, in which are united Dolman's Magazine and the Weekly and Monthly Orthodox, 1849–50.
Westminster Review, 1824–1914.

(2) *Books*

Acton, John E. E. Dalberg-, 1st Baron, *History of Freedom and other essays* (ed. J. N. Figgis and R. V. Laurence), London, 1907.
Essays on Church and State (ed. D. Woodruff), London, 1952.
Essays on Freedom and Power (ed. G. Himmelfarb), London, 1956.
Albites, Achille, *The Authors of France*, &c., London, 1839.
Allies, T. W., *Journal in France in 1845 and 1848*, &c., London, 1849.
The See of St. Peter, the Rock of the Church, the Source of Jurisdiction and the Centre of Unity, London, 1850.
Per Crucem ad Lucem, 2 vols., London, 1879.
Annual Register, or a view of the History and Politics for the Year, for 1841–51, London, 1842–52.
Arnold, Matthew, *Essays in Criticism*, 1st Series (1865), London, 1896.
Matthew Arnold's Notebooks, London, 1902.

The Works of Matthew Arnold, 15 vols., London, 1903-4.
The Complete Prose Works of Matthew Arnold, ii, Michigan, 1962.
Articles de L'Avenir, 7 vols., Louvain, 1830–1 (*A.A.*).
Berry, Miss M., *Extracts of her Journals and Correspondence 1783–1852* (ed. Lady T. Lewis, 1865), 3 vols., iii, London, 2nd ed., 1866.
Blanchard, L., *Life and Literary Remains of L.E.L.*, 2 vols., London, 1841.
Bowring, Sir John, *Autobiographical Recollections*, London, 1877.
Browne, E. G. K., *History of the Tractarian Movement*, Dublin, 1856.
Letters of Robert Browning and Elizabeth Barrett Browning, 2 vols., ii, London, 1899.
Bulwer, Henry Lytton, *The Monarchy of the Middle Classes. France, Social, Literary, Political*, 2nd series, 2 vols., London, 1836.
Butler, W. A., *Letters on the Development of Christian Doctrine*, Dublin, 1850.
Carlile, R., *Church Reform: the only means to that end. A letter to Sir R. Peel*, London, 1835.
A Report of the Public Discussion between the Revd. John Green and the Revd. Richard Carlile, London, 1837.
Carlisle, H. E. (ed.), *A selection from the Correspondence of Abraham Hayward, Q.C., from 1834 to 1884*, 2 vols., London, 1886.
Carlyle, A., *New Letters of Thomas Carlyle*, 2 vols., London, 1904.
Castle, Egerton (ed.), *The Jerningham Letters 1780–1843*, 2 vols., London, 1896.
(Challice, Annie), *French Authors at Home*, 2 vols., ii, London, 1864.
Church, R. W., *Essays and Reviews*, London, 1854.
The Oxford Movement, Twelve Years 1833–1845, London, 1891.
Cathedral and University Sermons, London, 1892.
Occasional Papers, 2 vols., i, London, 1897.
Churton, Edward (ed.), *Memoir of Joshua Watson*, 2 vols., Oxford, 1861.
Citizen of the United States, *Europe; or a general survey of the present situation of the principal powers, with conjectures on their future prospects*, London, 1822.
Coleridge, S. T., *On the constitution of Church and State, according to the idea of each*, London, 1830.
Craven, Mrs. Augustus, *A Sister's Story*, translated by Emily Bowles, 3 vols., London, 1868.
Croly, D., *An Index to the Tracts for the Times*, Oxford, 1842.
Davies, J., *First Impressions: a series of letters from France, Switzerland and Savoy*, London, 1835.
Dierlagh, Garrad, *Erin's Island*, Paris, 1834.
Digby, K. H., *Mores Catholici*, 9 vols., London, 1831–42.
The Broad Stone of Honour (1822–76), 5 vols., London, 1877.
Dowden, E., *Studies in Literature 1789–1877*, London, 1878.

Engels, F., *Die Entwicklung des Sozialismus von der Utopie zur Wissenschaft*, 6th ed., Berlin, 1919.

Faber, F. W., *Sights and Thoughts in foreign churches and among foreign peoples*, London, 1842.

Life and Letters (ed. J. E. Bowden), Derby, 1869.

Figgis, J. N. and R. V. Laurence (eds.), *Selections from the correspondence of the first Lord Acton*, London, 1917.

Firminger, W. K., *Some thoughts on the recent criticism of the life and works of John Henry Cardinal Newman*, Oxford, 1892.

and the Hon. W. Gibson, *The Idea of an Oxford Modern Ethical Society*, Oxford, 1891.

Fischer, W., *Die Briefe Richard Monckton Milnes' ersten Barons Houghton an Varnhagen von Ense, 1844–54*, Heidelberg, 1922.

Flint, R., *The Philosophy of History in Europe*, i (France and Germany), Edinburgh, 1874.

Historical Philosophy in France and French Belgium and Switzerland, London, 1893.

Forster, T. I. M., *Recueil de ma vie, mes ouvrages et mes pensées*, Bruxelles, 3rd ed., 1837.

Epistolarium or Fasciculi of Curious Letters, &c., Bruges, 1845.

Foster, Mrs. M. E., *A Hand-book of Modern European Literature*, London, 1849.

Foulkes, E. S., *Complaints of a Convert, or, Our religious relations with the Continent*, London, 1857.

Frost, Thomas, *Forty Years' Recollections: Literary and Political*, London, 1880.

Froude, R. H., *His remains*, 2 vols., London, 1838; Part 2, 2 vols., Derby, 1839.

Gasquet, F. A. (ed.), *Lord Acton and his circle*, London, 1906.

Gavazzi, A., *My Recollections of the last four Popes and of Rome in their times: an answer to Dr. Wiseman*, London, 1858.

Genoude, A. G. de, *Lettres sur l'Angleterre*, Paris, 1842.

Gibson, the Hon. W., *The Future of Political Economy*, Oxford, 1891.

The Abbé de Lamennais and the Liberal Catholic Movement in France, London, 1896.

Gladstone, W. E., *The State in its Relations with the Church*, London, 1st ed. 1838, 4th ed., 2 vols., 1841.

Church Principles considered in their Results, London, 1840.

Rome and the Newest Fashions in Religion; three tracts, London, 1875.

Gleanings of Past Years, 7 vols., London, 1879.

Goyau, G., *Le Portefeuille de Lamennais 1818–1836* (Collection Maurice Bucquet), Paris, 1930 (*Portefeuille*).

and P. de Lallemand, *Lettres de Montalembert à La Mennais*, Paris, 1932 (*M. à L.*).

Greenwell, Dora, *Lacordaire*, Edinburgh, 1867.

Guérin, M. de, *Œuvres complètes* (*texte établi et présenté par Bernard d'Harcourt*), 2 vols., ii (*Correspondance*), Paris, 1947.

Guiney, L. I., *Hurrell Froude: Memoranda and Comments*, London, 1904.

Haile, M. and E. Bonney, *Life and Letters of John Lingard 1771–1851*, 2 vols., London, 1912.

Hamilton, Sir William, Bart. (Preface, Notes, Supplement and Dissertations by), *The Works of Thomas Reid, D.D.*, Edinburgh, 1846 and (supplementary part) 1863.

Hanna, W., *Letters of Thomas Erskine of Linlathen from 1800 till 1840*, Edinburgh, 1877.

Hare, A. J. C., *Life and Letters of Frances, Baroness Bunsen*, 2 vols., London, 1879.

Hare, J. C., *Charges to the Clergy of the Archdeaconry of Lewes*, 3 vols., Cambridge, 1856.

The Victory of Faith (1840), 3rd ed., London, 1874.

and A. W. Hare, *Guesses at Truth, by two brothers* (1827), London, 1882.

Harper, G. H. (ed.), *Cardinal Newman and William Froude*, Baltimore, 1933.

Harring, Harro, *Worte eines Menschen—Dem Gläubigen von La Mennais gewidmet*, Strasburg [*sic*], 1834.

Skizze aus London, Strassburg [*sic*], 1838.

Historisches Fragment über die Entstehung der Arbeiter-Vereine und ihren Verfall in communistische Speculationen, London, 1852.

Henson, H., *Retrospect of an Unimportant Life*, i, London, 1942.

Holland, Bernard (ed.), *Baron Friedrich von Hügel, Selected Letters 1896–1924*, London, 1927.

Holyoake, G. J., *Life of Joseph Rayner Stephens, Preacher and Political Orator*, London, 1881.

Houghton, Lord (R. M. Milnes), *Monographs personal and social*, London, 1873.

Hunt, Leigh, *Autobiography* (1850), London, 1860.

James, J. T., *The Semi-Sceptic; or The Common Sense of Religion considered*, London, 1825.

Jephson, J. M., *Narrative of a walking tour in Brittany*, London, 1859.

Jerdan, William, *Autobiography*, 4 vols., London, 1852–3.

Jorgensen, J., *Travels through France and Germany in 1815, 1816, and 1817*, London, 1817.

Kaufmann, M., *Christian Socialism*, London, 1888.

Charles Kingsley, Christian Socialist and Social Reformer, London, 1892.

Socialism and Modern Thought, London, 1895.

Kaye, J. W., *Life and Correspondence of Major-General Sir John Malcolm*, 2 vols., London, 1856.

Kingsley, F. E., *Charles Kingsley: His Letters and Memories of his Life* (1876), London, 1899.

Knight, H. Gally, *Foreign and Domestic View of the Catholic Question*, London, 1828.

Latreille, C. (ed.), *Un Témoin de la Restauration et de la Monarchie de Juillet, Le Marquis de Coriolis, lettres à Lamennais 1825–1837*, Paris, 1912.

Laughton, J. K., *Memoirs of the Life and Correspondence of Henry Reeve, C.B., D.C.L.*, 2 vols., London, 1898.

Lear, H. L. Sidney, *Henri Dominique Lacordaire. A Biographical Sketch* (1882), London, 1905.

Lecky, W. E. H., *History of the Rise and Influence of the Spirit of Rationalism in Europe* (1865), 2 vols., London, 1875.

Leroy-Beaulieu, H. J. B. A., *Papacy, Socialism and Democracy*, translated by B. L. O'Donnell, London, 1892.

Lewes, G. H., *The History of Philosophy from Thales to Comte* (1845–6), 2 vols., 4th ed. London, 1871.

Lewis, G. Cornewall, *An Essay on the Influence of Authority in Matters of Opinion*, London, 1849.

Lilly, W. S., *Chapters in European History*, 2 vols., London, 1886.

Christianity and Modern Civilization, London, 1903.

Studies in Religion and Literature, London, 1904.

Lindesay, Harriot H. (ed.), *Memorials of Charlotte Williams-Wynn*, London, 1877.

Linton, W. J., *James Watson: a Memoir*, Hamden, Connecticut, 1879.

The Religion of Organization (an essay read to friends in Boston, 27 January 1869, reprinted from the *Boston Radical*), New Haven, Connecticut, 1892.

European Republicans, London, 1893.

Memories, London, 1895.

Ludlow, J. M., *Two Lay Dialogues*, Cambridge, 1861.

McAleer, E. C. (ed.), *Dearest Isa. Robert Browning's Letters to Isabella Blagden*, Austin, U.S.A., 1951.

MacHale, John, *The Evidences and Doctrines of the Catholic Church*, 2nd ed., London, 1842.

Letters, i, Dublin, 1888.

Mackintosh, Sir James, *Miscellaneous Works*, 3 vols., i, London, 1846.

Madden, R. R., *The Literary Life and Correspondence of the Countess of Blessington*, 3 vols., i, London, 1855.

The History of Irish Periodical Literature, 2 vols., ii, London, 1867.

Memoirs (ed. T. M. Madden), London, 1891.

Manning, H. E., *Caesarism and Ultramontanism*, London, 1874.
Marindin, G. E., *Letters of Frederic, Lord Blachford (Frederic Rogers)*, &c., London, 1896.
Marx, K. and F. Engels, *Historisch-kritische Gesamtausgabe* (ed. D. B. Goldendach), Frankfurt &c., 1927–36.
Maurice, F., *Life of Frederick Denison Maurice*, 2 vols., London, 1884.
Mazzini, J., *The Pope in the Nineteenth Century*, London, 1851.
Life and Writings, 6 vols., London, 1864–70.
The Metropolitan and Provincial Catholic Almanac, London, 1854.
Milner, J., *Letters to a Prebendary*, Winchester, 1801.
The End of Religious Controversy, London, 1818.
Morell, J. D., *An Historical and Critical View of the Speculative Philosophy of Europe in the Nineteenth Century*, 2 vols., London, 1846, 2nd ed. 1847.
Morgan, Lady (Sydney), *France in 1829–30*, 2 vols., London, 1830.
Morley, Edith J., *The Life and Times of Henry Crabb Robinson*, London, 1935.
Morley, John, *Life of William Ewart Gladstone*, 3 vols., London and New York, 1903.
Mozley, Anne, *Letters and Correspondence of J. H. Newman*, 2 vols., London, 1891 (Mozley).
Murray, J. Courtney, S.J., 'Leo XIII on Church and State';
'Leo XIII: Separation of Church and State';
'Leo XIII: Two Concepts of Government', in *Theological Studies*, xiv, 1953, pp. 1–30, 145–214, 551–67.
We hold these truths, London, 1960.
Nangle, E., *The Revd. Dr. M'Hale's Letter to the Bishop of Exeter, dissected, and the Established Church vindicated, in seven letters*, Dublin, 3rd ed., 1834.
Napier, Macvey, *Selections from the Correspondence of the late Macvey Napier, Esq.*, London, 1879.
Newman, J. H., *The Arians of the Fourth Century* (1833), 7th ed., London, 1890.
Sermons, bearing on Subjects of the Day (1843), London, 1869.
Fifteen Sermons preached before the University of Oxford (1843), 3rd ed., London, 1872.
Parochial and Plain Sermons (1834–42), 8 vols., London, 1868.
An Essay on the Development of Christian Doctrine (1845), 6th ed., London, 1888.
Discourses addressed to Mixed Congregations (1849), 6th ed., London, 1881.
Lectures on the Present Position of Catholics in England, London, 1851.
Certain Difficulties felt by Anglicans in Catholic Teaching (1850), 2 vols., London, 1918.

Apologia pro Vita Sua (1864), Oxford, 1913 (introduced by Wilfrid Ward), and London (Everyman), 1955.

Essays, Critical and Historical (1872), 2 vols., i, London, 1890.

An Essay in aid of a Grammar of Assent, London, 1870.

Normanby, Marquis of, *A Year of Revolution, from a Journal kept in Paris in 1848*, 2 vols., London, 1857.

Oakeley, Frederick, *Historical Notes on the Tractarian Movement 1833–1845*, London, 1865.

Oastler, R., *The Fleet Papers, being Letters to Thomas Thornhill, Esq., from Fleet Prison*, 2 vols., London, 1841–2.

Oliphant, Mrs. M. O. W., *Memoir of Count de Montalembert*, 2 vols., Edinburgh, 1872.

Ormsby, J. W., *Letters from the Continent in 1818*, London, 1819.

Ornsby, Robert, *Memoirs of James Robert Hope-Scott*, 2 vols., London, 1884.

Osborne, C. E., *The Life of Father Dolling*, London, 1903.

Palmer, Roundell (Earl of Selborne), *Memorials: Part 1, Family and Personal 1766–1865*, 2 vols., London and New York, 1896.

Palmer, W. (of Worcester), *A Treatise on the Church of Christ* (1838), 2 vols., 3rd ed., London, 1842.

A Narrative of Events connected with the Publication of the Tracts for the Times, Oxford, 1843.

Paul, H. (ed.), *Letters of Lord Acton to Mary, daughter of the Rt. Hon. W. E. Gladstone*, London, 1904.

Payne, J. *Songs of Life and Death*, London, 2nd ed., 1872.

Petre, M. D., *Autobiography and Life of George Tyrrell*, 2 vols., London, 1912.

Modernism: Its Failure and its Fruits, London, 1918.

George Tyrrell's Letters, London, 1920.

My Way of Faith, London, 1937.

Playfair, W., *France as it is, not Lady Morgan's France*, 2 vols., London, 1819–20.

Powell, Baden, *Tradition unveiled; or an Exposition of the pretensions and tendency of authoritative teaching in the Church*, London, 1839.

Pugin, A. Welby, *Church and State, or Christian Liberty*, London, 1875.

Purcell, E. S. (ed.), *Life and Letters of Ambrose Phillipps de Lisle*, 2 vols., London and New York, 1900.

Raikes, Thomas, *France since 1830*, 2 vols., London, 1841.

A Portion of a Journal 1831–1847, 4 vols., London, 1856–7.

Reid, T. Wemyss, *Life, Letters, and Friendships of Richard Monckton Milnes, first Lord Houghton*, 2 vols., 2nd ed., London, 1890.

Reynolds, G. W. M., *The Modern Literature of France*, 2 vols., London, 1839.

Rio, A.-F., *Épilogue à l'art chrétien*, 2 vols., Fribourg-en-Brisgau, 1870.

Robertson, J. B., *Lectures on some Subjects of Modern History and Biography*, Dublin, 1864.

Robinson, Henry Crabb, *Diary, Reminiscences and Correspondence* (ed. T. Sadler, 1869), 3rd ed., 2 vols., London, 1872.

On Books and their Writers (ed. Edith J. Morley), London, 1938.

Rose, H. J., *The State of the Protestant Religion in Germany* (1825), 2nd ed., London, 1829.

Notices of the Mosaic Law, London, 1831.

Russell, G. W. E., *Arthur Stanton: A Memoir*, London, 1917.

Smiles, S., *A Publisher and his Friends. Memoir and Correspondence of the late John Murray*, 2 vols., London, 1891.

Sotheby, William, *Lines suggested by the Third Meeting of the British Association for the Advancement of Science* (with a memoir of his life), London, 1834.

Stanley, A. Penrhyn, *Life and Correspondence of Thomas Arnold*, 2 vols., London, 1844.

Stern, Ludwig, *Die Varnhagen von Ensesche Sammlung in der Königlichen Bibliothek zu Berlin*, Berlin, 1911.

Sterling, John, *Letters to a Friend*, Brighton, 1848.

Stothard, C., *Letters written during a Tour through Normandy, Brittany and other Parts of France in 1818*, London, 1820.

Tennent, J. E., *Belgium*, 2 vols., London, 1841.

Thackeray, W. M., *The Paris Sketch Book* (1840), The Oxford Thackeray, ii, London, [1908].

Thirlwall, Connop, *A Charge delivered to the Clergy of the Diocese of St. Davids*, London, 1845.

Letters, Literary and Theological (ed. J. J. Stewart Perowne and L. Stokes), London, 1881.

Tierney, M. A., *A Reply to Cardinal Wiseman's Letter to his Chapter*, privately printed, London, 1858.

Trench, Maria, *Charles Lowder*, London, 1881.

Richard Chenevix Trench, Archbishop: Letters and Memorials, 2 vols., London, 1888.

Tristram, H. (ed.), *The Idea of a Liberal Education. A Selection from the Works of Newman*, London, 1952.

Trollope, Frances, *Paris and the Parisians in 1835*, 2 vols., London, 1836.

Trollope, T. Adolphus *A Summer in Brittany* (ed. Frances Trollope), 2 vols., London, 1840.

Tyrrell, G., *Faith of the Millions*, 1st and 2nd series, London, 1901.

Christianity at the Cross-Roads, London, 1909.

Ultramontane, An, *The Pope, the Press, and Napoleon III*, London, 1860.

Varnhagen von Ense, *Tagebücher*, i, Leipzig, 1861; x, Hamburg, 1868.

Ventouillac, L. T., *The French Librarian or Literary Guide*, London, 1829.

Ward, Mrs. J., *One Poor Scruple*, London, 1899.
The Light Behind, 2nd ed., London, 1903.
Out of Due Time, London, 1906.

Ward, Wilfrid, *W. G. Ward and the Catholic Revival*, London, 1893.
Life and Times of Cardinal Wiseman, 2 vols., London, 1897.
Problems and Persons, London, 1903.
Ten Personal Studies, London, 1908.
Life of John Henry, Cardinal Newman, 2 vols., London, 1912.
Last Lectures, London, 1918.

Ward, W. G., *Essays on the Church's Doctrinal Authority*, London, 1880.

Weitling, Wilhelm, *Garantien der Harmonie und Freiheit* (ed. F. Mehring), Berlin, 1908.

Wilberforce, S., *Essays contributed to the Quarterly Review*, 2 vols., London, 1874.

Williams, Helen Maria, *Letters on the Events which have passed in France since the Restoration in 1815*, London, 1819.

Williams, Rowland, *Life and Letters, edited by his wife*, 2 vols., London, 1874.

Wilson, James, *A Journal of Two Successive Tours upon the Continent in 1816–18*, 3 vols., London, 1820.

Wiseman, N., *Lectures on the Principal Doctrines and Practices of the Catholic Church*, London, 1836.
Funeral Oration on his Eminence Cardinal Weld, delivered at his Solemn Obsequies in the Church of S. Maria in Aquiro, 22 April, 1837, London, 1837.
Recollections of the Last Four Popes and of Rome in their Times, London, 1858.

Wordsworth, Christopher, *Diary in France, mainly on Topics concerning Education and the Church*, London, 1845.

D. SECONDARY SOURCES (ARTICLES, BIOGRAPHIES AND BACKGROUND MATERIAL)

Ahrens, L., *Lamennais und Deutschland: Studien zur Geschichte der französischen Restauration*, Münster, 1930.

Aldred, G. A., *Richard Carlile, Agitator: His Life and Times*, London, 1923.

Alison, Sir A., Bart., *History of Europe 1815–1852*, 8 vols., Edinburgh, 1853–9.
Altholz, J. L., *The Liberal Catholic Movement in England*, London, 1962.
Baldensperger, F., *Le Mouvement des idées dans l'émigration française*, 2 vols., Paris, 1925.
Balfour, A. J., *The Foundations of Belief*, London, 1895.
Barry, W., *Ernest Renan*, London, 1905.
The Papacy and Modern Times, a political sketch, 1303–1870, London, 1911.
Battistini, P., *J. H. Newman dans le mouvement d'Oxford, 1833–1839*, Paris, 1924.
Bertaut, J., *1848 et la seconde république*, Paris, 1948.
Bibliothèque Nationale, *Lamennais—Exposition organisée pour la centième anniversaire de sa mort*, Paris, 1954.
Binyon, G. C., *The Christian Socialist Movement in England*, London, 1931.
Bishop, Maria Catherine, *A Memoir of Mrs. Augustus Craven*, &c., 2 vols., London, 1894.
Boudou, A., *Le Saint-Siège et la Russie, 1814–1883, leurs relations diplomatiques au xix*[e] *siècle*, 2 vols., Paris, 1922–5.
Boutard, C., *Lamennais: sa vie et ses doctrines*, 3 vols., Paris, 1905–13.
Brandes, G., *Die Hauptströmungen der Literatur des xix. Jahrhunderts*, 4 vols., Berlin, 1872–6.
Bréhat, René, *Lamennais le trop chrétien*, Paris, 1941.
Brentano, Lujo, *Die christlich-soziale Bewegung in England*, 2nd ed., Leipzig, 1883.
Brightfield, M. F., *John Wilson Croker*, Berkeley, California, 1940.
Brilioth, Y., *The Anglican Revival*, London, 1925.
Broglie, Duchesse de, *Voyages de Miss Berry à Paris 1782–1836*, Paris, 1905.
Cambridge History of English Literature, xii and xiv, Cambridge, 1915 and 1916.
Carcopino, C., *Les Doctrines sociales de Lamennais*, Paris, 1942.
Carpenter, J., *Gore: a Study in Liberal Catholic Thought*, London, 1960.
Carpenter, S. C., *Church and People 1789–1889* (1933), London, 1959.
Chadwick, O., *From Bossuet to Newman: the Idea of Doctrinal Development*, Cambridge, 1957.
Chocarne, B., *Le R. P. H.-D. Lacordaire: sa vie intime et religieuse* (1866), Paris, 1873.
Cobban, A., *A History of Modern France*, ii (1799-1945), London (Pelican), 1961.
Cole, G. D. H., *Chartist Portraits*, London, 1941.
Richard Carlile, London, 1943.

Socialist Thought: the Forerunners 1789–1850, London, 1953.
and R. Postgate, *The Common People 1746–1946* (1946), London, 1961.
Cornu, A., *Karl Marx et Friedrich Engels*, 2 vols., Paris, 1955 and 1958.
Cross, F. L., *John Henry Newman*, London, 1933.
(ed.) *Oxford Dictionary of the Christian Church*, London, 1957.
Dansette, A., *Histoire religieuse de la France contemporaine*, 2 vols., Paris, 1952.
Dawson, C., *The Spirit of the Oxford Movement*, London, 1933.
Derré, J.-R., *Lamennais, ses amis et le mouvement des idées à l'époque romantique, 1824–1834*, Paris, 1962.
Devine, P., *Life of the Very Reverend Father Dominic*, London, 1898.
Dictionary of National Biography, London, 1908–9, and supplements.
Donovan, Marcus, *After the Tractarians (from the recollections of Athelstan Riley)*, London, 1933.
Driver, Cecil, *Tory Radical: The Life of Richard Oastler*, New York, 1946.
Dudon, P., *Lamennais et le Saint-Siège, 1820–1834*, Paris, 1911.
Duine, F., *La Mennais: sa vie, ses idées, ses ouvrages*, Paris, 1922.
Elliott-Binns, L. E., *English Thought 1860–1900: the Theological Aspect*, London, 1956.
Espinasse, F., *Life of Ernest Renan*, London, 1895.
Europe, February-March, 1954, numéro spécial: *Centenaire de la mort de Lamennais.*
Evans, D. O., 'French Romanticism and British Reviewers' in *French Quarterly*, ix, No. 4, December 1927, pp. 225–37.
Faber, G., *Oxford Apostles* (1933), London (Penguin), 1954.
Fairbairn, A. M., *Catholicism: Roman and Anglican*, London, 1899.
Farrar, A. S., *A Critical History of Free Thought in Reference to the Christian Religion*, Oxford, 1862.
Fasnacht, G. E., *Acton's Political Philosophy*, London, 1952.
Feugère, A., *Lamennais avant l'Essai sur l'indifférence*, &c., Paris, 1906.
Figgis, J. N., *Churches in the Modern State*, London, 1913.
Fisher, H. A. L., *A History of Europe*, London, 1936.
Fitzsimons, J. (ed.), *Manning: Anglican and Catholic*, London, 1951.
Fogarty, Michael P., *Christian Democracy in Western Europe, 1820–1953*, London, 1957.
Folghera, J. D., *Newman's Apologetic*, London, 1928.
Fonblanque, E. B. de, *Life and Labours of Albany Fonblanque*, London, 1874.
Foster, Joseph, *Alumni Oxonienses 1715–1886*, 4 vols., London and Oxford, 1887–8.
Foucher, L., *La Philosophie catholique en France au dix-neuvième siècle avant la renaissance thomiste et dans son rapport avec elle, 1800–1880*, Paris, 1955.

Fries, H. and W. Becker (eds.), *Newman-Studien*, Nürnberg, erste Reihe, 1948, zweite Reihe, 1954. (Valuable bibliographies of Newman.)

Gambaro, A., *Sulle Orme del Lamennais in Italia*, Turin, i, 1958.

'La Fortuna del Lamennais in Italia' in *Studi Francesi*, 1958, No. 5, pp. 198–219.

Gillow, J., *A Literary and Biographical History, or, Bibliographical Dictionary of the English Catholics from the Breach with Rome in 1534 to the Present Time*, 5 vols., London, 1885–1902.

Gosse, Edmund, *La France et l'Angleterre: l'avenir de leurs relations intellectuelles*, London, 1918 (reprinted from *Revue des deux mondes*, 1 October 1916).

Gougaud, L., 'François Rio' in *Revue Morbihannaise*, xvii, No. 10, October 1913, pp. 289–98.

'Alexis-François Rio et la Bretagne' in *Annales de Bretagne*, xxix, April 1914, pp. 439–63.

'Un disciple de La Mennais, gouverneur de Ceylan: Charles MacCarthy' in *Revue des facultés catholiques de l'ouest*, xxiii, 1914, pp. 476–80.

'Journal inédit de François Rio' in *Revue d'histoire ecclésiastique*, xxx, 1934, pp. 297–333, 559–86.

Grünberg, Carl, 'Die Londoner kommunistische Zeitschrift' in *Archiv für die Geschichte des Sozialismus und der Arbeiterbewegung*, ix, 1920–1, pp. 249–341.

Guibert, J., *Le Réveil du catholicisme en Angleterre au xix*[e] *siècle*, Paris, 1907.

Guillemin, H., *Histoire des catholiques français au xix*[e] *siècle*, Paris, 1947.

Guitton, J., *La Philosophie de Newman* (*La notion de développement chez Newman*), Paris, 1933.

Gwynn, D., *A Hundred Years of Catholic Emancipation*, London, 1929.

Father Dominic Barberi, London, 1947.

Haag, H., *Les Origines du catholicisme libéral en Belgique 1789–1839*, Louvain, 1950.

Hales, E. E. Y., *The Catholic Church in the Modern World* (1958), New York, 1960.

Harispe, P., *Lamennais et Gerbet*, Paris, 1909.

'Lamennais et les femmes' in *Nouvelle Revue*, xviii, 1910, pp. 154–70.

Lamennais: drame de sa vie sacerdotale, Paris, 1924.

Hayes, R. F., *Biographical Dictionary of Irishmen in France*, Dublin, 1949.

Healy, J., *Maynooth College: its Centenary History 1795–1895*, Dublin, 1895.

Hegarty, W. J., 'Was Lingard a Cardinal?' in *Irish Ecclesiastical Record*, lxxix, 5th series, February 1953, pp. 81–93.

Höffding, H., *A History of Modern Philosophy* (1895), 2 vols., London and New York, 1900.

Hoiss, A., *Histoire d'un livre: Affaires de Rome par F. de Lamennais, 1836. Étude critique*, Dijon, 1933.

Holdsworth, F., *Joseph de Maistre et l'Angleterre*, Paris, 1935.

Husenbeth, F. C., *Life of the Rt. Revd. John Milner, D.D.*, Dublin, 1862.

Inge, W. R., *The Platonic Tradition in English Religious Thought*, London, 1926.

Isambert, F., 'L'attitude religieuse des ouvriers français au milieu du xixe siècle' in *Archives de sociologie des religions*, iii, No. 6, July-December 1958, pp. 7–35.

Jakobson, R., *For Roman Jakobson: Essays on the occasion of his sixtieth birthday*, The Hague, 1956.

James, E., *Brief Memoirs of the late Right Reverend John Thomas James, D.D., Lord Bishop of Calcutta*, London, 1830.

[Jausions, Dom A.,] *Vie de l'abbé Carron, par un Bénédictin de la Congrégation de France*, 2 vols., Paris, 1866.

Jervis, W. Henley, *The Gallican Church and the Revolution*, London, 1882.

Jones, Ethel, *Les Voyageurs français en Angleterre de 1815 à 1830*, Paris, 1930.

Joye, D., *Théorie du Cardinal Newman sur le développement du dogme chrétien*, Paris, 1896.

Kelso, A. P., *Matthew Arnold on Continental Life and Literature*, Oxford, 1914.

Kenny, T., *The Political Thought of John Henry Newman*, London, 1957.

King, Bolton, *The Life of Mazzini* (1902), London (Everyman), 1938.

Knox, E. A., *The Tractarian Movement*, London, 1933.

Kridl, Manfred, 'Two Champions of a New Christianity: Lamennais and Mickiewicz' in *Comparative Literature*, iv, 1952, pp. 239–67.

Lallemand, P. de, *Montalembert et ses amis dans le romantisme 1830–1840*, Paris, 1927.

Montalembert et ses relations littéraires avec l'étranger jusqu'en 1840, Paris, 1927.

Laski, H., *Studies in the Problem of Sovereignty*, New Haven, 1917.

Authority in the Modern State (1919), New Haven, 1927.

Laugel, Auguste, 'Lamennais' in *International Review* (U.S.A.), ix, September 1880, pp. 281–97.

Lechler, G. V., *Geschichte des englischen Deismus*, Stuttgart-Tübingen, 1841.

Lecler, J., *The Two Sovereignties*, London, 1952 (translated from his *L'Église et la souveraineté de l'État*, Paris, 1946).

Leflon, J., *Histoire de l'église*, xx, 'La crise révolutionnaire 1789–1846', Paris, 1949 (very inaccurate).
Le Hir, Y., 'Mickiewicz et Lamennais' in *Annales de Bretagne*, 1948, pp. 47–58.
Leland, J., *A View of the Principal Deistical Writers that have appeared in England in the Last and Present Century* (1754), London, 1837.
Liddon, H. P., *Life of Edward Bouverie Pusey*, 4 vols., London, 1893–7.
Loisy, A., *George Tyrrell et Henri Bremond*, Paris, 1936.
Lovett, W., *Life and Adventures of William Lovett*, &c., London, 1876.
Maccoby, S., *English Radicalism 1832–52*, London, 1935.
MacDougall, H. A., *The Acton-Newman Relations*, New York, 1962.
Marchant, Sir J. (ed.), *The Future of the Church of England*, London, 1926.
Maréchal, C., *La Clef de 'Volupté'*, Paris, 1905.
La Famille de La Mennais, Paris, 1913.
La Jeunesse de La Mennais, Paris, 1913.
La Mennais: la dispute de l'Essai sur l'indifférence, Paris, 1925.
Martini, M., *La dernière amitié féminine de Lamennais*, Geneva-Lille, 1956.
Mathew, D., *Catholicism in England* (1936), 3rd ed., London, 1955.
Acton: the Formative Years, London, 1946.
Menczer, B. (ed.), *Catholic Political Thought 1789–1848*, London, 1952.
Merz, J. T., *History of European Thought in the Nineteenth Century*, 4 vols., Edinburgh, 1896–1914.
Mills, Lennox, A., *Ceylon under British Rule 1795–1932*, Oxford and London, 1933.
Monkhouse, Cosmo, *Life of Leigh Hunt*, London, 1893.
Moraud, M., *Le Romantisme français en Angleterre de 1814 à 1848*, Paris, 1933.
Une Irlandaise libérale en France sous la restauration: Lady Morgan 1775 1859, Paris, 1954.
Morley, J., *Critical Miscellanies*, London, 1871.
Life of Richard Cobden, 2 vols., London, 1881.
Biographical Studies, London, 1923.
Morse-Boycott, D. L., *Secret Story of the Oxford Movement*, London, 1933.
Mourre, M., *Lamennais, ou l'hérésie des temps modernes*, Paris, 1955.
'Lamennais, les Femmes et l'Ange' in *La Parisienne*, July 1955, pp. 752–8.
Mühlestein, Hans, 'Marx and the Utopian Wilhelm Weitling' in *Science and Society*, xii, 1948, pp. 113–29.

Nettlau, Max, 'Londoner deutsche kommunistische Diskussionen, 1845' in *Archiv für die Geschichte des Sozialismus und der Arbeiterbewegung*, x, Leipzig, 1921–2, pp. 362–91.

Newman, B., *Cardinal Newman: a Biographical and Literary Study*, London, 1925.

Nicolaievsky, B. and Otto Maenchen-Helfen, *Karl Marx, Man and Fighter*, London, 1936.

Nielsen, F., *The History of the Papacy in the Nineteenth Century* (German ed. 1880, translated under the direction of A. J. Mason), London, 1906.

Nippold, F., *The Papacy in the Nineteenth Century* (translated by L. H. Schwab), New York and London, 1900.

O'Broin, Leon, 'Dr. R. R. Madden, Historian and Public Servant' in *The Month*, October 1958, pp. 224–32.

Ollard, S. L. and F. L. Cross, *The Anglo-Catholic Revival in Outline*, London, 1933.

Omond, T. S., *The Romantic Triumph*, Edinburgh and London, 1900.

Oxenham, H. N., *Short Studies in Ecclesiastical History and Biography*, London, 1884.

Parsons, R., 'Lacordaire and Lamennais' in *American Catholic Quarterly Review* (Philadelphia), xxii, 1897, pp. 256–79.

Peck, W. G., *The Social Implications of the Oxford Movement*, New York, 1933.

Peigné, J. Marie, *Lamennais: sa vie intime à la Chênaie*, Paris, 1864.

Phillips, C. S., *The Church in France 1789–1848*, London, 1929.

Plamenatz, J., *The Revolutionary Movement in France, 1815–71*, London, 1952.

Pocquet du Haut-Jussé, B.-A., 'La Mennais. L'évolution de ses idées politiques jusqu'en 1832' in *Mémoires de la société d'histoire et d'archéologie de Bretagne*, xxxiv, 1954, pp. 101–31.

Poisson, J., *Le Romantisme social de Lamennais*, Paris, 1932.

Pope-Hennessy, J., *Monckton Milnes: the Years of Promise, 1809–1851*, London, 1949.

Monckton Milnes: the Flight of Youth, 1851–1885, London, 1951.

Poulet, Ch., *Histoire de l'église* (1926), 2 vols., Paris, 1947.

Pressensé, F. de, *Cardinal Manning*, London, 1897.

Prestige, G. L., *The Life of Charles Gore*, London, 1935.

Quilty, R. P., *The Influence of H. F. de Lamennais' Epistemology on his Theory of Democracy*, Washington, 1954.

Raphael, Paul, 'Lamennais et Fortoul' in *La Grande Revue*, cxv, 1924, pp. 265–80.

Raven, C. E., *Christian Socialism 1848–1854*, London, 1920.

Reckitt, M. B., *Maurice to Temple*, London, 1947.

Rémond, R., *Lamennais et la démocratie*, Paris, 1948.
Robertson, Priscilla, *Revolutions of 1848* (1952), New York, 1960.
Rodis-Lewis, G., 'L'esthétique de Lamennais' in *Annales de Bretagne*, lxii, 1955, pp. 33–61.
Roussel, J., *Félicité de Lamennais*, Paris, 1957.
Russell, G. W. E., *Mr. Gladstone's Religious Development: a paper read in Christ Church*, London, 1899.
Ryan, J. K. and E. D. Benard, *American Essays for the Newman Centennial*, Washington, 1947.
St. John, Henry, O. P., *Essays in Christian Unity 1928–1954*, London, 1955.
Salvan, Paule, 'La diffusion des Paroles d'un Croyant' in *Mercure de France*, cccxxviii, 1956, pp. 65–76.
Schenk, H. G., 'Lamennais 1782–1854' in *The Month*, January 1954, pp. 153–60, June 1954, pp. 332–8.
Schmidlin, J., *Papstgeschichte der neuesten Zeit*, 4 vols., Munich, 1933–9.
Schwab, R., *La Renaissance orientale*, Paris, 1950.
Sells, I. E., *Matthew Arnold and France*, Cambridge, 1935.
Sevrin, E., *Dom Guéranger et La Mennais*, Paris, 1933.
Simeon, A. B., *A Short Memoir of the Rev. Thomas Chamberlain, M.A.*, London, 1892.
Simon, A., 'Lamennais en Belgique' in *Revue belge de philologie et d'histoire*, xxxvii (1), 1959, pp. 408–17.
Simpson, W. J. Sparrow, *French Catholics in the Nineteenth Century*, London, 1918.
Review of C. S. Phillips's *Church in France*, in *Theology*, xxi, July-December 1930, pp. 297-9.
Religious Thought in France in the Nineteenth Century, London, 1935.
Smith, B. A., *Dean Church, the Anglican Response to Newman*, London, 1958.
Smith, H. Maynard, Review of C. S. Phillips's *Church in France* in *Church Quarterly Review*, April 1930, pp. 172–5.
Somerville, H., *Studies in the Catholic Social Movement*, London, 1933.
Spencer, P. H., *Politics of Belief in Nineteenth Century France*, London, 1954.
'Prophet without Dishonour' in *The Listener*, 25 March 1954, pp. 535 and 537.
'New light on Flaubert's youth' in *French Studies*, viii, No. 2, April 1954, pp. 97–108.
Starkie, E., *From Gautier to Eliot*, London, 1960.
Stearns, P. N., 'Nature of the *Avenir* Movement 1830–1831' in *American Historical Review*, July 1960, pp. 837–47.

Stephens, W. R. W., *The Life and Letters of Walter Farquhar Hook, D.D.*, 2 vols., London, 1878.
Stewart, H. L., *A Century of Anglo-Catholicism*, London, 1929.
Talmon, J. L., *Political Messianism: the Romantic Phase*, London, 1960.
Thureau-Dangin, P., *La Renaissance catholique en Angleterre au xixe siècle*, 3 vols., Paris, 1899–1903.
Tierney, M. (ed.), *A Tribute to Newman*, Dublin, 1945.
Trannoy, A., *Le Romantisme politique de Montalembert avant 1843*, Paris, 1942.
Trevelyan, G. M., *English Social History* (1942), London, 1946.
Trilling, L., *Matthew Arnold*, London, 1939.
Tristram, Henry, 'J. A. Moehler et J. H. Newman: la pensée allemande et la renaissance catholique en Angleterre' in *Revue des sciences philosophiques et théologiques*, xxvii, 1938, pp. 184–204.
(ed.) *John Henry Newman: Centenary Essays*, London, 1945.
Vallery-Radot, R., *Lamennais, ou le prêtre malgré lui*, Paris, 1931.
Versluys, J. C., *Essai sur le caractère de Lamennais*, Paris-Amsterdam, 1929.
Vidler, A. R., *The Modernist Movement in the Roman Church*, Cambridge, 1934.
Prophecy and Papacy: a Study of Lamennais, the Church and the Revolution, London, 1954 (Vidler).
The Church in an Age of Revolution, London (Penguin), 1961.
Villefosse, L. de, *Lamennais, ou l'occasion manquée*, Paris, 1945.
Vrijmoed, F. J. J., *Lamennais avant sa défection et la Néerlande catholique*, Paris, 1930.
Vulliaud, P., *Les Paroles d'un Croyant de Lamennais*, Amiens, 1928.
Wakeling, G., *The Oxford Church Movement*, London, 1895.
Wand, J. W. C., *A History of the Modern Church* (1930), London, 3rd ed., 1938.
Waninger, J., *Der soziale Katholizismus in England*, M.-Gladbach, 1914.
Ward, Bernard, *Catholic London a Century ago*, London, 1905.
The Eve of Catholic Emancipation 1803–1829, 3 vols., iii (1820–29), London, 1912.
The Sequel to Catholic Emancipation 1830–1850, 2 vols., i (1830–40), London, 1915.
Ward, Maisie, *The Wilfrid Wards and the Transition*, London, 1934.
Insurrection versus Resurrection, London, 1937.
Ward, Wilfrid, *The Oxford Movement*, London, [1913].
Watkin, E. I., *Roman Catholicism in England from the Reformation to 1950*, London, 1957.

West, Julius, *A History of the Chartist Movement*, London, 1920.

Widdrington, P. E. T., V. A. Demant, and M. B. Reckitt, 'The social mission of the Catholic Revival' in *Christendom*, ii, No. 6, June 1932, pp. 93–120.

Williams, N. P. and C. Harris, *Northern Catholicism*, London, 1933.

Willoughby, L. A., 'On Some German Affinities with the Oxford Movement' in *Modern Language Review*, xxix, No. 1, January 1934, pp. 52–66.

Wittke, C. F., *The Utopian Communist: a biography of Wilhelm Weitling*, Baton Rouge, Louisiana, 1950.

Woodgate, M. V., *Père Lacordaire: Leader of youth*, London, 1939.

Madame Swetchine, Dublin, 1948.

Woodward, E. L., *Three Studies in European Conservatism*, London, 1929.

Worley, G., *The Catholic revival of the nineteenth century*, London, 1894.

Wright, Thomas, *The Life of John Payne*, London, 1919.

Young, Urban, *Life and Letters of Fr. D. Barberi*, London, 1926.

INDEX